THE DIGITAL TRANSFORMATION OF SUPPLY CHAIN MANAGEMENT

THE DIGITAL TRANSFORMATION OF SUPPLY CHAIN MANAGEMENT

MICHELA PELLICELLI

Department of Economics and Management, University of Pavia, Italy

ELSEVIER

Elsevier
Radarweg 29, PO Box 211, 1000 AE Amsterdam, Netherlands
The Boulevard, Langford Lane, Kidlington, Oxford OX5 1GB, United Kingdom
50 Hampshire Street, 5th Floor, Cambridge, MA 02139, United States

Notices
Knowledge and best practice in this field are constantly changing. As new research and
experience broaden our understanding, changes in research methods, professional
practices, or medical treatment may become necessary.

Practitioners and researchers must always rely on their own experience and knowledge in
evaluating and using any information, methods, compounds, or experiments described
herein. In using such information or methods they should be mindful of their own safety
and the safety of others, including parties for whom they have a professional
responsibility.

To the fullest extent of the law, neither the Publisher nor the authors, contributors, or
editors, assume any liability for any injury and/or damage to persons or property as a
matter of products liability, negligence or otherwise, or from any use or operation of any
methods, products, instructions, or ideas contained in the material herein.

ISBN: 978-0-323-85532-7

For information on all Elsevier publications visit our
website at https://www.elsevier.com/books-and-journals

Publisher: Joseph P. Hayton
Acquisitions Editor: Kathryn Eryilmaz
Editorial Project Manager: Andrae Akeh
Production Project Manager: Stalin Viswanathan
Cover Designer: Vicky Pearson Esser

Typeset by TNQ Technologies

Working together
to grow libraries in
developing countries

www.elsevier.com • www.bookaid.org

Contents

PART 3   Global supply chain and global strategies

PART 4   The Effects on the Supply Chains of COVID-19 and the Russia's Invasion of Ukraine

PART 5   How businesses reacted to disruptions of supply chains

Introduction

Why this book now

For some time now, my research has focused on the progress made by Supply Chain Management (SCM), thanks to digital technologies and the ongoing evolution in global supply chains. I was preparing a publication when, in 2020, a phase of very strong change began that broadened my interests. The Fukushima nuclear disaster almost 10 years earlier had already highlighted the vulnerability of supply chains to unforeseen events, but the explosion of the coronavirus pandemic and Russia's subsequent invasion of Ukraine have changed the scene far more deeply.

While what supply chain managers had learnt during the coronavirus pandemic was becoming the 'new normal' and we were moving toward a humanitarian and economic crisis, a new mindset had emerged. Global supply chains had been strained, which made it urgent for policies that would lessen disruptions and intensify resilience. In the economic literature, new expressions have been used more and more frequently, such as reshoring vs. onshoring, inshoring vs. outsourcing, resilience vs. robustness, preparing for 'just-in-case' vs. 'just-in-time' delivery, and new words such as deglobalization have appeared. Companies have had to rethink most of their businesses and to develop new competencies. Old rules are not completely obsolete, but used on their own they are inappropriate for surviving and prospering in a fast-changing environment.

Starting from these premises, I decided to review what I had already written and explore the impact of new events on the challenges and policies posed by SCM.

What this book is about?

The purpose of this book is to review the foundation of SCM and discuss how it can deal with the recent waves of change by using digital technologies for more efficiency, profitability, and resilience. The book provides an understanding of the breathtaking shift in traditional industries and the resulting significant implications for SCM. The basic message is that the new social and economic environment requires a totally new strategic management mindset.

Key definitions and events

1. Digital transformation is the process of using digital technologies to reinvent a business to be more responsive to market demands. With digital transformation, the company "starts with a blank sheet", and by integrating new technologies it redesigns its activities, products, and services. It represents a path, a journey, with different objectives that depend on the industry to which the company belongs. The path must be accompanied by a process of change management both to overcome the normal resistance of the organization and adapt this to the transition.

2. "Supply chain management (SCM) is the handling of the entire production flow of a good or service to maximize quality, delivery, customer experience and profitability" (IBM, 2022). "By managing the supply chain, companies can cut excess costs and deliver products to the consumer faster" (Fernando, 2022). SCM has greatly benefited from digital transformation.

3. Digital transformation in SCM: It is not only the use of modern technology to increase efficiency and productivity, reduce risks, and leverage new opportunities; it is also a profoundly new way to drive the company. "Digital transformations are a long game" .. .. "The point of digital transformation isn't to become digital. It's actually to generate value for the business" (Smaje, Zemmel, 2022).

4. In recent years, some events have accelerated the digital transformation in SCM, which has taken center stage in business strategies. The Fukushima nuclear disaster (the earthquake and subsequent tsunami on the west coast of Japan), the coronavirus pandemic, and the war in Ukraine have had a common denominator in the disruption of supply chains, prompting the need to restore their resilience. A new age of SCM has begun in which a long journey toward resilience needs to continuously reconfigure business processes in a fast-changing environment.

5. Digital transformation has been ongoing for decades, but it got a boost when the coronavirus pandemic broke out and a lot of people around the world moved online. With Internet access, students and employees forced to stay home in isolation carried out their normal activities remotely. At the same time, many companies adopted digital business models to manage all stages of the value chain. Fast and

reliable connectivity facilitated interactions between machines, people, and organizations, prompting adaptation to the disruption of supply chains.

6. Just when the global economy was supposed to complete its recovery from COVID-19, the largest war on European soil for almost 80 years has undermined global economic prospects. Russia's invasion of Ukraine has contributed further to disrupt global supply chains in a more geographically limited way but with stronger consequences and a slower recovery of resilience than was the case at the end of the most acute phase of COVID-19, thereby accelerating the shift from global to regional, and even local, sourcing.

7. Globalization refers to the increase in the flows of trade, money, people, and ideas among countries beginning with the end of World War II. Globalization of supply chains means instead that, thanks to the ease of exchanges between countries, a product sold in one country can be the sum of components, modules, and services produced in various parts of the world, even when there is a great distance between the countries involved. The former is a powerful trend of international trade, while the latter is the "blood vessel system" that makes it possible. Globalization and supply chain are therefore strictly connected. Since the last decade, more frequent and intense supply chain disruptions have undermined globalization, leading to the widespread belief that globalization will suffer a decline, although the forces that support it will not be defeated.

The structure of the book

The book is organized into five key parts and nine chapters.

Part One (Chapter 1) is about the drivers of digital transformation and their effects on the supply chains; Part Two (Chapters 2 to 5) is about the digital technology solutions for managing the supply chains; Part Three (Chapter 6) deals with the evolution of the global supply chain and global strategies; Part Four (Chapters 7 and 8) discusses the effects on the supply chain of the recent wave of disruptions; and Part Five (Chapter 9) discusses how businesses have reacted to disruptions of supply chains.

Some chapters (such as Chapter 6) can be read as a stand-alone complete set of concepts, while others are closely connected with each other (such as

Chapters 2 to 5). Each chapter leads, one step at a time, toward a better understanding of the new tools available today and the need for a new approach.

Chapter 1 gives special attention to Digital transformation (DT) as an everlasting changing strategy. Amazon, Airbus, Dell, and Walmart have rewritten the rules of competition in their industries, demonstrating that the supply chain can be a strategic differentiator. For its part, the academic literature has identified four tiers of DT and five domains of strategy that DT is changing. To highlight the concepts introduced, the chapter recalls how Netflix's original DVD service defeated the leading position of Blockbuster. Facing an absolute dominator in the retail distribution of movie rentals, Netflix decided to attack Blockbuster by offering customers a completely new value proposition based on the introduction of new technologies, among which DT was the most important.

Chapter 2 focuses on the impacts of digital technology solutions and is divided into three parts. The first deals with the progress brought by the Digital Supply Network (DSN) and discusses its main capabilities. The second gives evidence of progress made possible by the rise of Industry 4.0, which involves a radical shift in how production currently operates and has many impacts on the supply chain. The process is driven by technologies such as Cloud computing, Big Data, the Internet of Things, Blockchain, Robotics, Additive Manufacturing and 3D printing, Autonomous Vehicles and Intelligent Transport Systems, Artificial Intelligence (AI), Co-Creation, and the Digital Value Chain (DVC). The third part warns that there is still a lot of hurdles to overcome in fully deploying automation in the supply chain. Industry 4.0 is still far from being fully realized. In fact, many companies are still at the early stages of exploring its possibilities and implementing the information sharing necessary to achieve sharp-witted SCM.

Chapter 3 examines how Supply Chain 4.0 technologies are rewriting the rules of SCM. One of the main advantages is overcoming the lack of transparency, in which a segmented supply chain is found in independent silos that do not communicate with each other. With Industry 4.0 technologies, the boundaries between silos disappear, and every link between them becomes visible to all players in the supply chain. Other main benefits of transitioning to a digitized, automated, and fully interconnected supply chain are identified. The adoption of digital technologies allows companies to obtain and analyze data in real time, providing relevant information to the production systems, which leads the way to advanced manufacturing, known as Smart manufacturing and Smart factory. Under Smart factory management, the traditional distinction between production planning and production management disappears since the machines constantly exchange information about the production process. An essential requirement to compete in the digital age is close cooperation among the various functions of the enterprise and communication among the various parts of the supply chain.

Chapter 4 surveys the evolution of transportation, warehousing, logistics, and procurement under Supply Chain 4.0 technologies, which bring many advantages. For instance, new technologies applied to trucking help in choosing the best routes to reach a destination, which is not a simple process as various elements need to be considered: speed limits that are different from one road section to another, the risks of traffic congestion, weather conditions, temporary road closures, and fuel costs. Warehouse transformation benefits from a wave of technological innovation that includes Robotics, Augmented Reality, Autonomous Vehicles, sensor technology, and the Internet of Things. In recent years, due to the introduction of Smart technologies, which are 'intelligent' systems capable of controlling processes autonomously, without human intervention, logistics has undergone a profound evolution from a simple operational function of the company to a means of carrying out advanced planning processes. Digital technologies have also brought significant advances in procurement made possible, thanks to the greater transparency of supplier/buyer transactions afforded by connecting the physical and digital worlds. Thanks to new technologies, strong advances have been made in the two parts of the procurement process: sourcing and purchasing.

Chapter 5 notes that the introduction of digital technologies in SCM has forced companies to review and reconsider all their operations. The amount of information about internal and external processes has grown dramatically, increasing the efficiency in all management areas, especially in SCM. Using the latest digital technologies — from Cloud computing to the Internet of Things, from Blockchain to Artificial Intelligence — to increase cost-effectiveness has become a must. This chapter examines the main features of, and the main advantages from, the use of digital technologies to manage the supply chains and making them a competitive weapon.

Chapter 6 provides a historical perspective on outsourcing and offshoring and on recent waves of disruptions. Over the past 30 years, globalization has been at the center of interest of many companies attracted by the rapid development of demand in some countries, especially China and India. Thanks to the low cost of labor in developing countries, these companies have made significant profits. Offshoring has quickly become a vital part of global strategies. However, starting from the financial crisis of 2008-2009, the scene has changed. Rising protectionism, the trade war between China and the United States, and recent radical changes to industries and markets have slowed the pace of growth. Reshoring has become a buzzword and the nature of globalization has changed, requiring managers to change their entire approach to the design and management of supply chains.

Chapter 7 explores the role of the coronavirus pandemic on the management of supply chains. The rapid spread of the epidemic throughout the world has been an unprecedented phenomenon, which has rapidly created a mismatch between supply and demand challenging the management of supply chains. Factory closures have stopped production by creating bottlenecks and shortages at various points in the supply chains, and the transport crisis has exacerbated the situation. Many firms have shifted their production closer to home and raised prices.

Chapter 8 addresses the key challenges that Russia's invasion of Ukraine poses to the global supply chains. This chapter was written when the Russia-Ukraine conflict had been going on for about three months. It was difficult to predict how the conflict would evolve, but some effects on supply chains were already evident and destined to last. Many companies have been forced to rethink their supply chains built over decades. The war has brought to the surface the vulnerability of supply chains and accelerated the shift of the critical phases of their activities from global to regional, and even to local. Global supply chains in some sectors are closely intertwined and feed production that has difficult-to-replace components. The invasion added further pressure to the global logistics and transportation network, also creating a spillover effect.

Chapter 9 looks at how businesses have reacted to various types of supply chain disruptions. The process is no different for anyone facing risk and uncertainty: first, identify the vulnerability, and second, be more resilient. There are many key strategies to make supply chains more resilient without weakening their competitiveness, such as building inventories faster than building factories, reshoring or onshoring, diversifying supply bases, devising a new business model, accelerating technological innovation, and rethinking the trade-off between product variety and flexible production capacity. This chapter distinguishes between 'resilience' and 'robustness'. Resilience refers to the ability to return to normal operations after a disruption, while robustness refers to the ability to maintain operations during a crisis. It also distinguishes between 'just in time' and 'just in case', the former being more appropriate in times of intense supply chain disruptions. At the end, a question is asked: why do disasters often find the MNCs unprepared? Psychologists have an answer. The problem is often not the inability to predict but the inability to react to the perception of a risk. This may explain why organizations, that have considerable means to scrutinize the horizon and protect themselves from large risks, have been slow to react to the effects of the pandemic, thereby worsening the effects of supply chain disruptions.

References

Fernando, J. (2022). *Supply Chain Management (SCM), Investopedia, January 29.* https://www.investopedia.com/terms/s/scm.asp#:~:text=of%20a%20product.-,By%20managing%20the%20supply%20chain%2C%20companies%20can%20cut%20excess%20costs,the%20inventories%20of%20company%20vendors.

IBM. (2022). *What is supply chain management?* https://www.ibm.com/topics/supply-chain-management.

Smaje, K., & Zemmel, R. (2022). *Digital Transformation on the CEO agenda, May 12.* https://www.mckinsey.com/business-functions/mckinsey-digital/our-insights/digital-transformation-on-the-ceo-agenda.

PART ONE

Drivers and effects of digital transformation on the supply chain

CHAPTER ONE

Toward a new way of thinking

1.1 Platforms and network effects

What is the secret to the success of Uber, Airbnb, Amazon, and Apple? All these companies disrupted their markets when they entered them and started their path to becoming industry leaders. These pioneering businesses are built on platforms. What each of them has in common is that the value they provide to customers increases as they take off and bring in more users. The concept of the platform has become a fundamental one for the innovation of business processes, having a radical impact on the way product development as well as the entire innovation process is conceived, including relationships with suppliers and customers (Clark & Fujimoto, 1991).

1.1.1 Definition of platform

The platform concept is considered an essential foundation to improve new production opportunities through new automation forms and new organizational structures; to increase market orientation and innovation; and to achieve additional quality improvements (Wilhelm, 1997).

Researchers (Robertson & Ulrich, 1998) define a platform as a collection of assets, components, processes, knowledge, people and relationships shared by a set of products.[1]

---

[1] The platform concept has been widely discussed in the literature, leading to many definitions with only small variations. According to Schenkl et al. (2011), "A platform is defined as a set of corporate values of the category's components (parts, production tools, electric circuits and software), processes (development processes and production processes, supply-chain), knowledge (developmental know-how and production technologies) as well as humans and networks. A platform can be used in several generations of products". As the authors argue, it can be considered as "a technical system for standardization including both technical and organizational aspects. It is a module that can be used in a wide range of products. The platform has degrees of freedom to be adapted to application specific requirements". Meyer and Lehnerd (1997) define a product platform as "a set of subsystems and interfaces that form a common structure from which a stream of derivative products can be efficiently developed and produced". "A platform is a group of technologies that are used as a base upon which other applications, processes or technologies are developed. In personal computing, a platform is the basic hardware (computer) and software (operating system) on which software applications can be run" (Techopedia, 2020).

The Digital Transformation of Supply Chain Management
ISBN: 978-0-323-85532-7
https://doi.org/10.1016/B978-0-323-85532-7.00006-2

In IT, a platform is any hardware or software used to host an application or service. An application platform, for example, consists of hardware, an operating system, and coordinating programs that use the instruction set for a particular processor or microprocessor. In this case, the platform creates a foundation that ensures the object code will execute successfully (Bigelow & Rouse, 2021).

A platform strategy provides advantages for the globalization process, such as greater flexibility between plants, cost reduction achieved by using resources on a global scale, increased use of plants, and a reduction in the number of platforms on a world-wide basis (Muffatto, 1999). The ability to get products to market faster is a key competitive advantage. "An effective method for gaining this advantage is to develop product platform architectures" (Martin and Ishii, 2000).

The development of products based on the platform approach is considered an important success factor in many markets. "By sharing components and production processes across a platform of products, companies can develop differentiated products efficiently, increase the flexibility and responsiveness of their manufacturing processes, and take market share away from competitors that develop only one product at a time" (Robertson & Ulrich, 1998). "The benefits include increased engineering efficiency, higher solution reliability and reduced direct costs" (Karandikar & Nidamarthi, 2007).

Some other researchers (Cusumano et al., 2019), after stating that a platform "connect[s] individuals and organizations for a common purpose or to share a common resource", distinguish three types of platforms.

- 'Ideological platforms': "ideas or policies that bring people together for a common goal".
- 'Physical platforms': "on which people catch trains, designated areas that bring people together to access a shared mode of transportation".
- 'Product platforms': that companies create with "common components and subsystems that different engineering groups within the firm and its supply chain (such as automakers or aircraft manufacturers) can use to build 'families' of related products more efficiently than building each product from scratch". The usefulness of an industry platform can grow through the power-of-network effect.

At least three factors are driving the industry's move to platforms: new infrastructure and technology, richer and more visible logistics data, and relentless pressure to reduce costs.

1.1.2 What is the network effect?

"The network effect is a phenomenon whereby increased numbers of people or participants improve the value of a good or service".

(Banton, 2021).

The standard definition refers to "an increase in consumer benefits due to an increase in the number of others consuming the network good" (Spulber, 2008).

The Internet is an example of the network effect. Initially, there were few users on the Internet since it was of little value to anyone outside of the military and some research scientists. As more people started using the Internet, the content of the information and services exchanged increased, and this attracted more users. The more their number grew, the more value of the exchanges increased.

E-commerce sites such as eBay have gradually grown in importance by accessing online networks and attracting consumers to their products and services. The willingness to pay for a service offered by eBay increased as the number of buyers or sellers for the business rose.

According to the "Economics of Managers" course at *Harvard Business School*, the term network effect refers to any situation in which the value of a product, service, or platform depends on the number of buyers, sellers, or users who leverage it. Typically, the greater the number of buyers, sellers, or users, the greater the network effect, and the greater the value created by the offering. "In other words, the willingness to pay, for a buyer, increases as the number of buyers or sellers for the business grows", says *Harvard Business School* Professor Bharat Anand.

Many of today's most prominent companies and startups are powerfully backed by network effects, such as eBay, Amazon, Alibaba (e-commerce); Uber, and Lyft (ride-sharing); and Facebook, Twitter, Instagram, LinkedIn (social media). What each of these companies has in common is that the value they provide to customers increases as they scale and acquire more users. eBay offers much more value to users as more sellers use their platforms. Uber and Lyft provide many more benefits to riders when more drivers join their platforms. As for social media, users find the service significantly more attractive as more people sign up.

There are two types of network effects: (1) direct and (2) indirect.

(1) 'Direct network effects' take place when the value of a platform increases because the service's value grows as a result of attracting more users. This is the case with social media platforms.

(2) Conversely, 'indirect network effects' take place when the value of a platform depends on two or more user groups, such as buyers and sellers. When the use of a platform by one group increases so, too, do the advantages for other groups. With ride sharing (arranged by means of a website or app), if there is an increase in the number of passengers that want to travel with a private vehicle driven by its owner for a fee, the number of those who offer to transport others with their own vehicles will also increase. Parker et al. define this rule as the 'two-sided network effect', and underscoring that "the importance of these effects for stimulating network growth is so great that platform businesses often spend money to attract participants to one side of the market" … "They know that, if they get one side to join the platform, the other side will follow" (Parker et al., 2017).

To better explain this latter concept, the Authors remind us that humanity has known for millennia the advantages of bringing together in the same place both producers and consumers, thereby creating value for both. "After all, what is the traditional open-air marketplace found in villages and cities from Africa to Europe if not a platform in which farmers and craftspeople exchange sell the wares to local consumers?". The fundamental difference between the traditional platform business and modern platforms is the breaking in of digital technology, which has greatly increased both the speed of execution and efficiency.

According to the *Harvard Business School* course, the underlying principles of network effects imply that the business, Website, or platform with the highest market share will be more successful in the long run. This means that its market share is likely to grow more substantially. For this reason, it is customary to say that when network effects take on significant weight in a market, the best performers acquire dominant positions at the expense of the also-rans.

1.1.3 How platforms change competition

The development of platforms has changed the nature of competition. For example, publishers used to compete against other publishers in the market, but now they have a formidable opponent in Amazon. Netflix has forced Blockbuster, once a dominant player, to abandon the market. "The result is a series of seismic upheavals that are making one business landscape after another almost unrecognizable", observes Parker et al. citing Alibaba's record IPO as proof (Parker et al., 2017).

How was it possible for the Chinese giant to suddenly become the first major threat to U.S. Internet dominance, defeat eBay in China, successfully bring Chinese products to world markets, and open up the Chinese consumer market to global companies such as Nike and Apple? Various factors have contributed to this. In addition to the strategic prowess of CEO Jack Ma, the explosion of demand from the Chinese middle class, and the Chinese government protection from foreign competition for Alibaba that allowed it to grow while sheltered from the foreign competition have all contributed. However, the speed and size of growth were in great part a function of the new reality of platform competition.

Alibaba's dizzying growth in international markets is due to fierce network effects and economies of scale. Companies from all over the world have been able to source goods, products, and parts from Chinese manufacturers through Alibaba.

Another advantage of platforms is that they can quickly incorporate the resources and connections of outside partners and of logistics, warehousing, and shipping companies. In previous decades, success in retail required strong investments and years of competition, with timing and results not even remotely comparable to the speed with which Alibaba has gained positions in the market.

The Authors consider the development of platforms (thanks to advances in technology) as a radical change in competition. For years, they argue, Porter's 'five forces' model has dominated the world of strategic thinking. According to the model, the goal of corporate strategy is to control five forces above all: (1) the threat of new entrants to the market, (2) the threat of substitute products or services, (3) the bargaining power of customers, (4) the bargaining power of suppliers, and (5) the intensity of competitive rivalry in the industry. For decades, businesses have used this model to decide and support their strategies. However, over the years, competition has become much more complicated than the Porter model shows.

According to the Authors, many of the forces remain valid, "but two new realities are now shaking up the world of strategy" (Parker et al., 2017).

(1) First of all, companies that can act through platforms can manipulate network effects to recreate markets, not just respond to them. It is no longer a question of devising strategies to divide a cake of roughly the same size among competitors (as in the Porter model), but often of dividing a larger cake. The action on the Airbnb and Uber marketplaces is proof of this: because of the use of platforms, these two markets, hospitality, and car riding, have grown in size.

Box 1.1 Lego

The Danish toy maker has announced it has overcome the effects of the coronavirus pandemic on its global supply chain and to have strengthened its position as a leader in the industry. "Investments in Lego's digital platforms and the opening of hundreds of new physical stores are behind the improvement in company performances", said CEO Chief Executive Niels Christiansen. "Those investments over recent years have prepared the company for both the pandemic and the subsequent return of shoppers to malls and high streets", he added (Moss, 2021). The switch in digital technology has caused far-reaching disruptions across many industries, including the toy industry.

(2) Secondly, the platforms transform companies internally by shifting managerial influence from inside to outside the firm's boundaries. The platform is the ecosystem in which a company seizes the best opportunities while at the same time sharing with partners the value they have created together. Competition in this sphere is much more complex, taking place on three levels: platform against the platform, platform against partner, and partner against a partner.

A significant example is Lego (Box 1.1).

The effectiveness of platforms grows with the growth in the applications of new technologies, such as the introduction of Blockchain (Box 1.2).

Box 1.2 TradeLens: platform in action

TradeLens is a Blockchain-based platform for managing global shipments arising from an alliance between Maersk and IBM involving multiple stakeholders. In the platform, the documentation regarding events is written on the Blockchain, which creates a single source of truth that all can observe. Contract signing, arrival at the port, credit checks, payment, and other events along the shipping life cycle can be recorded publicly. When a given event is recorded, the corresponding contracts encoded in the Blockchain are put into operation automatically, thus avoiding possible errors. "Logistics platforms like TradeLens scale through a combination of network effects, learning effects, and coordination effects. As more fleets, ports, warehouses, and containers become instrumented, the value of these platforms increases via network effects as partners create value for one another" (Choudary et al., 2019).

1.2 The evolution of digital transformation

1.2.1 A three-stage process

What is the difference between (1) 'digitization', (2) 'digitalization', and (3) 'digital transformation'?

(1) **'Digitization'** is the process of converting information from analog to digital. When we are converting a paper report to a digital file, such as a PDF, the data itself is not changed but simply encoded in a digital format. Digitization can reap efficiency benefits but does not seek to optimize the processes or data. "Digitisation will have the impact on supply chains that steam and electricity had on manufacturing", declared a manager at Bain. "Companies in many industries are experimenting with a variety of new technologies and methods that promise to improve how they plan, source, make and deliver. These innovations are making supply chains smarter by increasing their predictability, transparency and speed of delivery" … "Digitisation is helping to deliver goods faster" (The Economist, 2019).

(2) **'Digitalization'** uses digitized information to simplify how we work and make it more efficient, such as by using digital technology to transform reporting processing and the collection and analyses of data. Digitalization does not change how we do business or create new types of businesses. Rather, it deals with making our work faster and better. It is a transformation that moves beyond digitization. While digitization is a conversion of data and processes, digitalization is a transformation.

(3) **'Digital transformation'** **(DT)** "is changing the way business gets done and, in some cases, creating entirely new classes of businesses. With digital transformation, companies are taking a step back and revisiting everything they do, from internal systems to customer interactions both online and in person" (GEP, 2021). In one of its articles, McKinsey defines digital transformation as "an effort to enable existing business models by integrating advanced technologies" (Bughin et al., 2019).
Digital transformation involves the redesign of processes, the introduction of automation and other technologies, and the development of new products and services. It must be accompanied by a change management process both to overcome the normal resistance of the organization and adapt this to the transition.
Netflix is frequently used to show the advantages of digital transformation. After having started as a mail-order service, it successfully disrupted

the brick-and-mortar video rental business. Later, when digital transformation made the streaming video possible, Netflix successfully challenged the traditional broadcast and cable television networks by offering an extended library of on-demand content at outrageous prices. Before Netflix, people went to a store, chose from the various offers on the shelves, and decided if and what to buy. After Netflix, a digital library became available on the PC, with suggestions about its use, the range of preferences expressed by previous customers, and reports of similar products or accessories (see also below).

Digital transformation has changed the way services are sold to customers. Previously, the model was to promote the service to convince the potential buyer, and in case of success to start the sale in person or by email. The development of social media has changed the offer of services as well as advertising, marketing, and customer service.

Digital transformation is not simply a further advancement of technology but "a new way of thinking", and more importantly, "a mindset".

An important example concerns the investments of BMW to create the best customer experience in the premium automotive industry (Box 1.3).

In defining digital transformation, some researchers (Perkin & Abraham, 2017) assert that (1) digital transformation is inevitable: "change is happening whether you like it or not"; (2) digital transformation is about more than technology. "It is also about strategy, process, culture, behaviors and people"; and (3) digital transformation involves fundamental and comprehensive change. "It is the reinvention of the way in which a company operates".

Box 1.3 Looking for the best customer experience

BMW has committed to an investment of hundreds of millions of euros until 2025 to digitize its sales and marketing operations. The goal is to create the best customer experience in the premium automotive sector. Customers have experienced the new platform for the first time with the launch of the iX and i4 electric models. Pieter Nota, Member of the Board of Management of BMW AG, says the digital system will enable it to precisely target customers. "A very important element in our marketing strategy is to generate a high amount of highly qualified leads, customers that are interested in our vehicles", he explains. "We can play the right messaging to them personally" (Valentine, 2021). In a flawless customer journey, BMW now lets customers buy individually configured vehicles entirely online and have them delivered to their homes. However, its dealer network still plays an important role in sales and service.

> **Box 1.4 B2B digital supply chain transformation**
>
> Digital transformation is not limited to retailers. The pandemic catalyzed digital transformation in many business-to-business (B2B) supply chains as well. A survey by GEP revealed that many CEOs said their business changed more in the first few months of the pandemic than it had in the previous decade. Artificial Intelligence (AI), the Internet of Things (IoT), predictive analytics, and other transformative technologies have given support to business enterprises in responding to sudden shifts in demand and supply trends. The report about the ability to positively manage the digital transformation of supply chains concluded with an optimistic view and a call to arms, stating: "Disruptions like the pandemic are no longer rare and unpredictable 'black swan' events. The high threat of natural disasters, political unrest, economic crises, and pandemics will continue, so enterprises must build the capabilities they need to mitigate such disruptions" (GEP, 2021).

A case in point concerns the B2B digital supply chain transformation (Box 1.4).

1.2.2 The four tiers of digital transformation

Technologies have many advantages for firms that want to introduce digital transformation, argued Subramaniam, the Author of a seminal article that appeared in the *Harvard Business Review* (Subramaniam, 2021). The challenge is to fully capture the different kinds of value these technologies offer. To demonstrate the full range of value that digital technologies can offer and the strategic advantages available at a different tier of digital transformation, Subramaniam identifies four tiers, represented from the simplest to the most complex: (1) "operational efficiencies"; (2) "advanced operational efficiencies"; (3) "data-driven services from value chains"; (4) and "data-driven services from digital platforms". For each of the four tiers, the Author gives examples to highlight the strategic advantages.

- **Tier One: "operational efficiencies"**. To inspect the degree of paint finishing in its plants, Ford adopts an Automated vision-based technology acting through Augmented and Virtual Reality, the Internet of Things (IoT), and AI. This has enabled the company to reduce the number of paint defects in its cars. The new technology generates data, which AI uses to detect defects in real-time.

- **Tier Two: "advanced operational efficiencies"**. Caterpillar installs sensors in its construction equipment to control how this is used in its construction sites. For example, customers use motor graders more frequently to level lighter gravel than to level heavier dirt. Using this information, Caterpillar can bring to market the product that offers the most requested performance, thereby improving cost efficiency for the customer. While in the case of Ford the greatest efficiency is obtained through data from sensors applied to its own manufacturing plant asset (paint plant), the benefits for Caterpillar come from sensors activated by customers who use its products.
- **Tier Three: "data-driven services from value chains"**. General Electric tracks product-sensor data from their jet engines installed on the fuselage wings of the aircraft of client airlines. Using AI, GE analyzes data and offers real-time instruction for pilots to fly in ways that optimize fuel efficiencies. Airlines pay GE a part of what they save in fuel efficiency, in addition to what they pay for the product. The business model here differs from the first two cases: it is not a model "designed to produce and sell products" but one that "provides data-driven services to digital customers". GE provides a tangible product (jet engine) as well as a service (data concerning the use of the jet engine). "Because this drives new revenue streams, it does more than just enhance operational efficiency" (Subramaniam, 2021).
- **Tier Four: "data-driven services from digital platforms"**. Peloton employs a digital platform to connect a community of users of its exercise equipment (mainly bikes) and to connect individual users with suitable trainers. Sensors applied to the exercise equipment transmit data to the platform. AI algorithms match individual users to suitable trainers, analyzing data generated by product-user interaction. Like GE in the previous example, Peloton is generating new revenues from its data-driven services "by extending its products into digital platforms" (Subramaniam, 2021).

The four Tiers and the strategic advantages can be summarized as follows (Table 1.1).

1.2.3 Drivers of digital value

To adequately assess the four tiers of transformation, it is needed first of all to recognize two noteworthy value drivers that modern digital technologies have: (1) data in its new expansive role; and (2) emergent digital ecosystems.

Table 1.1 The four tiers of digital transformation.

The four tiers	The strategic advantages
Tier one	"Operational efficiencies" is a must, as most firms can benefit from operational efficiencies. The vast majority of digital-transformation initiatives take place in this tier, which is especially important if operational efficiencies are a big part of a firm's strategic thrust.
Tier two	"Advanced operational efficiencies" is imperative for companies selling products that have the potential to access interactive data from users, which can be leveraged for strategic advantage beyond what is available at tier one.
Tier three	"Data-driven services from value chains" is for companies that recognize that they can generate data-driven services from products and value chains.
Tier four	"Data-driven services from digital platforms" is strategically important for any firm whose products have emerging consumption ecosystems. Firms that stay within their production ecosystems in such scenarios risk being commoditized. Extending products into digital platforms is their key challenge.

"Data used to be 'episodic'" (generated by events with a finite number of outcomes such as the shipment of a component from a supplier), "but increasingly it is becoming 'interactive'" (generated continuously by sensors and by other tools to track information, i.e.: Website performance tracking).

Interactivity reverses the roles of products and data. Data was traditionally the basis for decisions about products, but now products are increasingly generating data. To manage the amount of data from sensors and IoT-enabled connectivity, companies need to have networks of data generators and data recipients. The latter refers to data that has been organized so that it has meaning and value for the recipient. Such networks give life to digital ecosystems.

From progress in data and digital connectivity, two types of digital ecosystems have emerged. One type is the 'production ecosystem', which embraces the existing digital linkages within the various parts of the value chains of firms. A second type is the *consumption ecosystem*, which encompasses networks existing outside the firm's value chain.

To build an optimal digital-transformation strategy, Subramaniam suggests: (1) evaluating what is needed to compete in each of the four tiers shown in the figure and diagram below; (2) identifying investments that can help management make the most of the benefits from digital ecosystems and their interactive data. Every firm should decide in which of the four tiers to engage in transformation. Not all companies want, or are, able to implement a digital transformation in all four tiers; nevertheless, the Author concludes that: "every firm must nonetheless remain aware of the expanding universe of new possibilities".

1.3 Digital transformation is an everlasting changing strategy

"Digital transformation is not a destination; it's a permanent state of evolution".
"Digital transformation is the CEO's job. Only the CEO can make the fundamental changes required for a successful transformation".

(Carey et al., 2021).

The main reason is that to reinvent a business model coordinated action is needed regarding all the functions of the organization, and this can only happen successfully if the necessary changes and investments start from the top down. "The point isn't to become digital; it's to generate value for the business". "Digital transformation can only happen if CEOs act as digital guardians of their companies' transformations and are clear on how they can best effect the change that will embed digital DNA into their organizations", write Carey et al. (2021) in the *Harvard Business Review*.

1.3.1 Five domains of strategy

The academic literature has identified five domains of strategy that digital transformation is changing (Rogers, 2016).

(1) Digital technologies (DT) change how firms connect with and create value for their customers. The world of the digital age is best described not by mass markets but by customer networks.

(2) DT transforms how firms need to think about 'competition'. More and more frequently firms are competing not only against rival companies inside their industry but also with companies outside their industry that, with their new digital offering, can take away customers from them. Moreover, the competitive assets may no longer be inside an organization but in a network of partners with whom the organization is linked through a system of relationships.

(3) DT has changed the way firms think about 'data'. Today data is produced at an extraordinary rate by companies and by everyone else. In addition, cloud-based systems to store data cost less and are increasingly easy to use. The more serious problem is transforming the large mass of data into useful and timely information.

(4) DT is also transforming the ways businesses deal with 'innovation'. Not an expensive, high-stakes process, in which testing ideas is difficult and costly, but one in which experimentation is quick and the prototypes can be developed at low costs.

(5) DT forces companies to change the value they deliver to their customers, their 'value proposition'. Traditionally, the value a business offered to its customers was assumed to be constant. In the digital age, relying on a constant value proposition is inviting disruption from new competitors. Since consumer expectations can change rapidly, competitors can constantly identify and seize new opportunities by subtracting demand from other companies. The offer must therefore constantly adapt to changes in consumer expectations and respond to new offers from competitors.

To successfully adapt and grow in the digital age, businesses need a new framework to face transformation in each of these five domains. Rogers identifies a set of strategic themes and key concepts that he calls: "The digital transformation playbook" (Rogers, 2016), which can be summarized as follows (Table 1.2).

Table 1.2 The digital transformation playbook.

Domains	Strategic themes	Key concepts
Customers	Harness customer networks	• Reinvented marketing funnel • Path to purchase • Core behaviors of customer networks
Competition	Build platform, not just Product	• Platform business models • (In)Direct network effects • (Dis)Intermediation • Competitive value trains
Data	Turn data into assets	• Templates of data value • Drivers of Big Data • Data-driven decision-making
Innovation	Innovate by rapid experimentation	• Divergent experimentation • Convergent experimentation • Minimum viable prototype • Path to scaling up
Value	Adapt your value proposition	• Concepts of market value • Paths out of a declining market • Steps to value proposition evolution

The following case illustrates how changing the value proposition can represent a formidable weapon of massive disruption for an industry.

1.3.2 How Netflix's original DVD service defeated the leading position of blockbuster

Netflix faced an absolute dominator in the retail distribution of movie rentals. It decided to attack Blockbuster by offering customers a completely new value proposition (Table 1.3).

In the Blockbuster retail model, customers would pick up a movie and pay a lump sum for a fixed number of rental days. If they held the movie for a longer period, they were charged a late fee. Netflix overcame this very hated practice with a flat monthly fee that gave the customer the right to have three movies at home contemporaneously and to change them as quickly as they wanted. The product was easily accessible: customers did not have to go to a retail store to exchange a movie; they simply selected the movies from the Netflix website. In a few days, they arrived by mail with a handy return envelope. Since Netflix shipped from a centralized warehouse, it was able to offer 100,000 movies to customers, far more than they could find in a Blockbuster store. Netflix also offered a very sophisticated system of information about the content of the offer. The combination of these value proposition features made Netflix the preferred renter.

Blockbuster reacted by trying to imitate their rival's model, but the obstacle represented by the differences between the two value networks did not make this possible. Blockbuster could build an e-commerce website, but it did not have the massive data sets and technology to make movie recommendations that could match the service offered by Netflix. Another

Table 1.3 Business model disruption Netflix DVD service (disrupter) versus blockbuster (incumbent).

Value proposition differential	Value network differential
• No late fees	• Subscription pricing model
• Easy access (products come to you)	• E-commerce website
• Wider choice	• Data assets and recommendation engine
• Personalized recommendation	• Warehouse and mail distribution system
	• No retail costs

difference was in the warehouse and mail distribution system. Blockbuster managed to build its own system, but the long experience of Netflix in maximizing automation and minimizing errors, lead times, and costs turned out to be far superior to Blockbuster's. Finally, Netflix did not have to bear the very high fixed costs of a chain of 9000 stores. For some time, Blockbuster managed to offer a value proposition compared to that of Netflix at the same prices but incurring higher costs. The decline in a few years became unstoppable. The last Blockbuster store closed in 2014 (Rogers, 2016).

1.3.3 Less complex, less costly, less time wasting than first imagined

How long does a digital transformation take and how much does it cost? It is widely believed that digitizing a major corporation's supply chain can cost tens of millions of dollars and that to complete it requires a strong commitment of management for at least three to 5 years. Investments range from cloud technology to new instruments on machines.

Based on their research, Mueller and Lauterbach identified three levers for accelerating digitalization projects "that will help organizations of any size reap the benefits of true transformations" (Mueller & Lauterbach, 2021). First, conduct preimplementation due diligence; second, design a step-by-step transformation plan; and third, develop tailor-made transformation measures.

Some other researchers (Simchi-Levi & Timmermans, 2021) suggest an alternative based on their experience in modernizing the supply chain in a number of companies. The experience gained in these companies has shown, according to the two Authors, that it is possible to obtain substantial advantages with an investment of a few million dollars over a period of between one and 2 years.

The proposed approach consists of three actions.

(1) In the first action, the company replaces the consensus forecast "with a unified view of demand", as the Authors outline. The consensus forecast is a method of forecasting used in a number of sciences, ranging from econometrics to meteorology. According to Wikipedia, consensus forecasts are "predictions of the future that are created by combining together several separate forecasts which have often been created using different methodologies".

(2) The second action is to switch from an approach to digitization that embraces the entire activity of the company toward a segmentation strategy.

(3) The third action is to develop a plan that constantly follows changes in the balance between supply and demand, identifying and responding to deviations from what is planned or to any disruptions. This action is based on the principle that in a free market the price mechanism pushes supply and demand toward equilibrium. During the pandemic this did not occur in the short term since, due to shortages, supply did not respond promptly to demand, pushing prices up.

Research has shown that the variability in customer demand is significantly lower than the variability in retail orders; this is the well-known bullwhip effect in supply chains. The Authors observe that this means that predicting consumption should be easier than predicting retail orders.

1.3.4 Defenses against threats. Adjusting to the new reality

How to defend against the threats of disruption from new technologies?

When digital transformation made its first appearance in the middle of the last decade, many thought that Hollywood's major motion-picture studios would "shrivel up and die", notes Smith, as the newcomers to the industry — Amazon, Netflix, and Google — showed their disruptive capabilities (Smith, 2021). However, this did not happen. Why? According to the Author, the explanation indicates how much needs to be done by the management of companies in other industries engaged in introducing digital transformation.

Compared to other transformations faced by companies, digital transformations have two important characteristics. The first is that they "tend to create abundance where there was once scarcity", says the Author. For example, the encoded information can be repeated many times without adding costs. The second is that digital transformations often involve multiple areas of the company at the same time. The multiple digital changes, which must be done in a combined way, often confuse management, which is generally accustomed to responding selectively to the competitive shocks from the environment.

Why have studios been able to respond to the threat posed by new digital technologies?

The Author (Smith, 2021) gives a masterful explanation of the motion picture industry (Box 1.5).

According to Smith, companies facing DT must draw three lessons from the experience of the motion picture industry.

Box 1.5 The motion picture industry

For over 100 years, six Hollywood studies have dominated the industry, during which time they have successfully dealt with the massive changes in all aspects of the 'content' of their product: how it is created (how to make a movie), distributed (how to distribute a movie), and consumed (how a movie is 'consumed' by customers). The question is: if none of these elements had changed in all these years, why has the digital transformation faced by the studios since 2015 been able to create changes through its 'disruptive power'? The answer is that this transformation is creating new types of abundance and a new, faster rate of change to which the studios have been able to respond. Throughout the 20th century, the six studios have retained their power because they have been able to control three key scarce market resources, as outlined by Smith: (1) "the financial and technological means of creating content, (2) the channels necessary to distribute content, and (3) the ability to use copyright law to control how consumers accessed content".

When the digital transformation process started, the studios were aware that digital technologies were making each of the three scarce market resources abundant by threatening the business model. In fact: (1) new digital technologies have facilitated access to tools to create content; (2) new digital channels have given content producers the ability to reach their audiences without going through television networks, the cinema, and brick-and-mortar store shelves; and (3) digital piracy has given free access to content.

While creating abundance in hitherto scarce resources, digital transformation also created a new scarcity: customer attention. Why have motion-picture studios been able to respond to the threat created by new technologies? Because: (1) they gave up defending their business model and returned to their corporate mission: "creating great entertainment and getting it in front of the right audience"; and (2) they have embraced new technologies and changed the business model.

(1) Verify if in one's sector digital transformation has replaced the scarcity of certain resources with abundant resources. An example can be that of Encyclopedia Britannica, in which DT changed the nature of the product by replacing printed paper with digital material.

(2) Verify if digital transformation is creating new scarce resources that are not under the control of the company, and determining the changes needed to acquire them.

(3) Verify if and how the new digital technologies can be useful in accomplishing the firm's mission.

Each of the three lessons is relevant, but the third is fundamental, Smith observes: "Leadership has the charge to consider digital transformation primarily as a threat without forgetting that it can underlie an opportunity to be seized".

1.3.5 Success factors in digital transformation

Digital transformation means several things at once. "Without a clear understanding, the wrong people are often put in charge, with the wrong resources, and the wrong KPIs, setting the digital transformation project up for failure" (Furr et al., 2022).

Digital transformation, the Authors argue, is not a monolithic concept but a path, a journey with different objectives according to the industry the company belongs to and the degree of evolution that digitization has achieved. It is therefore clear that digital transformation can be different for different companies even in the same sector. Based on research conducted on companies that have started a digital transformation, researchers have identified four pillars: Information Technology uplift; digitizing operations; digital marketing; and digital businesses. "All four are part of most companies' digital transformation journey", as the Authors outline. For each of the four pillars, the following aspects are indicated: (1) what it entails; (2) expected benefits; (3) capabilities required; (4) C-suite sponsor, and (5) KPIs.

- **IT uplift.** For most companies, digital transformation begins with the upgrading of Information Technology (IT) infrastructures. The first result is usually the access to up-to-date tools such as the platforms that modernize IT. To go further, however, there is a need for IT architectural capacity, change management capacity, and investments in new technologies, including Artificial Intelligence. Typically, the CIO or CTO should lead this pillar of digital transformation. KPI: new tools, reduced costs, improved capabilities, improved customer satisfaction.
- **Digitizing operations.** The second pillar is the use of digital technologies such as AI, 5G, and IoT to optimize existing businesses to improve efficiency and reduce costs. In the most basic form, this phase consists of switching from analog activities to digital ones. Digitizing operations is a fundamental test bench where the company puts into play its superiority over other companies. Since an in-depth understanding of the functioning of the company as expressed by the data is required, this phase should be led by the Chief Financial Officer or the Chief Operation

Officer. KPI: savings in personnel, time, and money, improved customer satisfaction.

- **Digital marketing.** Dealing with digital solutions to win clients, build brand awareness, and understand customers' expectations are the main objectives of the digital marketing pillar: who are the customers by age, gender, life stage, location, hobbies, and what is their past buying behavior? Global retailers are using digital channels, AI, and predictive analytics to identify potential customers. The Chief Marketing Officer is the natural leader of this phase. KPI: return on marketing, leads (potential customers), client acquisition.
- **Digital businesses.** Digital transformation provides opportunities for established companies, mainly through new business models and products. The payoffs are new revenue sources and growth opportunities. The capability required: business creation, innovation processes, and innovation leaders. The CEO, or head of sales, typically leads such initiatives. KPI: new products, new markets.

1.4 The definition of "supply chain"

What is a "supply chain"? In literature, the definition of "supply chain" has obtained a lot of proposals compared to the definition of "Supply Chain Management" (SCM) (Cooper & Ellram, 1993) (Londe & Masters, 1994; Lambert et al., 1998).

Quinn defines the supply chain as "all of those activities associated with moving goods from the raw-materials stage through to the end user. This includes sourcing and procurement, production scheduling, order processing, inventory management, transportation, warehousing, and customer service. Importantly, it also embodies the information systems so necessary to monitor all of those activities" (Quinn, 1997).

Lummus and Vokurka indicate that the supply chain includes all activities involved in delivering products, from sourcing raw materials and parts, manufacturing and assembly, warehousing, logistics, and procurement, to distribution through the different channels up to the sale to customers, including the information systems necessary to monitor all of these activities (Lummus & Vokurka, 1999).

According to Beamon, a supply chain may be defined as "an integrated process wherein a number of various business entities (i.e. suppliers, manufacturers, distributors, and retailers) work together in an effort to: (1) acquire raw materials, (2) convert these raw materials into specified final products, and (3) deliver these final products to retailers" (Beamon, 1998)[2].

Car industry. The automotive supply chain is among those that contribute the most to the final product, accounting for 70%–75% of a vehicle released to the market. The end manufacturers — Volkswagen, Toyota, Stellantis, Ford, and many others, known as the Original Equipment Manufacturers (OEM) — supply the remaining 25%–30% of the final product by assembling parts, components, and modules produced by an extensive supply chain that mainly consists of three levels: Tier 1, Tier 2, and Tier 3 (Fig. 1.1).

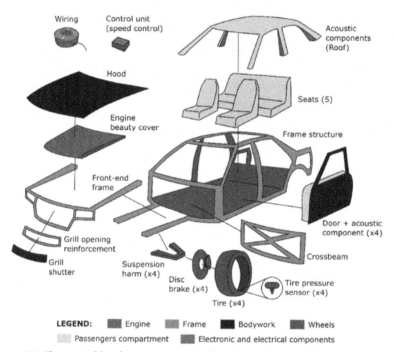

Figure 1.1 *The assembly of car components.* The figure describes the car assembly of all its main components. *From Spreafico, C. (2021). Can modified components make cars greener? A life cycle assessment.* Journal of Cleaner Production 307, 1–18. *https://doi.org/ 10.1016/j.jclepro.2021.127190.*

[2] There are various definitions in the literature. Lambert et al. (1998) defines a supply chain as "the alignment of firms that brings products or services to market". Mentzer et al. (2001) defines it as "a set of three or more entities (organizations or individuals) directly involved in the upstream and downstream flows of products, services, finances, and/or information from a source to a customer".

Tier 1 suppliers, such as Bosch and Continental, develop solutions adapted to the finished product without major modifications, such as airbags or air conditioners. Those firms that supply Tier 1 are called Tier 2 suppliers, and often have authority in their specific domain, but they also support a lot of non-automotive customers. Tier 2 must use raw materials, parts, and components provided by the next layer, namely, Tier 3. All these elements of the supply chain are linearly dependent on each other.

Amazon, Airbus, Dell, and Walmart have rewritten the rules of competition in their industry, demonstrating that the supply chain can be a strategic differentiator.

If a transformation company (usually represented as the OEM) is part of the supply chain, then we can distinguish between the upstream links of the material flows toward manufacturing and the downstream links of the final products toward the customer. In reality, this is not a linear link of relationships but a highly complex network of relationships among the participating companies. Companies participating in the global supply chain can be independent entities in any country in the world. The network epitomizes how the company members in the chain are interconnected.

Today, a supply chain is more frequently a network of interconnected firms with a web of relationships represented by three flows: (1) the flow from raw materials at the beginning of the supply chain to the finished product delivered to the customer; (2) the flow of information on demand, design, production, and distribution between participating companies both upstream and downstream; (3) the financial flows from the end-customer in the supply chain upstream to the material suppliers (Gilchrist, 2019).

Scholars have offered more specific definitions that highlight the upstream and downstream aspects of the final producer. "A supply chain is the network of organizations that are involved, through upstream and downstream linkages, in the different processes and activities that produce value in the form of products and services delivered to the ultimate consumer" (Christopher, 1998). In other words, a supply chain consists of multiple firms, both upstream (i.e. supply) and downstream (i.e.: distribution), and the ultimate consumer.

The concept of the supply chain should not be confused with that of logistics. Logistics is an activity, a process, a function carried out within the same company, while a supply chain is a network of companies that, coordinated by one of them, collaborate to bring a product to market. The supply chain moves and flows between independent companies united by a chain in which, hopefully, each link adds value to the others. In times of stability, the supply chain was considered an ancillary function to production. However, the earthquake and subsequent tsunami that caused problems in the reactor in Fukushima, and more recently the policies to deal with the COVID-19 pandemic and the war in Ukraine, have shown how important it is to avoid the vulnerability of supply chains, making their resilience today a strategic differentiator (see below in Chapter 4 on Transportation, Warehousing, Logistics and Procurement 4.0).

1.4.1 The drive toward shorter supply chains

Starting in the 2020s, a deep transformation began in global supply chains. Global trade growth has fallen, global regulatory harmonization has given way to local approaches, cross-border investment has dropped, and "soaring wages and environmental costs are leading to a decline in the 'cheap China' sourcing model".

Supply chains were already becoming shorter and faster before "politicians started taking a hammer to the trading system". The main force for change is technology. Multinational corporations must modify and modernize their supply chains in response to new technologies such as Artificial Intelligence (AI), Data Analytics, and Robotics, which are changing "how factories, warehouses, distribution centers and delivery systems work". The trend toward shorter supply chains will continue to gain in strength (Vaitheeswaran, 2019).

Three trends that suggest actions made by companies to shorten supply chains have been evidenced by the outbreak of the COVID-19 pandemic.

(1) The obsessive search for lean management and lower costs has increased the risk of supply chain disruptions. Many companies do not know all the suppliers operating in their supply chain, especially those in the links at the end of the chain and in distant countries.

(2) Over the past decade, international trade in services has grown more than 60% faster than the trade in tangible products. Moreover, services now account for a significant and increasing share of the value created in international trade (telecommunications, information technology, etc.). For companies with a significant share of services in their production processes, it is better to be in closer proximity to customers rather than to search the world for countries where labor and raw material costs are the lowest.

(3) Continuous shocks are coming from politics. Tensions between the U.S. and China, and the resulting increase in tariffs, have increased

the costs of products imported from the Asian giant. Moreover, Brexit has disrupted some supply chains that linked Great Britain and Western Europe, leading many multinational companies to reduce or close their businesses in Great Britain.

1.5 Supply Chain Management

Supply Chain Management (SCM) is considered: "an integrating philosophy to manage the total flow of a distribution channel from supplier to ultimate customer" (Ellram & Cooper, 1993).

Monczka and Morgan state that "integrated supply chain management is about going from the external customer and then managing all the processes that are needed to provide the customer with value in a horizontal way" (Monczka & Morgan, 1997). Lambert et al. define SCM as "the integration of business processes from end user through original suppliers that provides products, services, and information that add value for customers" (Lambert et al., 1998)[3].

A basic model for SCM is sometimes represented as Plan, Source, Make, Deliver and Return.

- **Plan.** "Supply chain planning (SCP) is the forward-looking process of coordinating assets to optimize the delivery of goods, services, and information from supplier to customer, balancing supply and demand" (Gartner Glossary, 2021).
- **Source.** The source function is procurement, the process of buying goods and services: (1) determining what is needed for manufacturing, from raw material to packaging; (2) selecting suppliers; (3) deciding whether and what to outsource from transport to warehousing.
- **Make.** Manufacturing of the product. The process that transforms raw materials, parts, and components into the finished product.
- **Deliver.** The processes that provide the final product to the customer, from distribution to warehousing to transport.

---

[3] There are other significant definitions that can be mentioned. According to Sherman (1998) SCM is the "dynamic process of managing the flow of material and information across distributed business processes for the purpose of profitably responding to and satisfying market demand". It is: "the coordination of activities, within and between vertically linked firms, for the purpose of serving end customers at a profit" (Larson & Rogers (1998); and "the delivery of enhanced customer and economic value through synchronized management of the flow of physical goods and associated information from sourcing to consumption" (LaLonde and Bernard, 1998).

- **Return.** The product can return to the manufacturer. Reverse logistics can be viewed as part of the supply chain process involving the business of returning, repairing, exchanging, refurbishing, or remarketing products. Return can occur for quality reasons, for recycling, or for postsales customer support (Gilchrist, 2019).

Representing the supply chain as consisting of several phases in sequence may seem static, but in reality, it is dynamic, since it reacts to changes in the environment. For example, management checks the level of stocks to assess the risk of being out of stock or accumulating excess inventory. To do this, it must follow the trend in demand and in the external factors that act on it (such as interruptions in transport) and react accordingly by modifying the stock volumes and/or its composition.

Many events have enhanced the importance of SCM as a way to maximize customer value and gain a competitive advantage over rivals in the marketplace. It is now regarded as a new way of managing the business and relationships with other members of the supply chain.

1.5.1 The evolution of SCM

The evolution of Supply Chain Management has been well-described by Lambert et al.: "One of the most significant paradigm shifts of modern business management is that individual businesses no longer compete as solely autonomous entities, but rather as supply chains. Business management has entered the era of Internet work competition. Instead of brand versus brand or store versus store, it is now suppliers-brand-store versus suppliers-brand-store, or supply chain versus supply chain" … "Strictly speaking, the supply chain is not a chain of businesses with one-to-one, business-to-business relationships, but a network of multiple businesses and relationships" (Lambert & Cooper, 2000).

Gilchrist summarizes in five phases the profound evolution SCM has undergone from the impetus of digital technologies (Gilchrist, 2019).

(1) "From a functional to a process perspective". The starting point for business management to build and manage a supply chain was based on the structure of the enterprise by functions, but today the SCM considers problems from the perspective of constantly evolving processes.

(2) "From an operational to a strategic viewpoint". In the early years, managers considered SCM as an operational tool to reduce costs and improve the efficiency of purchasing and of logistics. Gradually, however, their actions took on a strategic objective.

(3) "From a single enterprise to an extended one". The field of action of the supply chain today is by definition the extended enterprise. From the concept of competition among companies, we have gradually moved to that of competition among supply chains. In this way, management has been enriched by the contribution of ideas from several companies and not only those of the company of origin.

(4) "From transactional to relationship-based engagement". The relationships between suppliers and buyers were based in the past on transactions and economic analysis. Purchasing and procurement evaluated a transaction based on pricing, volumes, and delivery terms. Today these assessments have been accompanied by a "much wider consideration of knowledge exchange, long term commitment, incentives and rewards".

(5) "From local to regional, from regional to global". In recent decades, the links between the supply chains of companies have moved from a local to a regional scale, and for some companies to a global horizon, a trend driven by the search for lower labor and raw material costs. The pandemic, bottlenecks, and shortages in 2021−22 have slowed down this process, and many companies have switched to reshoring; however, the underlying tendency to broaden the geographical horizon of choices remains.

A meaningful example concerns Amazon's supply chain (Box 1.6).

According to Alicke et al. digitization is bringing about a Supply Chain 4.0, which will be faster, more flexible, more granular, more accurate, and more efficient (Alicke et al., 2016).

- **Faster,** because new product distribution approaches reduce the delivery time. Moreover, new technologies and their application provide a much more precise forecast of customer demand.
- **More flexible,** as real-time planning allows a flexible reaction to changing demand or supply situations. Planning becomes a continuous process that can react in an innovative manner to changing internal and external conditions. For example, once the products leave the factory, increased flexibility in the delivery processes allows companies to send shipments along a different route if a more convenient destination than that offered by the previous plan emerges.
- **More granular,** since customers' demand is becoming more detailed. Large segments are no longer beneficial. In many markets, companies must offer a much more granular set of products and a broad range of tailored products. In addition, in the last mile delivery companies have more than one option that precisely fits customers' needs.

Box 1.6 Amazon

Through new innovative technologies applied to Supply Chain Management, Amazon has changed retail distribution and left competitors trying to catch up. The innovative supply chain is one of the main factors in its rapid development. By using new technologies, Amazon has consistently anticipated competitors. Initially, its superiority was established by the introduction of 2-day delivery. When major competitors responded by mimicking Amazon and offering their own free 2-day shipping, Amazon revived the competition by offering another revolutionary solution: "a 1h delivery" with its Amazon Prime Now service.

Amazon's supply chain is considered among the most efficient among all the major companies in the world. The speed of deliveries is Amazon's main competitive advantage. The supply chain is based on the integration of advanced information technology, a wide network of warehouses distributed throughout the territory, efficient inventory management, and a first-rate transportation system. Through high economies of scale and efficient Supply Chain Management, Amazon has managed to significantly lower unit delivery costs, allowing it to compete with rivals who have lower sales volumes and a smaller network of warehouses (Leblanc, 2020).

- **More accurate,** since the new generation of technologies enhances "performance management systems that 'learn' to automatically identify risks or exceptions and will change supply chain parameters in a closed-loop learning approach to mitigate them". The integration of data from many sources ensures that all stakeholders drive from the 'control tower' and decide based on the same facts, which allows companies to be more correct in all details.

- **More efficient,** since automation and the ability to handle a broad spectrum of exceptions without human involvement boost efficiency. For example, robots handle the material automatically along the warehouse process and autonomous trucks can sense their environment and operate without human involvement in transporting the products within a precisely defined network.

1.5.2 SCM on a global scale

The global business environment is also evolving. The convergence of markets in countries toward the same set of similar products and services has been underway for some time. As a result, companies that have dominated and dominate regional markets (the U.S., Brazil, Russia, Western Europe, and others) tend to extend their commercial superiority to other areas as well. Some world markets are thus dominated by well-established global companies.

For these companies, national borders, with rare exceptions, are no longer a limit to the development of supply chains. We can find parts of the same supply chain for the same brand in Europe as well as in China, in an African country, or in Latin America. "The strength of globalization is that now everybody knows what everybody else is doing".

However, these global companies face some strategic challenges (Gilchrist, 2019).

(1) They must be able to integrate their supply chain all over the world (supply integration).

(2) They must be able to adapt products to the specific needs of different markets while maintaining first-class economies of scale. This means making the supply chain more capable of satisfying the divergent demand of the world market (divergent product portfolio).

(3) They must develop a competitive advantage for world excellence. To succeed as world-class companies, they must excel in four areas: (a) operational excellence; (b) strategic fit; (c) capability to adapt; (d) creating a unique voice for the supply chain (pursuing world excellence).

The COVID-19 pandemic is cited as the driving force by most executives and experts (Box 1.7).

These effects are developed extensively in Chapter 6 dedicated to globalization and in the concluding chapters.

1.5.3 The bullwhip effect

The supply chain must be able to react to the pressures of the external environment that threaten the coordination between the various phases. New

---

Box 1.7 COVID-19: the supply chain crisis

COVID-19 has further propelled a movement toward regionalization, and therefore a rethink on the globalization of many supply chains. "The supply chain crisis unleashed by the pandemic will inflict permanent damage on the globalization driven by multinationals", said a senior executive at UPS, one of the world's largest delivery companies (Dempsey, 2021).

Shifts in consumer demand, the passenger air transport crisis, and disruptions to global shipping have created "the deepest crisis in years for the supply chains of global companies". Many companies have realized that the longer (and more countries in) the supply chain, the greater the risks. As such, multinational retailers and manufacturers were making a 'big push' toward regionalizing their supply chains, said the senior executive. The range of sectors affected by the logistics crunch is increasing, with computer, furniture, and car makers struggling to source supplies quickly enough. Various factors are at play, but "most executives and experts cite the pandemic as the driving force".

Box 1.8 An example of the bullwhip effect

As a new season approaches, in one of the last links of the supply chain a retailer, due to a sudden change in demand, makes an adjustment in the orders of a given brand by increasing the units ordered from 10 to 30 per day. This propagates a wave (ripple effect) that step by step, from the wholesaler to production, reaches the raw materials orders at the other end of the supply chain. For example, the wholesaler receives an order of 30 from the retailer, glimpses a trend in the growth of final demand, and in order not to risk losing a further possible increase in demand might order 50 units from the manufacturer. This will further overstate the demand along the supply chain and so generate a second wave of demand increase.

For his part, the manufacturer, seeing the increase in demand from the wholesaler and fearing his final products may be out of stock, also reacts by increasing its manufacturing level to 80 units, thus generating a third wave in the amplification of demand. If the retailer loses sales because the manufacturer cannot deliver what is requested, he could change suppliers and shift to another brand (brand B), creating even more severe effects on the supply chain. The retailer would not repeat all or part of the orders from brand A (the original supplier), thereby creating excess stocks of this finished product and proving false the manufacturer's forecasts.

technologies are of great help in avoiding spikes and stabilizing the process, as evidenced by the progress made in attenuating the bullwhip effect (Box 1.8).

There are various techniques to mitigate or avert the bullwhip effect, including: (1) improving the exchange of information along the supply chain; (2) building up safety stocks to isolate the phases from each other; (3) reducing the batch size of the order and possibly increasing their frequency. All these measures lead to increased costs. More safety stock means more working capital investment and reducing the lot size means negatively affecting economies of scale in production and transportation[4].

---

[4] There is extensive literature on how to defend yourself against the bullwhip effect. What Sheffi (2022) wrote deserves mention here. "Although every disruption, whether volcano or virus, boom or bust, brings unique challenges, the fundamentals of preparing for and responding to disruptive conditions such as a recession remain the same. It entails understanding a company's specific supply chain vulnerabilities, determining what can be done about them beforehand, monitoring the situation for disruptions, and implementing countermeasures as needed". Sheffi proposes four steps: (1) identifying essential partners; (2) assessing partners' financial 'resilience'; (3) monitoring partners and the situation; (4) supporting threatened partners.

1.5.4 Giving efficiency and flexibility to the supply chain

Various measures can be adopted to give efficiency and flexibility to the supply chain. The most frequently used are: (1) 'lean supply chain', (2) 'just in time', (3) 'agile supply chain'.

(1) To be 'lean' stands for identifying and eliminating waste, cutting the costs of operations that do not add value, lessening and even culling 'dead times', and focusing on improving products and services based on what customers want and value.

(2) 'Just in time' (JIT) is a concept similar to lean management, but with some differences. JIT stands for organizing the production process so that it involves the supply of raw materials and components awaiting transformation exactly at the time when it is required by production in order to reduce the costs and risks associated with the accumulation of stocks. In JIT, production should be 'pulled through' rather than 'pushed through', which means producing only what is required by specific order, and thus not producing for warehouse stocks waiting to be processed or sold. The effects of the pandemic have convinced more companies to abandon this concept and switch to 'just-in-case'. The advantages and disadvantages of the two rules are discussed further in the paragraph on 'just-in-time' versus 'just-in-case' (see below in Chapter 9).

(3) Lean management has been particularly successful in areas where economies of scale, reliability, and reducing costs are priority objectives, in which the main driver is efficiency. Today, in many industries the primary objective is a fast response to demand variability, and the ability to move quickly. As Zara teaches, being able to give a quick response to a volatile customer-driven demand can be the main competitive advantage. Therefore, more 'agile supply chains' are needed.

References

Alicke, K., Rachor, J., & Seyfert, A. (October 27, 2016). *Supply chain 4.0: The next - generation digital supply chain*. McKinsey & Company. https://www.mckinsey.com/business-functions/operations/our-insights/supply-chain-40-the-next-generation-digital-supply-chain.

Banton, C. (November 30, 2021). *Network effect*. https://www.investopedia.com/terms/n/network-effect.asp#:~:text=The%20network%20effect%20is%20a,military%20and%20some%20research%20scientists.

Beamon, B. M. (1998). Supply chain design and analysis: Models and methods. *International Journal of Production Economics, 55*(3), 281–294. https://doi.org/10.1016/S0925-5273(98) 00079–6

Bigelow, S., & Rouse, M. (2021). *Platform definition*. https://searchservervirtualization.techtarget.com/definition/platform.

Bughin, J., Deakin, J., & Beirne, B. (2019). *Digital transformation: Improving the odds of success*. McKinsey Quarterly. https://www.mckinsey.com/business-functions/mckinsey-digital/our-insights/digital-transformation-improving-the-odds-of-success.

Carey, D., Charan, R., Lamarre, E., Smaje, K., & Zemmel, R. (2021). *The CEO's playbook for a successful digital transformation*. Harvard Business Review. https://hbr.org/2021/12/the-ceos-playbook-for-a-successful-digital-transformation.

Choudary, S. P., Alstyne, M. W. V., & Parker, G. G. (2019). *Platforms and blockchain will transform logistics*. Harvard Business Review. https://hbr.org/2019/06/platforms-and-blockchain-will-transform-logistics.

Christopher, M. (1998). Logistics and supply chain management: Strategies for reducing cost and improving service. In *Financial times* (2° Edition). Pitman Publishing.

Clark, K., & Fujimoto, T. (1991). *Product development performance*. Harvard Business School Press.

Cooper, M. C., & Ellram, L. M. (1993). Characteristics of supply chain management and the implication for purchasing and logistics strategy. *The International Journal of Logistics Management, 4*(2), 13−24. https://doi.org/10.1108/09574099310804957

Cusumano, M., Gawer, A., & Yoffie, D. (2019). *Business of platforms*. Harper Business.

Dempsey, H. (2021). UPS warns of lasting scar on supply chains. *Financial Times*. https://www.ft.com/content/6c127633-9825-4921-9a11-71518591e2f3.

Ellram, L., & Cooper, M. (1993). Characteristics of supply chain management and the implications for purchasing and logistics strategy. *International Journal of Logistics Management, 4*(2), 1−10.

Furr, N., Shipilov, A., Rouillard, D., & Hemon-Laurens, D. (2022). *The 4 pillars of successful digital transformations*. Harvard Business Review. https://hbr.org/2022/01/the-4-pillars-of-successful-digital-transformations#:~:text=The%20framework%20outlines%20the%20four,most%20companies%20digital%20transformation%20journey.

Gartner Glossary. (2021). *Gartner® magic QuadrantTM for multienterprise supply chain business networks*. https://www.gartner.com.

GEP. (2021). *How disruption accelerated digital supply chain transformation*. Harvard Business Review. https://hbr.org/sponsored/2021/08/how-disruption-accelerated-digital-supply-chain-transformation.

Gilchrist, A. (2019). *Supply chain 4.0. Fueled by industry 4.0*. Copyright Alasdair.

Karandikar, H., & Nidamarthi, S. (2007). Implementing a platform strategy for a systems business via standardization. *Journal of Manufacturing Technology Management, 18*(3), 267−280. https://doi.org/10.1108/17410380710730602

Lambert, D. M., & Cooper, M. C. (2000). Supply chain management: Implementation issues and research opportunities. *Industrial Marketing Management, 29*(1), 65−83. https://doi.org/10.1016/S0019-8501(99) 00113−3

Lambert, D., Stock, J. R., & Ellram, L. M. (1998). *Fundamentals of logistics management*. Irwin/McGraw-Hill.

Leblanc, R. (2020). *How Amazon is changing supply chain management*. https://www.thebalancesmb.com/how-amazon-is-changing-supply-chain-management-4155324.

Londe, La, B. J., & Masters, J. M. (1994). Emerging logistics strategies: Blueprints for the next century. *International Journal of Physical Distribution & Logistics Management, 24*(7), 35−47. https://doi.org/10.1108/09600039410070975

Lummus, R. R., & Vokurka, R. J. (1999). Defining supply chain management: A historical perspective and practical guidelines. *Industrial Management and Data Systems, 99*(1), 11−17. https://doi.org/10.1108/02635579910243851

Monczka, R. M., & Morgan, J. (1997). What's wrong with supply chain management? *Purchasing, 122*(1), 69−73.

Moss, T. (2021). *Lego builds on its position as world's No. 1 toy maker.* https://www.wsj.com/articles/lego-builds-on-its-position-as-worlds-no-1-toy-maker-11632843755?mod=itp_wsj.

Mueller, B., & Lauterbach, J. (2021). *How to speed up your digital transformation.* Harvard Business Review. https://hbr.org/2021/08/how-to-speed-up-your-digital-transformation.

Muffatto, M. (1999). Introducing a platform strategy in product development. *International Journal of Production Economics, 60,* 145–153. https://doi.org/10.1016/S0925-5273(98)00173-X

Parker, G., Alstyne, V., & Choudary, S. (2017). *Platform revolution.* Norton.

Perkin, N., & Abraham, P. (2017). *Building the agile business through digital transformation.* Kogan Page.

Quinn, F. J. (1997). What's the buzz? *Logistics Management, 36*(2), 43–47.

Robertson, D., & Ulrich, K. (1998). Planning for product platforms. *MIT Sloan Management Review, 39*(4), 19–31.

Rogers, D. (2016). *The digital transformation playbook.* Columbia Business School Publishing.

Simchi-Levi, D., & Timmermans, K. (2021). *A simpler way to modernize your supply chain.* Harvard Business Review. https://hbr.org/2021/09/a-simpler-way-to-modernize-your-supply-chain.

Smith, M. (2021). *Lessons from Hollywood's digital transformation.* Harvard Business Review. https://hbr.org/2021/12/lessons-from-hollywoods-digital-transformation.

Spulber, D. F. (2008). Consumer coordination in the small and in the large: Implications for antitrust in markets with network effects. *Journal of Competition Law and Economics, 4*(2), 207–262. https://doi.org/10.1093/joclec/nhm031

Subramaniam, M. (2021). *The 4 tiers of digital transformation.* Harvard Business Review. https://hbr.org/2021/09/the-4-tiers-of-digital-transformation.

The Economist. (2019). *Digitisation is helping to deliver goods faster.* https://www.economist.com/special-report/2019/07/11/digitisation-is-helping-to-deliver-goods-faster.

Vaitheeswaran, V. (2019). *Supply chains are undergoing a dramatic transformation.* The Economist. https://www.economist.com/special-report/2019/07/11/supply-chains-are-undergoing-a-dramatic-transformation.

Valentine, M. (January 15, 2021). *BMW invests 'hundreds of millions' in digital transformation.* MarketingWeek, 15 January https://www.marketingweek.com/bmw-invests-hundreds-of-millions-in-digital-transformation/.

Wilhelm, B. (1997). *Platform and Modular Concepts at Volkswagen - Their Effects on the Assembly Process,* 146–156. https://doi.org/10.1007/978-3-642-60374-7_12

Digital technology solutions for managing the supply chain

CHAPTER TWO

A long road to maximizing efficiency

2.1 The Digital Supply Network (DSN)

While recently the foundations of the competition were in supply chains built on linear sequences, today in digital markets they are built on interconnected open systems through, which companies compete. "The digital supply chain is a new media term which encompasses the process of the delivery of digital media, be it music or video, by electronic means, from the point of origin (content provider) to destination (consumer)" (Wikipedia, 2022).

Disruptive technologies, including new sensors and Artificial Intelligence, create the foundation for conversion between the physical and digital worlds, transforming traditional linear supply chains into digital supply networks (DSN) that are connected, intelligent, and have the power to be resized or scaled, can be modified to suit a particular individual or task, and are agile. DSN refers to an interconnected, open web of relationships that collect and integrate "information from many different sources and locations to drive the physical act of production and distribution" (Mussomeli et al., 2016).

2.2 A digital thread

As Deloitte clearly explains "Digital supply networks establish a 'digital thread' through physical and digital channels, connecting information, goods, and services in powerful ways" (Deloitte, 2022).

There are three steps in this connection, commonly known as the 'physical-to-digital-to-physical loop' (Mussomeli et al., 2016).

- **Physical to digital**: This loop captures signals and data from the physical world to create a digital record. Basic transactions that occur in any enterprise are digitally captured. Data is collected into a central location in which it is stored and processed to create a digital fingerprint of the physical environment and made ready for analytics.

The Digital Transformation of Supply Chain Management
ISBN: 978-0-323-85532-7
https://doi.org/10.1016/B978-0-323-85532-7.00009-8
37

- **Digital to digital**: This is a rapidly changing space accessible to companies now more than ever before. The goal is to exchange and enrich information using new technology-enabled capabilities such as Advanced Analytics, Artificial Intelligence, and Machine Learning to drive meaningful insights.
- **Digital to physical**: Here the information is delivered in automated and more effective ways to generate actions and changes in the physical world. Therefore, staff that manages operation processes can advance from passive dashboards to action guided in real-time by business decisions.

"Supply chains traditionally are linear, with a discrete progression of design, plan, source, make and deliver. Today, however, many supply chains are transforming from a staid sequence to a dynamic, interconnected system" (Parrott et al., 2020). This shift could lay the foundation for how companies compete in the future.

Far from a traditional supply chain model, digital supply networks are dynamic, integrated, and distinguished by a continuous flow of information resulting from the systematic analysis of data or statistics. Many organizations are committed to embracing DSN, moving away from managing and optimizing unconnected distinct parts from procurement to manufacturing, and logistics to distribution.

2.3 The rise of industry 4.0 and the DSN

In recent years, the emergence of Industry 4.0 and Digital Supply Networks (DSN) has radically changed the competitive ecosystem driven mainly by four elements: (1) cloud computing, which has delivered lower computing costs; (2) cheaper storage; (3) ubiquitous network access since computing facilities can be accessed from anywhere over the network; and (4) the Internet of Things (IoT), which has accelerated full-scale process automation.

The availability of digital technologies has lowered costs, reduced capital needs, allowed companies to invest less for the same results, and at the same time benefit on a broad scale.

The confluence of those technologies has led to the combination of information technology (IT) and operation technology (OT). The merger of IT and OT has brought the real world - sensors, machines, and processes - into convergence with the virtual world of advanced data analytics and process control. The ability to process a large mass of data in real-time has laid the foundations for the era of Industry 4.0, and the two worlds have evolved differently due to their different characteristics. While OT is machine- and process-oriented, IT is human-on-demand oriented. In practice, the latter might be considered the opposite of the former.

2.4 Impacts of technology disruption

In recent years, increasing computing power and lower costs have generated substantial technological and digital developments that have made an impact on the traditional supply chain in several important ways, among which: reduction in transaction costs, strong innovation in production, and the shift from linear to dynamic networks.

(1) Reducing transaction costs. The integrated process of design-execution-production and handling has remained virtually the same, but sensor systems and other technologies now provide real-time information about the situation at the various nodes along the supply chain, which, in addition to ensuring greater security regarding the control of times and flows, increases efficiency and therefore lowers production costs.

(2) Innovation in production. Innovation is driven by advances in technology. One of the most obvious advances is the greater flexibility in production processes, which has reduced the need for capital by lowering the minimum efficient scale and making it more convenient to decentralize the stages of production by bringing them closer to the final markets. Lowered barriers have also favored the birth and entry into the market of new lean and nimble companies that are reevaluating the criteria to optimize their supply chain and developing new ways to deliver more value.

(3) The shift from linear to dynamic networks. In traditional supply chains, each phase is linked to the previous one. As a result, inefficiencies in even one of these can transmit negative effects to subsequent ones. The more branched the supply chain, the more difficult it is to be informed in a timely manner about deviations from what was planned. In fact, the flow of information is linear, flowing from each phase to the next, therefore management has limited control capabilities.

This interconnected, open system is called a digital supply network (DSN). DSNs integrate information from many different sources and locations to drive the physical act of production and distribution. The result can be a virtual world, which mirrors and informs the physical world (Sinha et al., 2020).

For example, since the DSN is 'continuously accessible', sensors and other tools can continuously transmit data to provide integrated analyses of the supply chain with little to no latency. In a network, latency measures the time it takes for data to get to its destination across the network. It is usually measured as a round trip delay, the time taken for information to get to its destination and back again (Box 2.1).

2.5 The DSN capabilities

To manage the most advanced DSN models, according to Deloitte (Sinha et al., 2020) a company must have six main capabilities, which can be summarized as follows (Table 2.1).

According to the Authors, the main reasons for adopting digital transformation in a DSN context are based on four factors: customer expectation, efficiency, revenue, and stakeholder expectations.

Customer expectations are constantly changing. Therefore, firms must be able to constantly reinvent themselves. There are many companies that recently have not been able to reinvent themselves in the transition phases, from Nokia to Blockbuster to Kodak. The Authors state that: "The first

Box 2.1 The need to reduce latency

A large retail company also sells products (such as sun lotion and ice cream) whose demand depends significantly on weather trends. The aim is to adapt stocks as quickly as possible to actual needs while minimizing capital investment and unsold risks. In traditional systems, the adjustment of stocks in the event of a change in demand forecasts inevitably occurs with a certain latency (involving the point of sale, logistics, and the procurement chain). In a network, latency measures the time it takes for data to get to its destination across the network.

Suppose that the forecasts are not respected and the weather is going to get worse. The retailer reduces latency by feeding the new weather data into its Predictive Analytics model (being part of a smart DSN) to forecast the demand for weather-dependent products. The smart DSN "automatically adjust inventory and supply orders in advance on a store-by-store basis" to minimize the effects of missed revenue (Gilchrist, 2018).

Table 2.1 How to enhance DSN capabilities.

DSN capabilities	How to enhance capabilities
Digital development	Optimize product lifecycle management with advanced digital tactics. This reduces R&D expenses and product maintenance costs and increases manufacturing flexibility. Reduction in manual intervention results in fewer errors, delays, and inefficiencies.
Synchronized planning	Provide significant efficiencies through synchronization. This aligns strategic business objectives with financial goals and operational plans, thus helping to effectively anticipate customer demand and optimize inventory.
Intelligent supply	Reduce costs through new advanced technology models and capabilities. By adopting advanced electronic platforms, companies can more effectively collaborate with strategic partners and improve the customer and supplier experience.
Smart factory	Unlock new efficiencies by a more connected, agile, and proactive factory. Sensor data, image recognition, and collaborative robots can optimize the overall production efficiency, which involves a proactive approach to maintenance that helps in making informed trade-off decisions to identify opportunities.
Dynamic fulfillment	Boost customer service through new levels of speed and agility. This is a capability that enables companies to deliver the right product to the right customer at the right time, enhancing customer experience. It utilizes new technologies to provide real-time visibility and improve responsiveness.
Connected customers	Create seamless customer engagement from inspiration to service, allowing companies to move from traditional transaction-based relationships to seamless customer engagement throughout the entire customer lifecycle, permitting the identification of customer consumption patterns.

reason you should care is because your customers care, and there is no business without customers!"

The second factor is efficiency. The company's goal is to create value for customers and other stakeholders. Companies aim to achieve this through operating processes. Therefore, it is natural that they have the goal of maximizing the efficiency of these processes, which means better use of inputs to create value. For a long time, businesses have harnessed the benefits of the trade-off between economies of scale and scope to create efficiency. As a rule, to increase economies of scale they had to decrease the economies of scope or variability.

In the digital age, the trade-off between scale and scope is approached in a radically different way than in the past, having today become much less relevant since the return on the scale can continue to climb to unprecedented levels the more production increases.

The third factor concerns revenue growth. Adopting new digital technologies has a substantial effect on the pace of revenue growth. Agile supply networks capable of providing customers with products and services can reach a large customer base, thus multiplying the value of the network and consequently magnifying revenues. The use of platforms has been decisive, the most famous example being Amazon, which is capable of aggregating buyers and sellers on the same platform.

Stakeholders' expectations are the fourth factor. Platforms facilitate collaboration in networks, which in turn generates value in meaningful ways. In addition to serving the customer, the network creates a positive impact on other stakeholders in the company. The digital transformation adds value to employees (improving the efficiency of their work and freeing them from repetitive operations) partners (using a connected ecosystem), and to society (empowering the optimal use of resources).

2.6 Industry 4.0 or The Fourth Industrial Revolution

Industry 4.0 refers to the transformation of industry through the intelligent networking of machines and processes with the help of information and communication technology (ICT). The term is used interchangeably with the Fourth Industrial Revolution.

The First Industrial Revolution was driven by mechanization through water and steam power and the Second was by the electricity used for mass production and assembly lines in modern factories. Industry 3.0 was the Third Revolution, a period disrupted by the introduction of two new technologies: the computer and automation.

Where the Third Industrial Revolution focused on switching mechanical and analog processes to digital ones, the Fourth Industrial Revolution focuses on deepening the impact of our digital technologies by making our machines more self-

sufficient, able to 'talk' to one another, and to consider massive amounts of data in ways that humans simply can't - all in the name of efficiency and growth.

Immerman (2020).

2.6.1 A radical shift

The Fourth Industrial Revolution, widely known as Industry 4.0, involves a radical shift in how production shop floors currently operate and has many impacts on the supply chain. It is driven by technologies such as Cloud computing, Big Data, the Internet of Things, Blockchain, Robotics, 3D printing, Autonomous Vehicles, Artificial Intelligence (AI), Co-Creation, and the Digital Value Chain (DVC). The main technologies will be treated in depth in Chapter 5.

The basic concept behind Industry 4.0 was born in the early years of the 21st century in Germany from an initiative backed by the government[1]. Industry 4.0 is one of the major trending topics in both the professional and academic fields (Liao et al., 2017), and the effective implementation of Industry 4.0 technologies is still a subject of research (Babiceanu & Seker, 2016; Dalenogare et al., 2018; Lee et al., 2015).

Industry 4.0 is defined as: "a system that gathers and analyzes data from the floor to make intelligent decisions in an automated manner" (Ahuett-Garza & Kurfess, 2018).

The intended aim of Industry 4.0 is to enable the delivery of greater customer value through customized solutions using fewer resources.

Christopher (2021).

Industry 4.0 has been inserted into a changing configuration of customer demand characterized by growing demand for customized solutions both in business-to-consumer (B2C) and business-to-business (B2B) markets. The change was gradual but profound. From targets of homogeneous markets, we have moved to heterogeneous markets that have posed serious challenges

---

[1] The term was introduced by German scientists at the Hannover Messe (2011) with the aim of sensitizing the public and policymakers to a new high-tech strategy. In 2013, the Acatech (National Academy of Science and Engineering), a working group set up in Germany, presented its final report to the public: "Recommendations for implementing the strategic initiative INDUSTRIE 4.0" (Kagermann et al., 2013). Within a few years, other European countries followed this initiative, and some examples of the documents drafted are: "Piano Nazionale di Industria 4.0" in Italy (MISE, 2017), "Smart Industry - a strategy for new industrialization for Sweden" in Sweden (Government Offices of Sweden, 2016), "Industrie 4.0 Österreich" in Austria (Verein Industrie 4.0 Österreich, 2014), and "Industria Conectada 4.0" in Spain (Gobierno de España, 2017).

to logistics and distribution. From the concepts of economies of scale, large volumes to reduce unit costs, large batch sizes, and of maximum utilization of capacity, we have shifted to the concepts of economies of scope, customized products, and 'batch size of one'.

Industry 4.0 has contributed to significant advances in various fields, helping to increase safety at work, efficiency in production, and predictive ability. Industry 4.0 has required companies in many industries to redesign their supply chain. Several technologies have changed the way of working. One of the biggest advantages for manufacturers is that Industry 4.0 technologies help to break down data silos, thereby bridging the gap between what were once separate processes to create a more transparent, visible view across the entire organization.

It is important to point out that it "has created new opportunities and vulnerabilities that must be managed and governed to positively impact both business and society" (Büchi et al., 2020).

Industry 4.0 covers the entire supply chain and creates value at various stages. Value creation manifests itself in various ways from greater efficiency to better quality, from driving innovation to operational flexibility. Careful implementation of all this can result in lower costs.

2.7 Industry 4.0 technologies: the main categorizations in the literature

Recently, many research studies have identified different categorizations related to 4.0 technologies, which are also used as a basis for many national Industry 4.0 programs. Among the first and most cited is the Boston Consulting Group report: "Industry 4.0: The future of productivity and growth in manufacturing industries" (Rüßmann et al., 2015), which identifies the technologies that, more than others, are transforming industrial production (Table 2.2): (1) Big Data and Analytics, (2) Autonomous Robots, (3) Simulation, (4) Horizontal and Vertical System Integration, (5) The Industrial Internet of Things, (6) Cybersecurity, (7) The Cloud, (8) Additive Manufacturing, and (9) Augmented Reality. According to the Authors, even if many of these nine pillars of technological advancement are already used in manufacturing, "with Industry 4.0, they will transform production: isolated, optimized cells will come together as a fully integrated, automated, and optimized production flow, leading to greater efficiencies and changing traditional production relationships among suppliers, producers, and customers- as well as between human and machine" (Rüßmann et al., 2015).

Table 2.2 The nine pillars of technological advancement.

The nine pillars	Their main application in industry 4.0
(1) Big Data and Analytics	Analytics based on large data sets, thanks to the collection and evaluation of data from different sources (e.g., production equipment and systems, enterprise and customer management systems), allows companies to optimize the quality of production, save energy, and improve equipment service, and will emerge as a standard to support real-time decision making.
(2) Autonomous Robots	Robots are evolving, becoming more autonomous, flexible, and cooperative. They will be able to interact autonomously with each other and with humans and will have greater capabilities, at the same time becoming more affordable than present-day robots.
(3) Simulation	The 3D simulations of products, materials, and production processes will be increasingly used in manufacturing in the future. The simulations will in fact be able to exploit the data in real-time to reflect the physical world in a virtual model, reducing the setup time of machines and increasing the quality of products.
(4) Horizontal and Vertical System Integration	The universal data integration networks between and within companies are evolving (e.g., across business functions or in the case of engineering itself: from products to plants to automation). They will lead to truly automated value chains and also allow companies, suppliers, and customers to be more strongly connected.
(5) The Industrial Internet of Things	Thanks to the Internet of Things, sensors and machines will be enriched with embedded computing and connected using standard technologies. This will allow field devices to communicate and interact with each other and with more centralized controllers, and enable them when needed to respond in real-time, thereby decentralizing analysis and decision-making.
(6) Cybersecurity	The ongoing requirement to protect critical industrial systems and production lines from cybersecurity threats is currently a relevant issue due to the increase in connectivity and the use of standard communication protocols. Industry

(Continued)

Table 2.2 The nine pillars of technological advancement.—cont'd

The nine pillars	Their main application in industry 4.0
	4.0 will enable more secure and reliable communications, sophisticated identity management, and machine and user access control.
(7) The Cloud	To increase data sharing across sites and company boundaries, manufacturing companies will require increasingly advanced cloud-based software and analytics applications. Thanks to Industry 4.0, machine data and functionality will be increasingly distributed in the cloud, enabling more data-driven services for manufacturing and control systems.
(8) Additive Manufacturing	Thanks to Industry 4.0, companies will be able to use increasingly specialized, high-performance, and decentralized AdditiveManufacturing systems, such as 3D printing, enabling them to produce small batches of customized products that will offer construction advantages: for example, complex, lightweight designs, and reduce transportation distances and warehouse inventories.
(9) Augmented Reality	In the future, augmented reality-based systems that support a variety of important services, such as selecting parts in a warehouse and sending repair instructions to mobile devices, will be increasingly in demand by companies. The development of this technology will enable real-time information useful in improving decision-making and work procedures.

A very detailed study by Mc Kinsey (2015) titled: "Industry 4.0 - How to navigate digitization of the manufacturing sector", identified the key enabling technologies related to the manufacturing value chain (McKinsey & Company, 2015). They are accelerating through different drivers, which can be categorized into four clusters as follows (Table 2.3).

In the study titled: "Industry 4.0+: The Next Level of Intelligent and Self-optimizing Factories", Rauch identifies the two levels of Industry 4.0 (Rauch, 2020).

Table 2.3 The key enabling technologies.

---

(1) Data, computational power, and connectivity:
  * Big Data/Open Data
  * Internet of Things/Machine-to-Machine (M2M)
  * Cloud technology
(2) Analytics and intelligence:
  * Digitization and automation of knowledge work
  * Advanced Analytics
(3) Human-machine interaction:
  * Touch interfaces and next level Graphical User Interfaces (GUIs)
  * Virtual and Augmented Reality
(4) Digital-to-physical conversion:
  * Additive Manufacturing (i.e., 3D printing)
  * Advanced Robotics (e.g., human-robot collaboration)
  * Energy storage and harvesting

---

* **'Technology-Driven Innovation'**. The first level of I4.0 is primarily technology-driven and is the foundation for the second level. The main technologies are essentially the same as those proposed by the Boston Consulting Group (Rüßmann et al., 2015), explained in this sequence: (1) Autonomous Robots, (2) Additive Manufacturing, (3) Virtual and Augmented Reality (VR/AR), (4) Simulation, (5) Horizontal and Vertical Integration, (6) Industrial Internet of Things, (7) Cybersecurity, (8) The Cloud, and (9) Big Data and Analytics. "All these technologies have fundamentally contributed to the creation, storage, protection, exchange, processing, 'simple' analysis and visualization of information or data, as well as to give people in the manufacturing system the opportunity to interact with the virtual world" (Rauch, 2020). They are a prerequisite for advancing to the second level.

* **'Data and Intelligence-Driven Innovation'**. The second level of Industry 4.0 will be more focused on data and intelligence. This stage, also called I4.0 +, is intelligence-driven because it incorporates Artificial Intelligence (AI).

Recently, intelligent manufacturing systems and self-optimizers have been developed, using nature as a source of inspiration in addition to advances in Artificial Intelligence (AI), including Machine Learning (ML) and Deep Learning (DL). These terms are differentiated inside the Artificial Intelligence field: Machine Learning is a subset of Artificial Intelligence and Deep Learning is a subset of Machine Learning.

Artificial Intelligence in manufacturing might have many applications in different domains, such as in supply chain management as well as in automated or assisted engineering design, manufacturing system reconfiguration, production planning, predictive maintenance, and quality inspection, which might lead to the creation of future intelligent and self-optimizing factories.

AI would enable manufacturing systems to become more resilient, and therefore self-aware, self-comparing, self-predicting, and self-optimizing (Lee et al., 2015).

It would be capable of being used to improve data to develop autonomous intelligence and biological transformations to learn from nature how to solve complex problems and intelligently adapt principles from nature to various fields, such as manufacturing (Rauch, 2020).

The biological transformation can be seen as a parallel process to digital transformation (van Brussel & Valckenaers, 2017), and it can be transferred over three levels to industrial production: (1) Bio-inspired manufacturing, entailing the imitation or transfer of phenomena from nature to complex technical problems; (2) Bio-integrated manufacturing, involving the integration of technological and biological processes into industrial value-added processes; and (3) Bio-intelligent manufacturing: the combination of technical, informatics, and biological systems to create robust and self-sufficient value creation systems (Rauch, 2020).

These two different levels and the main technologies can be summarized as follows (Table 2.4).

According to some other researchers (Agrawal et al., 2020), Industry 4.0 is characterized by four foundational technologies applied along the value chain, which can be summarized as follows (Table 2.5).

In the literature, a different domain emerges from the categorization of technologies as Industry 4.0 by researchers, which can be divided into two main groups: (1) Data Management technologies, which focus on the ability

Table 2.4 The levels of Industry 4.0.

The two levels	Main technologies
Technology-Driven Innovation	(1) Autonomous Robots; (2) Additive Manufacturing; (3) Virtual and Augmented Reality (VR/AR); (4) Simulation; (5) Horizontal and Vertical Integration; (6) Industrial Internet of Things; (7) Cybersecurity; (8) The Cloud; (9) Big Data and Analytics
Data and Intelligence-Driven Innovation (I4.0+)	Artificial Intelligence (AI), including Machine Learning (ML) and Deep Learning (DL), might lead to the creation of future intelligent and self-optimizing factories. AI would be capable of learning from nature how to solve complex problems and intelligently adapt principles from nature to various fields; for instance, the biological transformation can be transferred in three levels to industrial production: **(1)** Bio-inspired manufacturing; **(2)** Bio-integrated manufacturing; **(3)** Bio-intelligent manufacturing.

Table 2.5 The foundational technologies applied along the value chain.

The four foundational technologies	The technologies applied
(1) Connectivity, data, computational power	• Sensors • Internet of Things • Cloud technology • Blockchain
(2) Analytics and intelligence	• Advanced Analytics • Machine Learning • Artificial Intelligence
(3) Human-machine interaction	• Virtual and Augmented Reality • Robotics and automation (collaborative robots, Autonomous Guided Vehicles - AGVs) • Robotic Process Automation - RPA, chatbots
(4) Advanced engineering	• Additive Manufacturing (e.g. 3D printing) • Renewable energy • Nanoparticles

to manage and analyze large quantities of data, and (2) Cyber-Physical Systems (CPS), which focus on the combination of hardware and software to automate manual processes (Kim et al., 2018). In this perspective, the application of Industry 4.0 in manufacturing companies consists mainly of the technical integration of Cyber-Physical Systems into production processes and the use of the Internet of Things and services in industrial processes (Kagermann et al., 2013; Pereira & Romero, 2017), where intelligent objects constantly communicate and interact with each other. The technological advancements, particularly the advent of the Internet of Things (IoT), Cloud services, Big Data, and Analytics, enable the creation of these kinds of systems.

Cyber-Physical Systems are based on the interaction between the physical and virtual environments and, operating as 'processing systems', are defined as 'intelligent central control units' (Fatorachian & Kazemi, 2018). CPS allows machines and devices to autonomously exchange information and oerate and control each other; more precisely, they integrate, control, and coordinate processes and operations, while simultaneously providing and utilizing data access and processing.

Smart objects communication embedded with sensors or actuators, in cybernetic physical environments, and their interconnectivity is enabled by the application of the Internet of Things, where Internet operates as a connectivity center for smart devices, machines, and systems.

The integration of CPS with the manufacturing environment will enable interconnection along the entire supply chain, potentially transforming today's manufacturing factories into completely innovative Industry 4.0 factories.

The notion of Cloud supply chain introduced by Ivanov et al. (2022) integrates concepts and technology of Industry 4.0 and digital operations emerging in the 'supply chain-as-a-service' (Fig. 2.1). "Cloud supply chain combines all the operational processes (e.g., logistics, warehousing, manufacturing, procurement, sales, and returns), all the supply chain flows (i.e., material, informational and financial), and all the supply chain actors (i.e., suppliers, manufacturers, distributors, and customers) within digital platforms and ecosystems" (Ivanov et al., 2022).

2.8 Progress made possible by Industry 4.0

Some examples of the major advances in supply chain management made possible by Industry 4.0 are as follows.

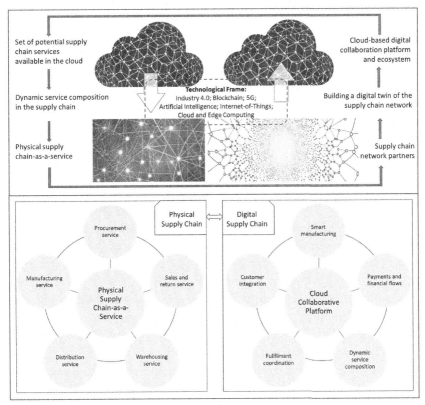

Figure 2.1 *Cloud supply chain framework.* The Figure illustrates the cloud supply chain framework emerging in the 'supply chain-as-a-service'. *From Ivanov, D., Dolgui, A. & Sokolov, B. (2022). Cloud supply chain: Integrating Industry 4.0 and digital platforms in the "Supply Chain-as-a-Service."* Transportation Research Part E: Logistics and Transportation Review, 160, 1−11. https://doi.org/10.1016/j.tre.2022.102676.

- **Identify opportunities.** The large mass of data made available by Industry 4.0 is analyzed by connected machines to identify patterns and insights in a way that would be impossible for a human to do in a reasonable time frame. Industry 4.0 gives manufacturers greater ability to identify what deserves the most attention.
- **Enhance logistics and supply chains.** A connected supply chain can elaborate data and adjust planned operations to new conditions. If a sudden change in weather delays a shipment, a connected system can take action to control the situation rather than just respond to it after it has occurred and adjust to the new reality by modifying manufacturing sequences.

- **Autonomous equipment and vehicles.** In the mining industry, for example, the use of autonomous cranes and trucks to transport raw materials streamlines operations and increases productivity.
- **Robotics.** Autonomous Robots can quickly and safely support manufacturers, handling products in a warehouse or optimizing any production process that could prove overly dangerous or repetitive for workers. They can also reduce costs and allow better use of floor space. Once used only by companies with large budgets, today they are within reach of even smaller companies.
- **Additive Manufacturing (AM).** Greater design freedom, with little or no added cost and less waste overall, are the advantages of Additive Manufacturing. This technology, by creating objects layer by layer, has made considerable progress. Once used to build prototypes, it has now entered actual production. It is reasonable to predict that Additive Manufacturing will serve as a complement to traditional manufacturing (), rather than as a substitute. Over time, AM will likely continue to close the gap with traditional manufacturing and expand its influence on the global manufacturing industry, creating a gap in economic advantage between Traditional and Additive Manufacturing. According to Gupta and Taufik in order to "facilitate part production decisions, the key qualities of a part from a manufacturing aspect are complexity, customization and production volume" (Gupta & Taufik, 2022). The Figure illustrates an example where the cost per part is compared with the complexity of the part for traditional manufacturing and Additive Manufacturing. From this perspective, it is evident that if the complexity level is above the break-even point, it will be cost-effective to build the part with manufacturing (Fig. 2.2).
- **Big Data and Analytics.** Big data are wide and complex data sets, especially from new data sources. They are marked by great volumes that traditional data processing software packages just cannot manage. With modern machines, it is a fully different approach. Using up-to-date advanced computing capabilities, those huge streams of data can be transformed into accurate, useful information that can drive decision-making for manufacturing management. The higher quantity of data used in a proper and intelligent way, the greater the level of effectiveness. A significant example of Big Data and Analytics in Manufacturing concerns Predictive Manufacturing (Box 2.2).
- **Augmented Reality.** Augmented Reality (AR) applications are increasingly providing solutions to a multitude of robotic applications,

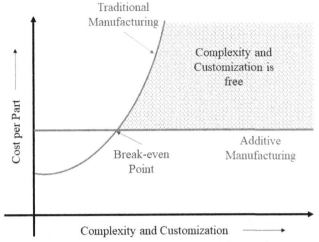

Figure 2.2 *Comparison of costs for traditional manufacturing and AM process.* The Figure illustrates an example where the cost per part is compared with the complexity of the part for traditional manufacturing and Additive Manufacturing. *From Gupta, A. K. & Taufik, M. (2022). The effect of process parameters in material extrusion processes on the part surface quality: A review.* Materials Today: Proceedings, 50(5), 1234–1242. https://doi.org/10.1016/j.matpr.2021.08.110.

including demystifying robot motion intent and enabling intuitive control and feedback (Bassyouni & Elhajj, 2021)[2].

A good example concerns Augmented Reality in Manufacturing (Box 2.3).

- **Blockchain.** "Blockchain is a system of recording information in a way that makes it difficult or impossible to change, hack, or cheat system. A blockchain is essentially a digital ledger of transactions that is duplicated and distributed across the entire network of computer systems on the blockchain. Each block in the chain contains a number of transactions, and every time a new transaction occurs on the blockchain, a record of that transaction is added to every participant's ledger" (Monroe, 2021).

---

[2] "Augmented reality (AR) is an interactive experience of a real-world environment where the objects that reside in the real world are enhanced by computer-generated perceptual information, sometimes across multiple sensory modalities" (Wikipedia, 2022). Augmented reality includes extra sensory input, usually visual, overlaid upon the actual world. Common examples include Google Glass and the game Pokémon Go.

Box 2.2 An example of Big Data and Analytics in Manufacturing: Predictive Manufacturing

"Imagine this: There's a shop floor somewhere in Wisconsin that has a small sensor (an industrial IoT sensor which we'll cover in greater depth momentarily) connected to each and every machine in that factory. That sensor is constantly logging and analyzing information both at the sensor site as well as in the Cloud. All the data from this little IoT sensor, including information like how much the machine has been used, is collected and fed into a machine learning algorithm". "That algorithm, or formula, spits out results regarding that equipment's maintenance schedule. It says, 'This machine's belt is likely to break in 2–3 weeks.' With that in mind, maintenance is scheduled in 'off' hours within a week and the machine maintains operational effectiveness during all working hours. That's called 'predictive maintenance' and it wouldn't work at all without big data. Big data helps this factory care for its assets, reduce costs, and limit the risk of downtime" (Immerman, 2020).

Box 2.3 An example of Augmented Reality in Manufacturing

In manufacturing, Augmented Reality can be used for worker training and maintenance alike. New employees can learn how to use machinery that could be dangerous in a safe, virtualized environment before entering the factory floor. AR can also be beneficial during maintenance tasks by offering tooltips, repair manuals, and other notations to become readily visible on-site, within the technician's field of vision. Augmented Reality also allows technicians to see inside dangerous and complicated machinery before they open it up, so they know exactly what they're looking for and what to do before they start (Ong et al., 2008).

2.8.1 What is blockchain? How does it help the supply chain?

The implications that blockchain has for a supply chain business have been widely discussed in recent years. Some relevant comments are provided by Walker as follows (Walker, 2021).

One of the main features of this technology is that buyers will have transparent access to key information across the tiers of the supply chain "without compromising the trade secrets of individual companies within it". Not everyone finds contemporary blockchain systems attractive. For someone, they might even represent a threat. Walker clears away many of the doubts and explains how blockchain technology will have a positive impact on the supply chain.

What is blockchain? There is some confusion about the word blockchain and what it means. For the Author, the word blockchain "refers to all platforms, whether public or private, that deliver the standard set of features of a blockchain".

We can think of a blockchain as a place where you can reduce the uncertainty associated with trading by declaring to thousands of people the terms agreed with your trading partner "who act like escrow, ensuring terms are met and who enact pre-agreed penalties automatically if one party reneges on the agreement".

Rather considering blockchain as a data store, like a database, consider it as a repository of verifiable truth. Blockchain records attested data only.

(Walker, 2021).

There are two types of blockchain: a public blockchain and a private blockchain. The first empowers anyone to play a part, the second empowers only authorized users to play a part. In the future, both types of public and private blockchains will be adopted with increasing intensity.

Public and private blockchains will provide information such as identity, product provenance, and ingredients. For example, they will allow anyone in the supply chain to verify where a product comes from, what raw materials were used, what the characteristics of its production process are, how it was transported, and so on. They thus offer guarantees about "the good behavior of all supply chain participants". Public blockchains "are too expensive to use, lack scalability and perform too slowly for modern supply chain business" while private blockchains already provide services to supply chain participants and when the problems of public blockchains are solved they will be able to connect, utilize and supply data to them.

How to motivate supply chain companies to participate in the new system when the benefits and resource commitment vary significantly between them? The questions are many: what additional costs need to be incurred? And are these costs commensurate with the benefits to be gained from the new system? In other words, what is the return on investment? Who should take the first step to start the system? Who in the supply chain will drive the project forward? For it to be possible to well organize and make the best of a management supply chain it takes a lot of commitment from many people more than in other supply chain management systems.

How does blockchain help the supply chain? As for the Author, the blockchain can assist the management of the supply chain in many ways. Three of these deserve special mention: customer service, budget versus result and managing risks (Walker, 2021).

(1) Customer service. In any supply chain, it is important to give effective communication about customer service. This principle is all the more important the greater the complexity and variety of information sources. Giving the right product, in the right quantity, delivered to the right place and at the agreed time means knowing where it is at any given time and who has control over it. A customer service representative is authorized to have access to attested data across the supply chain. The same information is accessible by all authorized users of the network such as the anchor buyer, their banks, and their distributors. This reduces the administrative effort to establish where products are, what their status is, and whether transit times in the supply chain are respected. This means improving the efficiency of operational management.

(2) Budget versus result. There are many factors that create uncertainty and pressure on supply chain participants. They range from rising costs to fluctuations in demand, from modernizing technologies to new regulations and rising labor costs. Blockchain enables cost reduction through error-free processes. This adds visibility to operational activities and accelerates the flow of products along the supply chain. Blockchain ensures an immutable record of the origin, movement, and status of products. Businesses use this information to prevent criminal activity and counterfeit products.

(3) Managing risk. Having the ability to withstand product flow disruption is important for every participant in the supply chain. The better they are able to cope with internal risks such as market changes, new technologies, new products, and credit availability, the better they are positioned to deal with external risks such as economic and political events. Blockchain diminishes the unnecessary links within a chain. In the future, it will be possible for consumers to scan a product with their smartphone and check the product's origin. This increases the ability to understand what we are buying and improves the efficiency of the choice process. In the food production sector, this process has already been tried out.

2.8.2 Governance, quality, and transparency

Walker emphasizes three aspects: (1) An important property of every blockchain project is its governance. Good governance can ensure support to improve performance across the whole supply chain and ward off possible friction among participants. (2) Quality control is an important duty for all participants. (3) Transparency is one of the main strengths of a blockchain. It has the ability to find reliable information practically instantaneously. For example, a shipping manager may have instant access to shipping volume availability at a given time and also for the future. A blockchain-driven supply chain system can be a formidable tool for corporate treasury to control and maximize liquidity as well as mitigate risk in the car industry blockchain can be used in supply chain logistics, as well as services in the area of warranty management, vehicle inspection or handling of short-term loans, as well as payment in the area of connected services (Walker, 2021).

Winkelhake points out that the goal of blockchain architecture in finance is to enable direct and secure business relationships between two parties without intermediaries, such as the transfer of money from A to B without the intervention of a bank (Winkelhake, 2017). The basic idea is to store in a transparent way a network of transactions for all parties involved and to update these in a chronological way. In financial relationships, verification mechanisms ensure that the payer is actually the owner of the funds at the time of the transaction. Each transaction is stored in a new blockchain attached to the previous block. This creates a chain of data blocks, which explains the name of the procedure.

Business solutions using blockchain have several advantages. Apart from the security aspect, there are cost advantages in that the intermediation of another organization can be avoided and the advantages of transparency of the transaction. The disadvantages are in the use of resources to complete the process, which includes storing, sending, and updating. For this reason, the procedure is considered by many to be more suitable for applications with individual business content and a small transaction volume, rather than for standardized mass processes.

2.9 The road ahead

According to McKinsey, the main reason why industry players are investing resources in Industry 4.0 is the deceleration of the traditional productivity levers: in the 1970s and 1980s, lean adoption was the enabling factor (McKinsey & Company, 2015). In the '90s, outsourcing and offshoring led to greater profitability by relocating the production to low specialization in low-cost countries (LCC), while in the 2000s, the benefits of offshoring began to diminish due to rising LCC wages and transportation costs.

Industry 4.0 is a relatively recent subject that will continue to be investigated in the future (Moeuf et al., 2018; Müller et al., 2018), although numerous studies have been conducted in relation to technologies 4.0. The progress in this field is evident and the technologies constantly evolving.

Although the concept of Industry 4.0 is enticing, there are still a lot of hurdles to be overcome in deploying automated outfitting in the supply chain. Industry 4.0 is still far from being fully realized. In fact, many companies are still at the beginning of exploring its possibilities and implementing the information sharing necessary to achieve smart logistics and supply chain management. New technologies, experts warn, are not enough on their own to prevent information silos from remaining between the various stages of the supply chain and from continuing to be disconnected from each other. All stakeholders need to work together to create the necessary flexibility.

2.10 Industry 4.0 technologies during the COVID-19 pandemic crisis

Industry 4.0 was achieving success before the COVID-19 pandemic, supporting companies in transforming their operations, from production efficiency to product customization, by improvements in speed to market, service effectiveness, and new-business model creation. The role of Industry 4.0 becomes even more critical in the backdrop of the pandemic.

The crisis brought on by COVID-19 has highlighted the critical role of Industry 4.0. Businesses adopting digital technologies have been at an advantage during the crisis compared to their low-tech competitors.

However, it should be highlighted that in dealing with the crisis, companies are subjected to two opposing forces: the need to develop resilience and agility, on the one hand, and spending constraints to preserve liquidity on the other.

According to the researchers (Agrawal et al., 2020), three archetypes of adoption pathways emerge:

(1) accelerated adoption irrespective of existing technology infrastructure;

(2) differential speed of adoption with an advantage to those with existing technology infrastructure;

(3) slowed adoption irrespective of existing technology infrastructure.

Companies may implement digital solutions that can reach across the entire end-to-end value chain to address planning challenges related to disruptions from suppliers or manufacturing facilities.

The archetypes of adoption pathways and the digital solutions can be detailed as described above (Table 2.6):

It should be noted that Russia–Ukraine war will also accelerate technological progress, particularly regarding weapons of war (as happened previously during World War I and World War II).

Table 2.6 The archetypes of adoption pathways.

The three archetypes	Main solutions
(1) Accelerated adoption irrespective of existing technology infrastructure	• Digital work instructions for operator assistance • Digital performance management using IoT • Operator assistance through Augmented Reality • Basic retrofit automation for loading, conveyors, etc. • Digital maintenance (condition-based) This solution is suitable for companies to respond quickly to their needs (e.g., to the new norms).
(2) Differential speed of adoption with an advantage to those with existing technology infrastructure	• Advanced Analytics (AI/ML) for operations • Robotic process automation for services • Automation of plant/warehouse logistics (as AGVs) • Digital-twin simulations for optimization • Operator training using Virtual Reality Differential adoption rates are suitable for solutions such as digital twins and logistics automation, which fall into a middle category requiring foundational information technology (IT), operations technology (OT), and data infrastructure.
(3) Slowed adoption irrespective of existing technology infrastructure	• full, end-to-end advanced robotic automation • 3D printing of spares, jigs, and product components • Blockchain for supply-chain traceability • Nanotechnology in manufacturing This solution is suitable in situations that require higher capital expenditure and have unclear or long-term payback periods.

The effects of the COVID-19 pandemic and Russia-Ukraine war on Supply Chain Disruption will be discussed below in the concluding chapters.

References

Agrawal, M., Eloot, K., Mancini, M., & Patel, A. (2020). *Industry 4.0: Reimagining manufacturing operations after COVID-19*. McKinsey & Company. Operations Practice https://www.mckinsey.com/business-functions/operations/our-insights/industry-40-reimagining-manufacturing-operations-after-covid-19.

Ahuett-Garza, H., & Kurfess, T. (2018). A brief discussion on the trends of habilitating technologies for Industry 4.0 and Smart manufacturing. *Manufacturing Letters, 15*, 60—63. https://doi.org/10.1016/j.mfglet.2018.02.011

Babiceanu, R. F., & Seker, R. (2016). Big data and virtualization for manufacturing cyber-physical systems: A survey of the current status and future outlook. *Computers in Industry, 81*, 128—137. https://doi.org/10.1016/j.compind.2016.02.004

Bassyouni, Z., & Elhajj, I. H. (2021). Augmented reality meets artificial intelligence in robotics: A systematic review. *Frontiers in Robotics and AI, 8*. https://doi.org/10.3389/frobt.2021.724798

van Brussel, H., & Valckenaers, P. (2017). Design of holonic manufacturing systems. *Journal of Machine Engineering, 17*(3), 5—23. http://www.not.pl/wydawnictwo/2017JOM/V3/1_BRUSSEL.pdf.

Büchi, G., Cugno, M., & Castagnoli, R. (2020). Smart factory performance and Industry 4.0. *Technological Forecasting and Social Change, 150*, 1—10. https://doi.org/10.1016/j.techfore.2019.119790

Christopher, M. (2021). In E. Aktas, M. Bourlakis, I. Minis, & V. Zeimpekis (Eds.), *Supply chain 4.0. Enabling market-driven strategies*. Kogan Page.

Dalenogare, L. S., Benitez, G. B., Ayala, N. F., & Frank, A. G. (2018). The expected contribution of Industry 4.0 technologies for industrial performance. *International Journal of Production Economics, 204*, 383—394. https://doi.org/10.1016/j.ijpe.2018.08.019

Deloitte. (2022). *Digital supply networks*. Deloitte, Services. https://www2.deloitte.com/global/en/pages/operations/solutions/gx-digital-supply-networks.html.

Fatorachian, H., & Kazemi, H. (2018). A critical investigation of industry 4.0 in manufacturing: Theoretical operationalisation framework. *Production Planning and Control, 29*(8), 633—644. https://doi.org/10.1080/09537287.2018.1424960

Gilchrist, A. (2018). *Supply chain 4.0. Fueled by Industry 4.0*. Copyright ©Alasdair Gilchrist.

Gupta, A. K., & Taufik, M. (2022). The effect of process parameters in material extrusion processes on the part surface quality: A review. *Materials Today: Proceedings, 50*(5), 1234—1242. https://doi.org/10.1016/j.matpr.2021.08.110

Immerman, G. (September 17, 2020). Real-world industry 4.0 technologies with examples. *Machine Metrics*. https://www.machinemetrics.com/blog/industry-4-0-technologies.

Ivanov, D., Dolgui, A., & Sokolov, B. (2022). Cloud supply chain: Integrating industry 4.0 and digital platforms in the "supply chain-as-a-service. *Transportation Research E: Logistics and Transportation Review, 160*, 1—11. https://doi.org/10.1016/j.tre.2022.102676

Kagermann, H., Helbig, J., Hellinger, A., & Wahlster, W. (2013). *Recommendations for implementing the strategic initiative INDUSTRIE 4.0: Securing the future of German manufacturing industry*. Berlin: Industrie 4.0 Working Group.

Kim, A. S., DiPlacido, M. P., Kerns, M. C., & Darnley, R. E. (2018). *Industry 4.0: Digitization in Danish Industry*. Worcester Polytechnic Institute.

Lee, J., Bagheri, B., & Kao, H. A. (2015). A cyber-physical systems architecture for Industry 4.0-based manufacturing systems. *Manufacturing Letters, 3*, 18—23. https://doi.org/10.1016/j.mfglet.2014.12.001

Liao, Y., Deschamps, F., Loures, E. D. F. R., & Ramos, L. F. P. (2017). Past, present and future of Industry 4.0 - a systematic literature review and research agenda proposal. *International Journal of Production Research, 55*(12), 3609—3629. https://doi.org/10.1080/00207543.2017.1308576

McKinsey, & Company. (2015). *Industry 4.0-how to navigate digitization of the manufacturing sector.* McKinsey Digital. https://www.mckinsey.com/ ~ /media/McKinsey/Business%20Functions/Operations/Our%20Insights/Industry%2040%20How%20to%20navigate%20digitization%20of%20the%20manufacturing%20sector/Industry-40-How-to-navigate-digitization-of-the-manufacturing-sector.ashx.

Moeuf, A., Pellerin, R., Lamouri, S., Tamayo-Giraldo, S., & Barbaray, R. (2018). The industrial management of SMEs in the era of Industry 4.0. *International Journal of Production Research, 56*(3), 1118—1136. https://doi.org/10.1080/00207543.2017.1372647

Monroe, A. (2021). New Request for Information: Blockchain Management, Department of Administrative Services, Connecticut States. https://portal.ct.gov/DAS/DasBlog/DAS-RFI-Blockchain-Management.

Müller, J. M., Kiel, D., & Voigt, K.-I. (2018). What drives the implementation of industry 4.0? The role of opportunities and challenges in the context of sustainability. *Sustainability, 10*(1), 247. https://doi.org/10.3390/su10010247

Mussomeli, A., Gish, D., & Laaper, S. (2016). *The rise of the digital supply network.* Deloitte University Press. https://www2.deloitte.com/content/dam/insights/us/articles/3465_Digital-supply-network/DUP_Digital-supply-network.pdf.

Ong, S. K., Yuan, M. L., & Nee, A. Y. (2008). Augmented reality applications in manufacturing: a survey. *International Journal of Production Research, 46*(10), 2707—2742. https://doi.org/10.1080/00207540601064773

Parrott, A., Warshaw, L., & Umbenhauer, B. (January 25, 2020). Digital twins: Bridging the physical and digital. *Deloitte Insights.* https://www2.deloitte.com/us/en/insights/focus/tech-trends/2020/digital-twin-applications-bridging-the-physical-and-digital.html.

Pereira, A. C., & Romero, F. (2017). A review of the meanings and the implications of the Industry 4.0 concept. *Procedia Manufacturing, 13*, 1206—1214. https://doi.org/10.1016/j.promfg.2017.09.032

Rauch, E. (2020). Industry 4.0+: The next level of intelligent and self-optimizing factories. *Lecture Notes in Mechanical Engineering*, 176—186. https://doi.org/10.1007/978-3-030-50794-7_18

Rüßmann, M., Lorenz, M., Gerbert, P., Waldner, M., Justus, J., Engel, P., & Harnisch, M. (2015). *Industry 4.0: The future of productivity and growth in manufacturing industries.* Boston Consulting Group. https://www.bcg.com/it-it/publications/2015/engineered_products_project_business_industry_4_future_productivity_growth_manufacturing_industries.

Sinha, A., Bernardes, E., Calderon, R., & West, T. (2020). *Digital supply networks. Transform your supply chain and gain competitive advantage with disruptive technology and reimagined processes.* McGraw Hill.

Walker, M. (2021). In E. Aktas, M. Bourlakis, I. Minis, & V. Zeimpekis (Eds.), *Blockchain in the supply chain.* Kogan Page.

Wikipedia. (2022). *Digital supply chain.* https://en.wikipedia.org/wiki/Digital_supply_chain.

Winkelhake, U. (2017). *The digital transformation of the auto motive industry.* Springer.

CHAPTER THREE

Supply chain 4.0. rewriting the rules

3.1 Enabling technologies

A wide range of digital technologies is supporting Supply chain 4.0, such as Big Data analytics, Artificial Intelligence, Machine Learning, Augmented and Virtual Reality, Cloud technologies, Cyber security, the Internet of Things (IoT), and Robotics. Big Data applications are especially seen as one of the most important areas in generating new capabilities and innovation in supply chains. These technologies make it possible to digitize products and services through the digitization of every link in the supply chain, from procurement to engineering, from customer service to digital sales channels, enabling companies to improve their supply chain performance. These new technologies have accelerated progress in various business areas, including the development of new products and services, with significant changes in supply chain management.

One of the main advantages of moving to Supply Chain 4.0 within Industry 4.0 is overcoming the lack of transparency, in which a segmented supply chain is found in independent silos that do not communicate with each other. Simplifying, we can imagine that the marketing manager makes a forecast of demand that includes a forecast of sales. He then communicates the sales forecast to production, which, considering the optimal size of the production batches, orders raw materials, parts, components, and modules from procurement, which in turn takes into account various constraints in deciding what and how much to buy. However, sales forecasts rarely come true exactly, and as we have seen when dealing with the 'bullwhip effect', errors propagate along the supply chain.

With Industry 4.0 technologies, the boundaries between silos disappear, and every link between them becomes visible to all players in the supply chain. The sudden increase or decrease in demand, the difficulties in supplying a 'critical' component, and the blackout in a 'critical' production plant represent information that all the players can have in real-time, based on which they can react accordingly.

The Digital Transformation of Supply Chain Management
ISBN: 978-0-323-85532-7
https://doi.org/10.1016/B978-0-323-85532-7.00007-4

The Figure summarizes the path from a 'customer-centric supply chain' to a 'supply chain 4.0', driven by advances in technology (Fig. 3.1).

To understand the role that technology plays in the Digital Supply Chain, Gilchrist proposes dividing this into eight key areas (Gilchrist, 2018), which can be summarized as follows (Table 3.1).

3.2 Supply chain 4.0 and market-driven strategies

In "Supply chain 4.0. Enabling market-driven strategies", Christopher identifies three evolutions toward Supply chain 4.0 that have raised efficiency: (1) the transition from a 'mass market' to a 'segment of one'; (2) the transition from 'forecast-driven' to 'demand-driven'; (3) a shifting center of gravity (Christopher, 2021).

- **From 'mass market' to 'segment of one'.** For much of the last century, the goal of large corporations was to serve the 'mass market' by offering a limited variety of products and taking advantage of economies of scale. Gradually, however, consumers, with the increase in incomes and shopping experiences, began to ask for more specific solutions for their needs, to which companies responded with the segmentation of supply.

1990. Customer centric supply chain. Then DRIVE 1 took place: Shift of focus from 'push' to 'pull', which has given way to:

1995. On-demand supply chain. Then DRIVE 2 took place: Digital optimization, which has given way to:

2005. Digital Supply Network (DSN). Then DRIVE 3 took place: Digital transformation, which has given way to:

2010. Smart Digital Network (SDSN). Then DRIVE 4 took place: Via Industry 4.0 Ecosystem, which has given way to:

2015. Supply Chain 4.0.

Figure 3.1 *Supply chain evolution: from customer-centric to supply chain 4.0.* The Figure summarizes the path moving from a 'customer-centric supply chain' (1990) up to a supply chain 4.0' (2015).

Table 3.1 The role of technology in the Digital Supply Chain.

Key areas	Roles
Integrated planning and execution	By integrating data from the entire supply chain, the agility of the entire supply chain can be increased, reducing delivery times and optimizing transport and inventory management.
Logistics visibility-seeing into the network	Visibility has become one of the most important elements. Opening up to all increases visibility and the ability to detect the many causes of disruption in both B2C and B2B markets. Track-and-trace technologies for tracking the movement of supplies and products have evolved significantly in recent years.
Procurement 4.0-sourcing on demand	The digitization of procurement is a priority in most companies. A digital supply chain has several key consequences for the procurement function.
Smart warehousing-robots at work	The warehouse and logistics functions have been at the forefront in the use of the IoT and advanced technologies, both of which have radically changed over the past decade. The transformation of the warehouse in the context of 4.0 begins with inbound logistics. Digitization has eliminated much of its inefficiency.
Efficient spare part management	Digitization has revolutionized the warehousing function and the distribution of spare parts. Analytics allows demand for spare parts to be forecast much more precisely.
Autonomous and B2C logistics-robotic transport	The most common use of Autonomous Vehicles in logistics will be in driverless vehicles. Autonomous Robotic Vehicles are routinely moving raw materials, parts, and components around the world. Another area for deploying process

(Continued)

Table 3.1 The role of technology in the Digital Supply Chain.—cont'd

Key areas	Roles
	automation is the last-mile delivery of products to the consumer.
Prescriptive supply chain analytics-decisional support for managers	Using Big Data and predictive algorithms allows companies to anticipate variations in demand through the supply chain. Prescriptive analytic systems provide decisional support to supply chain managers and can even act autonomously on routine decisions.

For each segment, they proposed different marketing mix strategies (products, pricing, distribution, and promotion). Initially, the segments were large, but over time consumers have increasingly demanded specific solutions. This need led to 'mass customization', which represents the combination of two contrasting concepts: the efficiency of economies of scale, on the one hand, and the 'granularity' of supply on the other. The most widely adopted solution was to maintain the common production process for multiple products destined for different segments and then adapt the last mile to the specific needs of the market as dictated by individual customer specifications. This brought the importance of the supply chain to the forefront. The product is divided into modules that are made in advance of the demand and are kept in stock until the demand becomes apparent. Once the 'decoupling point' (the node in the supply chain network where the downstream activities are driven by actual customer orders) is passed, the product is personalized. From an economy of scale objective, we shift to an economy of purpose objective. In the end, unit production costs are reduced and the final product meets specific needs.

These principles have been used by businesses for a long time, but Supply Chain 4.0 has changed the situation by expressing its full potential as "it provides the ability to respond more quickly and flexibly and to reduce the batch size" (Christopher, 2021).

- **Transitioning from 'forecast-driven' to 'demand-driven'.** It had long been the tradition for the supply chain to be designed from the factory to the customer, not vice-versa. This meant it was 'production-driven', and therefore efficient in the supply chain, not 'demand-driven', and therefore non-market effectiveness. This choice was due to the difficulty of predicting, and therefore the enterprise responded with production planning on the basis of a demand-level hypothesis (which involved scheduling orders for procurement, logistics, and so on). Mistakes were inevitable when reality began to manifest itself since the various parts of the supply chain did not communicate with each other. When Supply Chain 4.0 and IoT burst onto the scene, everything changed. The 'end-to-end' supply chain visibility became greatly enhanced and the horizon closer, making it easier to predict demand. Technologies such as Data Analytics, AI, and Machine Learning can anticipate the actual demand. "All in all, a powerful virtuous circle can be created that will provide a real foundation for the development of 'demand-driven' supply chain" (Christopher, 2021).

However, there are obstacles to overcome. While efficiency is greater, Christopher states that we need to change our conception of matching supply with demand. For decades companies reasoned on the basis of 'forecast-driven' management: because lead times were long, it was necessary to plan ahead to secure the necessary resources. Planning based on forecasts meant, for example, producing batches to feed warehouse stocks, resulting in increasing costs and the risk of obsolescence and of making other mistakes. The longer the forecast horizon, the greater the errors.

In recent years, two goals for management have become imperative: to reduce lead times and to collect data about demand "as close to real time as possible". Supply Chain 4.0 has also made significant contributions in this field. Meanwhile, the expectations of B2C and B2B customers have increased. "Seeking more customized solutions delivered in ever shorter time frames" means moving from a 'forecast-driven' business model to one "capable of responding when demand happens".

While the transition from 'forecast-driven' to 'demand-driven' is not easy, long-term planning is fundamental to acquiring the most appropriate resources; however, the day-to-day response to market demand should be informed by data able to anticipate customer expectations. According to the Author, the use of Big Data and Analytics "can dramatically improve forecast accuracy by enabling the faster interpretation of events and by aiding the understanding of the underlying drivers of demand."

- **Constantly shifting center of gravity.** Every supply chain has a center of gravity. Where this depends on the "relative strength of various supply-side and demand-side vectors". These vectors are beyond the control of management. Sometimes it is labor costs (e.g. the increase in labor costs in China that has caused many supply chains or their parts to be transferred to Vietnam), sometimes it is the availability of raw materials, and sometimes the risks of transport disruptions (which have brought the sources of supply closer to the places of final production).

On the demand side, the vectors that act are "changing demographics in the marketplace, changing customer preferences and levels of disposal incomes, and the rise and/or decline of industrial sectors". The great variability in the environment frequently shifts the center of gravity, necessitating a high level of agility and flexibility.

For companies that embrace Supply Chain 4.0, the picture could be different. Supply Chain 4.0, in fact, "has the potential to enable a much higher level of connectivity across the supply-demand network" (Christopher, 2021). This is a notable advantage. We must not forget that companies no longer compete as individual entities but rather as supply chains, hence the need for high "collaborative working across the network."

Finally, the Author recalls that many of the analyses and suggestions concern the use of new technologies, but to apply Industry 4.0 ideas to supply chain management "involves far more than technology". Success depends on a high level of end-to-end supply chain integration.

3.3 How the supply chain has been transformed

Digital transformation (DX) has opened a new phase in supply chain management, connecting suppliers and customers in a new way and breaking down the barriers between the digital and real worlds, cutting inefficiencies, and lowering costs.

Digital transformation is driven by the confluence of several different technological disruptions, including IoT, AI, Big Data and Analytics, Machine Learning, Automation and Robotics, Cloud computing, Blockchain, 3D printing, etc., and the explosive growth in smart devices. As digital technologies increase real-time visibility into every part of the value chain, companies can identify areas of potential risk in advance and be prepared to respond to potential disruptions. In the end, a suitable supply chain digitalization can be a source of competitive advantage.

According to BDO International, DX is transforming the traditional supply chain in six principal ways (BDO digital, 2021).

- **The Connected supply chain.** Done properly, a smarter supply chain connection can mitigate disruption, build resilience, and increase visibility and responsiveness across the entire supply chain. For instance, recent advancements in supply chain technology give companies real-time awareness of asset status and location and can detect supply chain disruptions or quality issues.

- **Demand-driven supply chain management.** The new technologies give management a powerful tool: the ability to quickly and accurately identify demand trends contained in a large mass of data. Traditional methods of forecasting were mainly based on historical analyses and their projections into the future and therefore did not interpret the current demand environment. Although not perfect, technologies such as Predictive Analytics and Machine Learning can now reliably predict demand, recognize patterns, and anticipate changes.

- **Formation of the digital thread.** The main goal of the digital thread is the keystone of the evolution from a supply network to an integrated value chain. The digital thread is a communication framework for sharing information upstream and downstream of the supply chain, creating a constant feedback loop between suppliers, the company (OEM), and customers.

- **Value Co-creation.** We define Co-creation as a form of innovation through the collaboration between people or organizations in which ideas are jointly shared and enhanced, as opposed to individuals or organizations keeping these ideas to themselves. An integrated value chain that allows transparency can increase efficiencies if the best practices are shared with internal and external stakeholders. "The idea is that the synthesis of data from all supply chain entities is more valuable than data input from a single network."

- **Evolving customer expectations.** Both Business-to-Consumer (B2C) and Business-to-Business (B2B) enterprises need to respond to demand more than ever before. This is because customers' expectations are higher, making them less likely to accept delays in deliveries or errors in order execution. Many companies have given up serving as intermediaries by switching to direct sales to customers to better control the 'last mile'. For consumer goods, this practice has been accelerated by the positive experience of the strong growth in online sales during the COVID-19 pandemic.

- **Cyber risk.** By breaking down the traditional barriers among those who collaborate in joint innovation projects to promote transparency and improve efficiency, new technologies have paved the way for criminal behavior, thus increasing cyber risk supply chains. Often attackers exploit third-party vulnerabilities to gain access to their ultimate target. "All suppliers should go through an evaluation process that identifies cyber risks", and risk exposures should then be addressed with contractual provisions.

A significant example of Supply Chain transformation concerns Walmart (Box 3.1).

3.4 Key benefits of supply chain 4.0

Companies have a lot to gain from improving their supply chain management under the umbrella of Industry 4.0. Aided by disruptive new technologies, such as IoT, AI, Big Data and Analytics, Machine Learning, Automation and Robotics, Cloud computing, Blockchain, and 3D printing, Industry 4.0 has fast transformed how businesses manage their key functions.

Supply chain management has made the most from going digital. A study, by the consulting company GEP, suggests that thanks to mutual connections, a digital supply chain can "lower operational costs by more than 30%, reduce lost sales opportunities by more than 60%, and even reduce inventory requirements by more than 70%, all while making companies faster, more agile, granular, accurate, and efficient" (GEP, 2021).

The GEP study summarizes the main benefits of transitioning to a digitized, automated, and fully interconnected supply chain as follows:

- **Greater transparency and accuracy.** The supply chain ecosystem of a global company may involve thousands of suppliers. In this instance, providing overall transparency and real-time asset tracking is of crucial importance. Going digital enables companies to track the integrated supply chain in real-time, which helps order accuracy, enhances inventory control, and lowers the working capital.
- **Leading to cost savings.** Advanced Machine Learning algorithms help enterprises accurately forecast both the demand for a particular item and the probabilistic distribution of its expected demand. Data-Backed Decisions help to estimate the maximum and minimum risk points of the quantities in stock. Furthermore, predicting demand more accurately helps companies in cost reductions.

Box 3.1 Supply chain transformation at Walmart

After 2020, eCommerce in the U.S. and in many developed countries has grown much faster than in-store sales, and online orders have remained high after COVID-19 forced many people to stay at home. Brick-and-mortar retailers that did not have a strategy to grow sales based on an 'omnichannel' strategy went out of business with increasing frequency. Walmart was in a good position to react to the changed situation since the giant retailer has been working to develop 'omnichannel' for several years to help speed growth. For Walmart, 'omnichannel' is defined as a customer-centric experience that seamlessly integrates eCommerce and retail stores into an offering that saves time for consumers. The store 'omnichannel' services include pickup at the store, shipping from the store, and digital pharmacy fulfillment options. The company has 7300 pickup and 5200 delivery locations globally.

At Walmart, the digital transformation of the supply chain has a high priority. In the U.S., investments in new eCommerce technologies and in new infrastructure represent about 70% of total investments for the 2020 and 2021 fiscal years. David Guggina, Senior Vice President for the Supply Chain at Walmart, said in an interview with Forbes: "For many of our customers, saving time is as important as saving money. That has led to growth in eCommerce. But Walmart will not abandon their strategy of being a low-cost provider: what the company calls 'everyday low prices'. Low prices translate into having a focus on cutting costs; this in turn means having an efficient supply chain" (Banker, 2021).

The use of demand management, inventory optimization, and replenishment applications can help this retail giant achieve much better inventory placement and fulfillment flexibility. Investing in supply chain applications, Mr. Guggina added, also helps them with their 'relentless cost focus': "The pandemic propelled our omni strategy ahead by 3—5 years". Pick-up at the store and home deliveries have increased rapidly due to the pandemic. In its distribution centers, Walmart has modernized its warehouse management system (WMS), paying particular attention to better inventory control. Walmart has made broad investments in warehouse automation, deployed autonomous mobile robots to move pallets, and also invested in the use of automation for picking/putting to and from containers. In transportation, Walmart has undertaken various experiments, some of which have already had useful applications: for example, it has experimented with trucks that can move about autonomously in their yards and with over-the-road autonomous trucks that move inbound from suppliers to their distribution centers.

- **Increased interconnectedness.** A fully interconnected supply chain fosters the flow of information between suppliers, manufacturers, and customers, strengthening transparency and efficiency. Since the information is exchanged on a shared platform, this interconnectedness breaks silos and transforms planning into an endless process. Stakeholders, especially in cases of non-competitive relationships, can look for joint planning solutions. Since suppliers can exchange perceived early warnings with each other, an interconnected platform can also lower lead times through better communication. Another advantage is the ability to integrate pricing decisions with demand and supply planning and to vary them in relation to demand, stock levels, and replenishment capacity.

- **Improved warehouse management.** Along the supply chain, both inventory management and warehouse and logistics management can greatly benefit from digitalization. For example, technology can communicate in real-time through sensors and determine where a product is located and how long it takes before it reaches the destination point. The advantages of such precision are in the savings of time in transport and in the greater efficiency with which plant managers can control the global flow of inventory.
- **'Intelligent' supply chain.** Supply chains that 'think' and can 'learn' to recognize risks have the power and 'skills' to change their supply chain parameters to mitigate such risks. Except for extraordinary events that require human intervention, those 'intelligent' supply chains continuously evolve and learn to handle many exceptions.
- **Greater Agility.** In a 'supply chain cloud', information converges from the various stakeholders of the supply chain regarding their advanced solutions. In this way, everyone can make decisions having the same data and knowledge. Such real-time visibility will enable companies to react more quickly and easily to disruptions and minimize risk.

An important example concerns the car industry shortage of chips (Box 3.2).

3.5 Toward Smart manufacturing and Smart factory

The Fourth Industrial Revolution has Smart manufacturing as its central element (Kagermann et al., 2013).

Industry 4.0 is rooted in Advanced Manufacturing (Smart manufacturing). The adoption of digital technologies allows companies to obtain and analyze data in real-time, providing relevant information to the production systems (Frank et al., 2019). In the industrial and manufacturing environment, the IoT will especially be able to provide

Box 3.2 Car industry shortage of chips

The global computer-chip shortage during the coronavirus pandemic has long hampered the world's largest car makers. Stellantis NV., the world's third-largest car company by sales, reported that the semiconductor shortage continuously hit production in 2021. The rival General Motors Co. said that the chip shortage has led to the idling of three North American factories that make large pickup trucks, the company's biggest moneymaker.

Semiconductors are of critical importance in cars, used in everything from engines and airbags to touch-screen displays. Various strategies have been adopted to mitigate the consequences of the shortage. For example, GM has largely avoided disruption to its pickup truck output by diverting chips from less-popular models. The shortage of parts is also having far-reaching effects on dealership sales, where inventory has become historically low.

A well-known precedent exists for this situation: the abrupt closure more than a decade earlier of the only factory making a vital pigment, due to its proximity to the tsunami-hit Fukushima nuclear plant in Japan, affected most of the world's big carmakers. The sudden unavailability of that pigment highlighted the vulnerability of the industry's global supply chain.

In 2021, a dearth of semiconductors left car firms unable to install the complex electronics that control entertainment systems, safety features, and advanced driving aids, causing many firms to cut assembly-line shifts and some to temporarily close factories. The shortage of chips was a consequence of the pandemic, which boosted demand from the makers of electronic devices for those stuck at home during the lockdowns. Car manufacturers also underestimated the rapid pace of recovery that has taken place during the first part of 2021. Expecting weak sales, in 2020 they pared backorders.

The initial response of car makers was to produce more vehicles that require resources to build their most profitable models. In these circumstances, two significant differences have emerged between fully Electric Vehicles (EV) and those propelled by Internal Combustion Engines (ICE): (1) Fully electric cars are packed with twice as many chips by value as ICE-fueled ones, and (2) software has become a critical source of profits as cars progress toward a central system connected to the internet that can be updated remotely (The Economist, 2021).

many opportunities for companies due to its possible use in different fields, such as automation, industrial production, logistics, business processes, process management, and transportation.

Smart manufacturing is an adaptable system in which flexible lines automatically adjust production processes, which can be adapted to different types of products, including large-scale customized products, in response to changing conditions (Wang, Wan, Zhang, et al., 2016; Schuh et al., 2017). Its application allows for increasing quality, productivity, flexibility, and improved resource consumption (Dalenogare et al., 2018). It considers the integration of the factory with the entire product life-cycle and with supply chain activities, also changing the way people work (Stock et al., 2018).

Companies will be expected to increase value creation through the development of emerging IoT applications with respect to three main pillars: (1) process optimization, (2) optimized resource consumption, and (3) the creation of complex autonomous systems (Pereira & Romero, 2017).

Industry 4.0, therefore, represents the new industrial phase in which production systems, by integrating the emerging and converging technologies, can add value to the entire product life-cycle (Wang, Wan, Li, et al., 2016).

An in-depth Smart manufacturing conceptual framework is illustrated by Frank et al. in which Industry 4.0 technologies are separated into two different layers according to their main focus, characterized by the 'front-end technologies' and the 'base technologies' of Industry 4.0. At the center of the framework are the 'front-end technologies', where four 'smart' dimensions that address operational and market needs are placed (Frank et al., 2019). The technologies concern:

(1) the transformation of manufacturing activities based on emerging technologies (Smart manufacturing);
(2) the ways in which products are offered (Smart products) (Dalenogare et al., 2018);
(3) the ways in which raw materials and products are delivered (Smart supply chain) (Angeles, 2009);
(4) the new ways in which workers perform tasks based on the support of emerging technologies (Smart working) (Stock et al., 2018).

The layer represented by 'base technologies' allows 'front-end technologies' to be connected into a complete and integrated manufacturing system (Tao et al., 2018; Thoben et al., 2017) by providing them with connectivity and intelligence based on four main elements: the Internet of Things, Cloud services, Big Data, and Analytics.

The Smart manufacturing technologies and their main purposes are discussed in the study by Frank et al. They can be details as follows (Frank et al., 2019): (a) Vertical Integration, (b) Virtualization, (c) Automation, (d) Traceability, (e) Flexibility and (f) Energy management (Table 3.2).

Table 3.2 Technologies for Smart manufacturing.

Smart manufacturing technologies	Main applications
Vertical Integration	• Sensors, actuators, and Programmable Logic Controllers (PLC) • Supervisory Control and Data Acquisition (SCADA) • Manufacturing Execution System (MES) • Enterprise Resource Planning (ERP) • Machine-to-Machine communication (M2M)
Virtualization	• Virtual commissioning • Simulation of processes (e.g. digital manufacturing) • Artificial Intelligence for predictive maintenance • Artificial Intelligence for planning of production
Automation	• Machine-to-Machine communication (M2M) • Robots (e.g. industrial robots, Autonomous Guided Vehicles, or similar) • Automatic non-conformities identification in production
Traceability	• Identification and traceability of raw materials • Identification and traceability of final products
Flexibility	• Additive Manufacturing • Flexible and autonomous lines
Energy management	• Energy efficiency monitoring system • Energy efficiency improving system

According to the Authors, Smart manufacturing includes intra-logistics processes with internal material tracking technologies, and self-driving vehicles and other technologies can connect factories to external processes.

Vertical Integration is achieved by digitizing all physical objects and parameters with sensors, actuators, and Programmable Logic Controllers (PLCs), which improves the efficiency of manufacturing processes. Data is collected for production control and shop floor diagnosis using Supervisory Control and Data Acquisition (SCADA). Successively, Manufacturing Execution Systems (MES) obtain the data and provide production status to the Enterprise Resource Planning (ERP) system. If the systems are fully integrated, they are also able to flow production order information in the reverse (downstream) direction, from ERP to MES, and then to SCADA (Jeschke et al., 2016).

Adaptability to different types of products can be improved through Machine-to-Machine (M2M) communication (Kagermann et al., 2013), as a result of which machines are connected and understand each other, thereby improving their adaptability in production lines.

Automation can improve productivity and efficiency through the implementation of robots that can provide greater accuracy and labor quantity than in the past (Thoben et al., 2017).

Artificial Intelligence can support Smart manufacturing with predictive maintenance to prevent downtime due to unexpected breakdowns during the manufacturing process, while also allowing systems such as ERP to be integrated and to predict long-term production requirements, turning them into daily production orders with the needed adjustments.

The internal traceability of raw materials and finished products can be organized using sensors, thus ensuring optimized inventory control, which in turn can provide support for recall actions by identifying specific components in lots of finished products.

Additive Manufacturing is a promising technology that enables the customization of products by adopting the 3D printing of digital models that can be modified for customization and by employing the same resources to produce different goods. In addition, it also provides sustainable production as it requires only a single process that generates less waste than traditional manufacturing.

The efficiency of manufacturing processes can also be improved through energy management by implementing monitoring and improving energy efficiency.

The Authors (Frank et al., 2019) also highlight how Smart manufacturing technologies are operating as a central pillar of internal operational activities (Ahuett-Garza & Kurfess, 2018), while Smart product considers the external added value of products when customer information and data are integrated into the production system (Dalenogare et al., 2018). Smart manufacturing is considered the beginning and first purpose of Industry 4.0, whereas Smart product is typically seen as its extension.

In the literature, many studies consider Smart products as the second main objective of Industry 4.0.

Smart products can provide data feedback for new product development as well as new services and solutions to the customer (Porter & Heppelmann, 2015), as well as enable new business models such as product-service systems, creating new opportunities for manufacturers and service providers (Zhong et al., 2017; Ayala et al., 2019).

The Smart products technologies and the other two 'smart' dimensions discussed in the study by Frank et al.: Smart supply chain and Smart working (Frank et al., 2019), can be summarized as follows (Tables 3.3 and 3.4).

3.5.1 Smart factory

The Smart factory is the keystone of the Fourth Industrial Revolution, a concept used to describe the use of different digital technologies. The goal is to collect data through connected machines, devices, and production systems in order to share it effectively. The Smart factory applies new developments in digital technologies such as Advanced Robotics and Artificial Intelligence, high-tech sensors, Cloud computing, the IoT, Data capture, and Analytics.

With the help of an integrated system of sensors, those who govern the Smart factory are constantly informed on the progress of the production

Table 3.3 Technologies for Smart products.

Smart products	Main applications
Capabilities of smart, connected products	• Product connectivity • Product monitoring • Product control • Product optimization • Product autonomy

Table 3.4 Technologies for Smart supply chain and Smart working.

Smart supply chain and Smart working	Main applications
Technologies for Smart supply chain	• Digital platforms with suppliers • Digital platforms with customers • Digital platforms with other company units
Technologies for Smart working	• Remote monitoring of production • Remote operation of production • Augmented Reality for maintenance • Virtual Reality for worker training • Augmented and Virtual Reality for product development • Collaborative robots

process as well as the ordering process and the availability of raw materials. The network information system allows independent autonomous production modules to communicate with each other without human intervention.

Consequently, the traditional distinction between production planning and production management falls under the management of the Smart factory since the machines constantly exchange information about the production process. An essential requirement to compete in the digital age is close cooperation between the various functions of the enterprise and communication between the various parts of the supply chain.

The aim is to create smart and connected factories that connect machines, people, products, and the entire value network by vertical and horizontal data integration (Rauch, 2020), thus creating a smart environment.

According to Kagermann, "Smart factories constitute a key feature of Industry 4.0 being capable of managing complexity, being less prone to disruption and able to manufacture goods more efficiently" (Kagermann et al., 2013). In this vision, Smart factories become intelligent factories capable of generating rapid and flexible adaptations through connected machines that exchange information with other machines, products, or people. They will move toward the creation of self-organizing manufacturing systems with production facilities that are autonomous, self-controlled, self-configuring, self-regulating, self-aware, and self-optimizing (Rauch, 2020).

Intelligent factories, thanks to the Internet connection, are capable of thinking, learning, memorizing, sharing data and knowledge, and reacting when necessary.

Intelligent manufacturing systems, being highly automated at the manufacturing level, are self-repairing, self-optimizing, and self-configuring by incorporating Artificial Intelligence and neural network technology (Juhás & Molnár, 2017).

The advantages of a Smart factory have been demonstrated. According to a Smart factory study: "Capturing value through the digital journey" (Deloitte, 2019), early adopters report average 3-year gains of 10% or better for factory output, factory capacity utilization, and labor productivity. More than 85% of study respondents believe Smart factory initiatives will be the main driver of manufacturing competitiveness in the next 5 years, and 83% say they will transform the way products are made in 5 years.

Transitioning to Smart factories is very difficult to do, particularly because in the past most companies, instead of building new factories, are updating existing ones. As for Deloitte's study (2020), Smart factory participants fall into three adoption groups: Trailblazers (18%), Explorers (55%), and Followers (27%).

- **Trailblazers** are at the vanguard of innovation inside the factory, spending 65% or more of their budget on Smart factory initiatives. They apply Smart factory initiatives along the value chain to build a connected ecosystem among factory personnel, suppliers, and customers. The results speak volumes: Trailblazers have reported a 20% average improvement in production output, factory capacity utilization, and employee productivity over the past 3 years.
- **Explorers** are engaged in the development of the Smart factory but to a lesser extent than trailblazers. They allocate no more than 20% of their global factory budget to innovation in Smart factories. As a result, they involve the ecosystem of factory personnel, suppliers, and customers to a modest extent. However, they have made substantial progress in factory capacity utilization and employee productivity.
- **Followers** are in the wait-and-see position until technologies achieve clear results. On average, they invest 13% of the global factory budget in the Smart factory. Only 20% of followers have fully connected ecosystems and, though they have obtained modest gains in productivity, they expect this to increase by 3% over the coming 3 years.

Unlike the other two groups, the Trailblazers' study responses provide interesting insights into what they do. As Deloitte remarks, they: "(1) identify concrete business outcomes, i.e., improved production capacity, increased throughput, greater visibility into performance, improved product or part quality: (2) show a higher propensity for multiple adoption approaches, for example, a combination of retrofitting and building new assets, enabling quick course corrections if one approach doesn't work; (3) engage leadership early; (4) start small and scale, some Trailblazers report 50 to 70 small use cases running simultaneously; (5) Tie multiple small projects to measurable business metrics and use these successes for additional funding approval" (Deloitte, 2019).

A case in point concerns a leading service provider of manufacturing businesses (Box 3.3).

Box 3.3 Bossard AG

Bossard is based in Zug, Switzerland, and is a leading service provider of manufacturing businesses that take advantage of new opportunities arising from Industry 4.0. Bossard has an extensive global network of service locations, logistic centers, and application engineering laboratories around the world. By means of this network, the factories of industrial companies are supplied with fastening technology products and services with high-quality standards and standardized systems and processes.

Bossard's business model was developed in Switzerland and neighboring countries where the costs of manual labor were high, so saving time spent by employees on routine tasks translated into hefty saving costs. Therefore, Bossard's solutions were more appreciated and more competitive in high-cost labor countries, while in low-cost countries its ability to compete was challenged.

Bossard's ability to deliver consistent quality and reliable local services at many locations in the world was an advantage in its becoming a supplier of multinational companies. Among Bossard's main customers are Altstom, Sneider Electric, ABB, General Electric, Bombardier, John Deere, Honeywell, and Siemens.

Core business. Bossard buys large volumes of basic components - screws, nuts, and bolts, which are base products ('C-parts') for manufacturing - from a variety of suppliers, repackages the items for its customers, and delivers them just in time to manufacturing sites worldwide. Bossard integrates the delivery by providing logistics solutions and participating in the customers' product development process.

Although these 'C-parts' are standardized mass-produced items and are not expensive, their quality is critical for the overall safety and reliability of the products in which they are assembled. An error in choice or defects in quality could have disastrous consequences for product affordability.

It was the morning of July 25th, 2000, at Charles DeGaulle Airport. Five minutes before the supersonic Concorde took to runway 26R, a Continental flight headed to Newark, using the same runway, lost a titanium alloy strip. During the following takeoff of the Concorde, a piece of this debris cut and ruptured one of the airplane's left tires. As the aircraft accelerated down runway 26R, this tire disintegrated and a piece of it struck the underside of the wing, where fuel tank five was located. Fuel poured from the tank and ignited. The Concorde had already reached a velocity where it could not stop safely by the end of the runway, and so it lifted off the runway with flames hanging from the left wing. The tragic crash that followed cost the lives of 113 and the image of a truly impressive airliner.

Bossard has gained a strong reputation and competitive advantage for the extensive testing of its 'C-parts', such as precise sizing, push and pull pressures, corrosion protection, surfaces, and coatings. Bossard's corporate slogan, 'Proven productivity', enhances the goal to help industrial customers to improve/upgrade their productivity.

A query: In a manufacturing world where commoditization puts suppliers' margins under constant pressure, how was it possible for a Swiss-based supplier to grow with profitability higher than the industry benchmarks?

Box 3.3 Bossard AG (*cont'd*)

The reply: the adoption of Industry 4.0, which refers to the Fourth Industrial Revolution as manufacturing converged with the digital economy, in particular with emerging "big collection systems and analytics". Bossard decided to ride this wave of revolution in manufacturing to become the most requested supplier for companies in the manufacturing sector willing to update their activities with Industry 4.0 technologies and profoundly innovate their logistics systems.

Bossard offered three types of services: product solutions, application engineering, and factoring logistics.

Product solutions. Bossard does not sell a mere tangible product like a fastener or a nut but a service. The approach starts with the analysis of the products and the production processes of the customer, whom Bossard can advise regarding the best solution for the safety and reliability standards required and for strengthening customer productivity. About half of Bossard's products sold are customized products.

Application engineering. Moving from its expertise in technology and logistics, Bossard advises customers regarding their product innovation process in the search for new products and new solutions and on how to bring both to the market faster.

Factory logistics. Bossard helps its customers upgrade their operation process through the management concepts of lean management, Smart manufacturing, and mass customization. Bossard's service named 'Smart factory logistics' enables customers to reduce inventory and procurement costs along their value chain and value.

To help its customers manage 'C-parts', including solutions that simplify ordering, Bossard introduced SmartBin, a fully automated ordering system. SmartBin constantly checks current stock levels. When the minimum level of stock is reached, a predefined order quantity is automatically shipped to the customer's warehouse or directly to the point of use. SmartBin was an instant success among Bossard's clients as it helps to optimize the ordering and supply processes, reducing supply complexity and excessive inventories, increasing production and providing data analytics.

In 2014, Boussard introduced SmartBin Flex, a wireless-enabled mobile solution, and the following year SmartLabel, which triggers the ordering of a predetermined quantity of products by pressing a labeled button.

These and other innovations enabled Boussard to implement the 'Smart factory logistics concept', by which computer systems monitored the physical processes and made decentralized decisions. This Internet of Things (IoT) solution empowers Bossard to communicate and cooperate in real-time with participants in the value chain of its clients, offering the company's services. Bossard's sales forces started to use these IoT solutions to provide Vendor-Managed Inventory (VMI).

References

Ahuett-Garza, H., & Kurfess, T. (2018). A brief discussion on the trends of habilitating technologies for Industry 4.0 and Smart manufacturing. *Manufacturing Letters, 15*, 60–63. https://doi.org/10.1016/j.mfglet.2018.02.011

Angeles, R. (2009). Anticipated IT infrastructure and supply chain integration capabilities for RFID and their associated deployment outcomes. *International Journal of Information Management, 29*(3), 219–231. https://doi.org/10.1016/j.ijinfomgt.2008.09.001

Ayala, N. F., Gerstlberger, W., & Frank, A. G. (2019). Managing servitization in product companies: The moderating role of service suppliers. *International Journal of Operations and Production Management, 39*(1), 43–74. https://doi.org/10.1108/IJOPM-08-2017-0484

Banker, S. (2021). *Walmart's massive investment in a supply chain transformation.* www.forbes.com/sites/stevebanker/2021/04/23/walmarts-massive-investment-in-a-supply-chain-transformation/?sh=6a8d5192340e.

BDO digital. (January 12, 2021). *Supply chain 4.0: 6 ways digital transformation is transforming the supply chain.* www.bdo.com/digital/insights/digital-transformation/6-ways-the-supply-chain-is-transforming.

Christopher, M. (2021). In E. Aktas, M. Bourlakis, I. Minis, & V. Zeimpekis (Eds.), *Supply chain 4.0. Enabling market-driven strategies.* Kogan Page.

Dalenogare, L. S., Benitez, G. B., Ayala, N. F., & Frank, A. G. (2018). The expected contribution of Industry 4.0 technologies for industrial performance. *International Journal of Production Economics, 204*, 383–394. https://doi.org/10.1016/j.ijpe.2018.08.019

Deloitte. (2019). *Capturing value through the digital journey.* Deloitte Insight - MAPI Smart Factory. https://www2.deloitte.com/content/dam/insights/us/articles/6276_2019-Deloitte-and-MAPI-Smart-Factory-Study/DI_2019-Deloitte-and-MAPI-Smart-Factory-Study.pdf.

Frank, A. G., Dalenogare, L. S., & Ayala, N. F. (2019). Industry 4.0 technologies: Implementation patterns in manufacturing companies. *International Journal of Production Economics, 210*, 15–26. https://doi.org/10.1016/j.ijpe.2019.01.004

GEP. (2021). *Impact of industry 4.0 on supply chains, all you need to know" March 08, Digital Supply Chain Transformation, Supply chain & Procurement.* www.gep.com/blog/strategy/impact-of-industry-4-on-supply-chain.

Gilchrist, A. (2018). *Supply chain 4.0. Fueled by industry 4.0.* Copyright ©Alasdair Gilchrist.

Jeschke, S., Brecher, C., Meisen, T., Özdemir, D., & Eschert, T. (2016). *Industrial Internet of Things and Cyber Manufacturing Systems*, 3–19. https://doi.org/10.1007/978-3-319-42559-7_1

Juhás, P., & Molnár, K. (2017). Key components of the architecture of cyber-physical manufacturing systems. *Industry 4.0, 2*(5), 205–207.

Kagermann, H., Helbig, J., Hellinger, A., & Wahlster, W. (2013). *Recommendations for implementing the strategic initiative INDUSTRIE 4.0: Securing the future of German manufacturing industry.* Industrie 4.0 Working Group.

Pereira, A. C., & Romero, F. (2017). A review of the meanings and the implications of the Industry 4.0 concept. *Procedia Manufacturing, 13*, 1206–1214. https://doi.org/10.1016/j.promfg.2017.09.032

Porter, M. E., & Heppelmann, J. E. (2015). *How smart, connected products are transforming companies.* Harvard Business Review, 2015(October) https://hbr.org/2015/10/how-smart-connected-products-are-transforming-companies.

Rauch, E. (2020). Industry 4.0+: The next level of intelligent and self-optimizing factories. *Lecture Notes in Mechanical Engineering*, 176–186. https://doi.org/10.1007/978-3-030-50794-7_18

Schuh, G., Anderl, R., Gausemeier, J., Hompel, & Wahlster, W. (2017). *Industrie 4.0 maturity index managing the digital transformation of companies.* www.utzverlag.de/catalog/book/44613.

Stock, T., Obenaus, M., Kunz, S., & Kohl, H. (2018). Industry 4.0 as enabler for a sustainable development: A qualitative assessment of its ecological and social potential. *Process Safety and Environmental Protection, 118,* 254—267. https://doi.org/10.1016/j.psep.2018.06.026

Tao, F., Cheng, J., Qi, Q., Zhang, M., Zhang, H., & Sui, F. (2018). Digital twin-driven product design, manufacturing and service with big data. *The International Journal of Advanced Manufacturing Technology, 94*(9—12), 3563—3576. https://doi.org/10.1007/s00170-017-0233-1

The Economist. (2021). *Semiconductors pose an unwelcome roadblock for carmakers".* The Economist. www.economist.com/business/semiconductors-pose-an-unwelcome-roadblock-for-carmakers/21803287.

Thoben, K. D., Wiesner, S. A., & Wuest, T. (2017). Industrie 4.0" and smart manufacturing-a review of research issues and application examples. *International Journal of Automation Technology, 11*(1), 4—16. https://doi.org/10.20965/ijat.2017.p0004

Wang, S., Wan, J., Li, D., & Zhang, C. (2016). Implementing smart factory of industrie 4.0: An outlook. *International Journal of Distributed Sensor Networks, 12*(1), 1—10. https://doi.org/10.1155/2016/3159805

Wang, S., Wan, J., Zhang, D., Li, D., & Zhang, C. (2016). Towards smart factory for industry 4.0: A self-organized multi-agent system with big data based feedback and coordination. *Computer Networks, 101,* 158—168. https://doi.org/10.1016/j.comnet.2015.12.017

Zhong, R. Y., Xu, X., Klotz, E., & Newman, S. T. (2017). Intelligent manufacturing in the context of industry 4.0: A review. *Engineering, 3*(5), 616—630. https://doi.org/10.1016/J.ENG.2017.05.015

CHAPTER FOUR

The need for a different approach

4.1 Transportation evolution

The impact of the evolution of Supply Chain 4.0 has been strong in all links, but especially in transportation, warehousing, logistics, and procurement 4.0. The war in Ukraine has had profound consequences on the procurement process of raw materials for many companies (Chapter 8). Evolution in transportation under Supply Chain 4.0 is particularly evident. Until a few years ago, for example, trucking logistics simply meant establishing where a truck in operation was at a certain time to compare what the position was with respect to the travel program. Subsequently, various advances were made including the use of GPS, but the main goal was always location tracking. With Supply Chain 4.0, logistics objectives have become much more than location and shipment tracking.

New technologies applied to trucking help to choose the best routes to reach a destination, which is not a simple process as various elements need to be considered: speed limits that are different from one road section to another, the risks of traffic congestion, weather conditions, temporary road closures, and fuel costs. The use of Artificial Intelligence and Machine Learning is being extended with the use of algorithms that consider several factors and can continuously monitor progress and variations. Operating in real time, these algorithms can send notifications and suggest routing adjustments along the way (Gilchrist, 2018).

- **Estimated time of arrival**. Transport logistic software allows companies to calculate, under given travel conditions, how long it will take for a vehicle to reach its destination. In the event of breakdowns or accidents, it can determine how long it takes to rescue a stranded vehicle.
- **Driver performance**. Using data produced by every tire via IoT embedded sensors and Big Data analytics, Michelin Solutions provides customers with relevant data about the vehicle, information that allows companies to measure the performance of drivers not only regarding on-time deliveries but also road safety. These are not only

The Digital Transformation of Supply Chain Management
ISBN: 978-0-323-85532-7
https://doi.org/10.1016/B978-0-323-85532-7.00003-7

technologies for performance control but also tools for collecting information in order to improve efficiency.

- **Other benefits of trucking logistics**. Modern trucking logistic technology allows many other forms of assistance such as knowing in real time the reason for a delay or how to schedule a multiple delivery in a certain period of time along the same trip.

Two significant examples of Supply Chain 4.0 concern the need to invest in infrastructure in transport and logistics (Box 4.1) and Maerks acquisition of LF Logistics (Box 4.2).

4.2 Warehouse transformation

Two trends are driving traditional warehouse transformation. The first is a shift in the characteristics of distribution, driven by a change in customer expectations and in the characteristics of orders and requested services. This trend has promoted the development of a new type of very agile warehouse that can optimize the capabilities of men and machines in a newly symbiotic relationship. The second trend is the wave of technological innovation that includes Robotics, Augmented Reality, Autonomous Vehicles, Sensor technology, and the Internet of Things. These two trends emerge clearly from various studies. Among them, a DHL global survey on Warehousing 4.0 (Harrington, 2022) found that 39% of participants indicate Robotics as the most important mechanical technology for managing their supply chain in the coming years.

Strong advances in computing power have also increased the ability of robots to operate, analyze their environment, and accelerate the speed at which information can be translated into action. Voos recalls that when, in the 1970s at Stanford University, one of the first autonomous self-driving robots was tested to analyze and understand the surrounding environment, it took more than an hour and a half to safely travel no more than a meter. To advance, it had to repeat the whole operation again. "Now the entire process takes milliseconds and includes far more complex tasks such as picking" (Voss, 2021). The operations to move the robot from A to B are smoother, but very complex calculations must be made in milliseconds, thanks to advances in computational power.

Progress is increasing rapidly, with new advancements and breakthroughs happening every day. According to various experts, we are entering a phase in which robots will become more visible and their impact on our lives more direct. By improving the capacity of robots and increasing

Box 4.1 The need to invest in infrastructure

COVID-19 has highlighted the fragility of many supply chains, particularly in transport and logistics. One of the reasons is that the boom in online shopping has increased the pressure on ports and their equipment. According to experts, digital transformation can significantly increase efficiency thanks to better coordination of various activities.

According to Plimmer and Dempsey: "Ports have always faced delays caused by waves, fog and storms, but the pandemic has brought the biggest disruption since the start of container shipping 65 years ago". The logjam has caused stock shortages and delays to deliveries and raised prices. Even before the pandemic, ports were under pressure to upgrade their infrastructure and build the facilities to handle the new generation of ever-larger ships. Added to this was the tendency to build larger and larger ships to increase economies of scale and reduce unit transport costs. As the Authors point out: "The biggest ships can carry up to 20,000 20 ft containers at a time, which, if loaded on to lorries, would stretch further than the distance between Paris and Amsterdam on a motorway lane. But they also require changes to the infrastructure, including deeper docks and bigger cranes" (Plimmer & Dempsey, 2021).

Shifting to new infrastructure takes time: for example, it is estimated that a crane can take 18 months from being ordered to installation. This has made it difficult to respond quickly to changes in demand. Larger ships also mean greater risks and limitations, as shown by the Evergrande affair, where a large container ship blocked the Suez Canal for weeks in 2021. However, improved infrastructure is only part of the story. The pandemic has highlighted the need for greater coordination, information exchange, and digitization throughout the supply chain, according to experts.

The other side of the coin is represented by a 'strange' effect of the pandemic, whereby shipping industry companies have been flooded with cash: 'an unimaginable bonanza'. The Danish group Moller Maersk has made rapid and significant progress in becoming a "global integrator of container logistics that ferries goods by sea, land and air". Maersk manages about a fifth of the world's containers with its fleet, benefitting from global supply strains that have pushed ocean freight rates to record levels. It has allocated part of the large profits earned during the early years of the pandemic to creating an inland logistics network.

our acceptance of their diffusion, they will enter the world of logistics at a faster rate than has been the case so far.

Two core trends will increase the pace of development in the near future. (1) Increasing demand, for example, from e-commerce, will require

> **Box 4.2 Maerks**
>
> In 2021, Maersk acquired LF Logistics for around $3.6 billion, acquiring a network of warehouses in Asia and boosting its footprint in inland logistics. By acquiring LF Logistics, Maersk has gained control of a network of 223 distribution centers across Asia and more than 250 customers globally, according to LF's website. Six months earlier Maersk had purchased two e-commerce logistics companies, one in the United States and one in Europe. The company's management explained why Asia is at the heart of their development plans: "In the next two or 3 decades you will see a lot of growth in Asia as hundreds of millions of people move from poverty into the middle class and consume more. The Maersk deal will be the springboard for more carriers buying inland logistics and more consolidation in the logistics industry" (Dummet & Paris, 2021).
>
> Another goal is to capture a larger share of the market for moving goods between Asian and U.S. ports, and then from American ports into warehouses or businesses and the "last mile to a person's home". Maersk has around 70,000 ocean customers that include U.S. retail chains, car makers, furniture suppliers, electronics makers, and clothing importers. However, less than a quarter of those customers use the company to move their goods from ports to warehouses and distribution centers.

meeting the needs of Supply Chain 4.0 in warehouses rather than in other parts of the supply chain, which will entail increasing operational capacity, especially to cope with peaks in demand. (2) Technology, in particular in robotics, already offers solutions and advances in productivity that help in coping with the growing demand for operational capacity in warehouses. According to experts, this technology and others like it will be developed further, and no doubt in ways that can go beyond what we can now imagine.

A good example concerns shortages and bottlenecks during the pandemic (Box 4.3).

4.3 Warehouse robotics

One of the main drivers of digital logistics and a core component of Supply Chain 4.0 is the automation of highly repetitive labour-intensive and, in some cases, physically intensive tasks.

Voss (2021).

Box 4.3 Chain reaction

People have experienced supply chain problems especially during the pandemic. As shortages and bottlenecks became more acute, supply chain tracking measures proliferated, all of which highlighted an unprecedented high level of disruption. An indicator published by Flexport, an American logistics firm, detects how long it takes a shipment "to move from the supplier warehouse to the departure gate of the destination port" (The Economist, 2022a) for two major freight routes out of China to Europe and America. Before the pandemic, the journey to Europe lasted less than 60 days and that to America less than 50. After the outbreak of the pandemic, times have risen considerably, though to a slightly different extent between the two routes. Those to Europe fluctuated around 108 days and those to America around 114.

A global supply chain index developed since the 1990s based on a variety of indicators by the Federal Reserve of New York before the pandemic, reached its highest level in 2011. The earthquake and tsunami in Japan pushed the index up to a standard deviation of 1.7 above its long-run average. In the spring of 2020, the measure soared higher to 3.9 standard deviations above the average, and in 2021 it rose further, reaching 4.4 in October.

The development of this automation technology is particularly popular in Europe and North America where, especially in some countries, there are difficulties in recruiting staff both for demographic reasons and because of attitudes contrary to certain types of work. Moreover, the increasing customization of products has led to a greater commitment to picking, packing, and shipping of products. The more people increase the 'customer experience', the more they ask for personalized products. The expansion of e-commerce-demand during the coronavirus pandemic (a trend that is set to persist in future years) has also increased the need for new solutions. This is reflected in the management of warehouses and other aspects of logistics. The more shipments move from business-to-business to business-to-consumer, the more e-commerce pushes the boundaries of the supply chain away from the retailer and places greater importance on warehouse management.

The development of this automation technology is particularly popular in Europe and North America.

Robotics has already largely entered logistics management under the pressure of technological progress and greater affordability. The development of e-commerce requires logistics service providers to process small orders quickly to meet customer expectations, while industries in the most economically advanced countries show increasing reluctance among workers to accept certain types of jobs. DHL's global survey on Warehousing 4.0 concludes that in the coming years the introduction of key mechanical warehousing technologies will accelerate rapidly and that the robotics warehouse will see the greatest development. Robotics is therefore considered a determining factor for the success of Supply Chain 4.0.

Progress in warehouse robotics and the difficulty of finding skilled workers in some countries have created a watershed moment in the logistics industries. On the one hand, COVID-19 has caused disruption in supply chains, while on the other remote work has increased home deliveries. According to McKinsey: "Automation in warehousing is no longer just nice to have but an imperative for sustainable growth", which means more robots are needed. McKinsey forecasts that "the warehouse-automation market will grow at a compound annual rate of 23% to be worth more than $50bn by 2030" (The Economist, 2022b).

Voss described how the DHL Supply Chain has introduced global cutting-edge robotics solutions, with reference to Europe and the United States, where demography and operating costs make the application of robotics technology particularly attractive (Voss, 2021). Therefore, it is in the warehouse that DHL Supply Chain believes automation, in particular the latest robotics technologies, will transform the ways in which the industry will respond to the growing demand of supply chains (Box 4.4).

4.4 Logistics

The ultimate goal of logistics "[is] about ensuring products desired are received by customers at the right place, at the right time" (Shippeo, 2021). The main objectives of logistics are to choose the most advantageous transport modes, to design and manage the warehouse system, to manage and control inventory, and to create a logistics network.

Logistics moves products from one place to another using a variety of land, air, and sea means of transport. It monitors the fleet management and shipments and exchanges information with partners along the supply chain to ensure speed and efficiency. At the end of the journey, goods are stored waiting to be delivered to distributors, retailers, or end customers.

Transformation companies have for decades considered logistics as a purely operational function that reported to sales or manufacturing, with the aim of supplying raw materials and components to production plants,

Box 4.4 DHL Supply Chain 4.0

The main advantages from robotic solutions are greater agility and elasticity of logistics in dealing with market fluctuations; an increase in asset utilization and productivity; the automation of repetitive tasks that require demanding physical effort with the possibility of assigning work resources to more complex tasks. There is no shortage of challenges to be faced in introducing new solutions: (1) legislative restrictions on the use of robots in the vicinity of people and (2) ethical and legal issues such as an appropriate level of automation versus human security.

DHL continuously monitors the development of new robotics technologies and assesses their applicability to logistics management. The DHL Supply Chain has a large team of engineers who evaluate warehouse solutions for their customers, and the company adopts a range of key performance indicators, including safety, costs, ROI, and productivity.

The main robotics solutions successfully tested and introduced in the management of warehouses by the DHL Supply Chain are the following: assisted pick-to-bin robots; automated bin point-to-point robot; autonomous goods-to-person robot; autonomous pallet point-to-point robot; assisted pick-to-pallet robot; semiautomated very-narrow-aisle forklift; and collaborative robotic arms. DHL has made many of these solutions available to customers by working in partnership with several robotics technology suppliers.

For example, regarding 'assisted picking robots', the DHL Supply Chain has pioneered the use of collaborative robots with Locus Robotics. The results from the collaboration between Locus Bots and the staff in the DHL warehouses are as follows: (1) a maximum peak of productivity increase: 180% in relation to all warehouse layout; (2) a reduction in training times by 80%; (3) a reduction in error rate; (4) better employee satisfaction; and (5) reduced picker fatigue.

Increased costs and the need to improve productivity as e-commerce pushes the supply chain to greater speed and higher volumes, together with the trend in demand, have led DHL to explore multiple potential warehouse robotic solutions (Voss, 2021).

where the products would be transported and delivered to customers. Operational logistics has often been outsourced to third parties. In recent years, logistics has undergone a profound evolution from a simple operational function of the company to carrying out advanced planning processes due to the introduction of smart technologies, which are 'intelligent' systems capable of controlling processes autonomously, without human intervention.

The terms supply chain and logistics are often used synonymously, but there are important differences. A supply chain is a succession of phases that go from sourcing to processing to the delivery of products to customers, while logistics refers more precisely to moving and storing goods all throughout the supply chain. There are also different meanings according to the geographical areas: the meaning of 'supply chain management' in the United States refers to what in Europe is understood as 'logistics management'.

Logistics is divided into two categories: 'inbound' and 'outbound'. 'Inbound' covers upstream activities relating to receiving, handling, storing, and transporting materials. 'Outbound' covers downstream activities such as the collection, maintenance, and distribution of products to customers.

Logistics efficiency is especially important when the company seeks to grow by entering new global markets. In these phases, acquiring the ability to compete requires the agility and flexibility that logistics can give, especially in the 'last mile delivery'. Process efficiency is being leveraged in logistics as well by advanced supply chain management systems, customer relationship management systems, and Big Data (Box 4.5).

Box 4.5 Big, bulky, and heavy

"Furniture has been one of the biggest casualties of the global shipping and supply chain crisis as costs to transport a sofa or table are much higher than a pocket-sized iPhone or a pair of trainers" (Johnston & Dempsey, 2022). In some cases, after the outbreak of the pandemic the cost of transporting containers for home furniture have risen as much as 1200%, forcing companies to face a choice: absorb the higher costs and therefore reduce profit margins, which can also mean less ability to make new investments, or increase prices and pass on the higher costs to customers, thereby making the offer less attractive with the risk of reducing the demand for their products.

For many companies, it was inevitable that production be brought closer to the sales markets. Some European retailers, under the pressure of rising transport costs but also long delivery times from Asia, have relocated production to countries such as Poland, Lithuania, and Latvia, which also present advantages due to the low cost of labor and the access to raw materials. Other chain retailers, such as Denmark's Jysk, use large distribution centers to stock goods close to its European customers, although they still maintain part of their production in China or in other Asian countries.

The effects of COVID-19 on logistics have been profound. The most obvious involves the redesign of the supply chains forced on many companies. The main reason for revising these plans was summarized by one manager during an interview: "The engineers have designed supply chains around predictability, and when that predictability goes away everything goes to hell in a handbasket" (Edgecliffe-Johnson, 2022).

During the pandemic, the conditions no longer existed for building supply chains extending to various countries and with numerous suppliers. A second reason concerned putting the search for efficiency and performance (lean management) first. "Most companies are realizing that they over-tuned their operation for performance versus resilience", commented the Boston Consulting Group's global Chair, who in an interview added that "clients were adopting more of a 'just in case' attitude". Giving up 'just in time' to shift to 'just in case' (accumulating more stock than necessary in the very short term) means prioritizing resilience.

Various factors therefore converge in redesigning the supply chain by shortening it and moving closer to customers, with the aim of giving maximum security to the continuity of operations. Locating inventory closer to customers is a fundamental step in this direction. Proximity to end markets has become a criterion for selecting suppliers. For example, the clothing group behind brands such as The North Face have moved some production to suppliers closer to their biggest markets.

4.5 Procurement 4.0

Procurement refers to all the business activities involved in obtaining products and services, from sourcing to all stages of the purchasing process, focusing on the strategic process of sourcing.

The difference with purchasing is significant, as the latter focuses instead on how products and services are acquired and ordered.

Procurement has become a critical business activity by being considered a boundary spanning function, where it is responsible for sourcing decisions and acts as a bridge between internal and external enterprises … Internally, procurement managers provide information (such as suppliers' capacity, logistics data, pricing and discounts and new products information) to other functions and internal customers taking responsibility to supply procurement with their needs … Externally, procurement is responsible for product or service cost, timeframes of delivery, product quality and general supply decisions, such as supplier selection and supplier relationship.

Pereira et al. (2014).

A case in point concerns procurement as the key factor for Apple (Box 4.6).

Digital technologies have also brought significant advances in procurement, including AI, Advanced Analytics, and Machine Learning, contributing above all with sourcing goods and services, selecting suppliers and best value, and prices. These advances were possible, thanks to the greater transparency of supplier/buyer transactions afforded by connecting the physical and digital worlds.

Three main technologies support procurement 4.0: (1) Cognitive computing and Artificial Intelligence. Machine Learning technologies, for example, help in pattern recognition. (2) Intelligent content extraction, which makes it possible to obtain data from unstructured documents that in the past "would have taken days or weeks to assemble". (3) Predictive and Advanced Analytics, which enables a planner to predict the probable scenario for cost/price fluctuations in demand and for risks, making it possible to control a situation rather than responding to it after the fact (Gilchrist, 2018).

The procurement process can be divided into two parts: (1) sourcing and (2) purchasing.

(1) Sourcing concerns the identification of the sources of the materials to verify they are relevant to the strategies adopted and legally compliant.

Box 4.6 Apple: Procurement as the key factor

The global supply chain has 200 suppliers that account for 98% of expenditures on materials, manufacturing, and product assembly across all products. Located in 43 countries and six continents, these suppliers had more than 800 total production location.

The cost of materials and components for the iPhone 11 Pro Max was estimated at $490.50, with a suggested retail price of $ 1099. Considering that annual production is around 200 million items, Apple wielded enormous clout with suppliers. Although each iPhone had approximately 1000 individual parts, there were about a dozen key components that were typically provided by single-sourced suppliers. Apple maintained strict control over its supply chain, negotiating discounts on material costs and insisting on flexible manufacturing capacity. Suppliers were expected to provide a detailed breakdown of the cost of labor, material and overhead, and their profit. Apple stretched its accounts payable to 90 days or more (Fraser, 2020).

The main criteria for selecting sources are the search for low cost, high quality, and low lead time. In recent years, the need to select sources based on the criterion of environmental sustainability has also increasingly emerged.

(2) The purchasing process begins when the source is confirmed and concerns the management of quantity and time negotiations and the receipt of deliveries. The choice to unify the two processes or to keep them distinct depends primarily on the size of the organization. COVID-19, in bringing to the surface the fragilities of many supply chains, has given growing importance to procurement.

4.6 The sourcing process

Sourcing is the process of selecting suppliers to provide the goods and services management needs to run its business. It may sound uncomplicated, but the process can be complex. Strategic sourcing involves a process that improves the efficiency and quality of production, contains costs, and minimizes risks through the careful selection of suppliers. It is defined as "the use of supplier competencies to achieve flexibility goals through: establishing relationships with suppliers with fast response capabilities to schedule or design changes; and formal incorporation of supplier technological capabilities in design, engineering, and manufacturing strategies" (Narasimhan & Das, 1999).

Two sourcing choices in recent years have required careful review because of both the progress of technologies and the vulnerabilities to supply chains created by the coronavirus pandemic: outsourcing and reshoring.

4.6.1 Outsourcing

Outsourcing refers to the process of obtaining raw materials, components, finished products and services from sources outside the organization. The decision by large companies to produce internally or buy from the outside is oriented to building and retaining within the organization the core competencies (defined as production 'in-house') and entrusting to the outside those activities considered to be non-core (Pellicelli, 2009a, 2009b).

In recent years, as the risks of vulnerability of supply chains have increased, these decisions have been carefully reviewed, and many companies have decided to shorten the chain by bringing back various in-house activities that were previously entrusted to the outside.

Often when it comes to decisions about the sourcing of materials, products, or services, the words 'outsourcing' and 'offshoring' are used synonymously. However, they are two different concepts because offshoring indicates that the company controls a production process that takes place in an offshore location, outside the national borders (Pellicelli, 2018). The main reasons for the choice are to take advantage of productions with lower costs, better quality, or shorter lead times. Other reasons for producing offshore may be the tax advantages offered by local authorities or the decision to locate a source of offshore activity near a new sales market.

4.6.2 Reshoring

More companies have shortened the supply chain by deciding to bring back to the country of origin part of their activities previously done outside the national borders (*reshoring*). These decisions were made to cope with rising costs in offshore locations, political turmoil, exchange rate fluctuations, and quality issues. Disruptions caused by the COVID-19 pandemic and the Russia—Ukraine war have accelerated the reshoring process.

This issue will be discussed in more detail in the concluding chapters.

4.7 The purchasing process

There are various methods to guide choices in purchasing strategies. Dani distinguishes three aspects in this regard: portfolio analysis, supplier segmentation, and supplier development (Dani, 2020).

- **Portfolio analysis**. One of the most used methods for analyzing the portfolio of relationships with suppliers is the Kraljic matrix, which classifies the products of companies in a two-dimensional matrix with the variable 'profit impact', on the one hand, and 'supply risk' on the other (Kraljic, 1983). The purchases or suppliers of a company are segmented by dividing them into four classes, based on the complexity (or risk) of the supply market (such as monopoly situation, barriers to entry, and technological innovation) and the importance of the purchases or suppliers (determined by the impact they have on the profitability of the company). The matrix can assist companies in analyzing their purchasing portfolio from a strategic point of view. The construction of the matrix is considered a good premise for setting up a purchasing strategy. A good example proposed by researchers (Nudurupati et al., 2015) is applied to the global health care companies (Fig. 4.1).

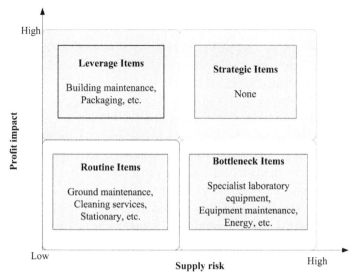

Figure 4.1 *The purchasing portfolio from the strategic point of view.* The Figure explains the purchasing portfolio from the point of view of the profit impact and the suppy risk, highlighting four categories: strategic items, bottleneck items, routine items and leverage items. *From Nudurupati, S. S., Bhattacharya, A., Lascelles, D. & Caton, N. (2015). Strategic sourcing with multi-stakeholders through value co-creation: An evidence from global health care company.* International Journal of Production Economics, 166, 248–257. https://doi.org/10.1016/j.ijpe.2015.01.008.

- **Supplier segmentation.** Another tool to manage relationships with suppliers is to distinguish them based on multiple criteria such as risk level, delivery times, stock policies, and costs. Regarding the level of risk, a frequent distinction is between: (1) strategic suppliers ("relationships that provide a definitive advantage and are heavily integrated into the buyer's supply chain"); (2) tactical supplier ("important for the day-to-day operations of the buyer"); (3) and transactional suppliers ("that provide spot-buying") in which the buyer does not have the power to set prices and terms and whose relationships "do not create any long-term working plan" (Dani, 2020).
- **Supplier development.** To maintain continuity, it is necessary to sustain and develop strategic suppliers. To achieve this goal, the buyer may need to invest in expansion or modernization programs regarding the supplier's production activities in the interest of the buyer itself.

4.8 Toward a new model of procurement

In one of its most recent reports, *Harvard Business Review* "calls for an innovative new operating model and predicts that procurement will evolve" in the following ways (Guernsey, 2021):

(1) Prioritizing Supplier Relationships. Not only focusing on cutting costs has critical importance, but also the ability to build and maintain deep supplier relationships. Procurement teams that can collaborate in real time with their suppliers are better positioned to face disruption and better able to mitigate risk and generate competitive advantage for the business.

(2) Leveraging automation for increased visibility. Digital technologies have automated many routine procedures in procurement processes by increasing the visibility of operations for all stakeholders. "By aggregating their contract, supplier, and project data, procurement leaders and key decision makers have a birds-eye view into the end-to-end sourcing process" (Guernsey, 2021). With the increased use of automation and digitalization, success in procurement choices has also acquired strategic importance, which can contribute to the success of the company.

(3) Building an agile and resilient sourcing function. Procurement can play a key role in bringing greater stability and agility to the sourcing process, and therefore contribute to giving resilience to supply networks, a role that has been enhanced by the growing uncertainty and supply chain disruptions caused by the pandemic.

(4) Supporting a purpose-driven organization. Increasing visibility regarding "suppliers, compliance, and resilience" increases the importance of procurement in creating value for the company, a goal that can be achieved through partnering with a more diverse set of suppliers. The supply chain disruption over the past year has fragmented the conventional supplier relationship by forcing major operators to enter into contracts with a wide variety of "smaller, more local vendors in order to shore up their supply chains".

An important example concerns the semiconductor shortage (Box 4.7).

Box 4.7 Why was the world running low on chips?

Not only were carmakers running out of semiconductors in 2021–22: even Microsoft, Nintendo, and Sony were running out of semiconductors for their gaming consoles. Samsung, one of the world's leading chip manufacturers, has warned that smartphone production has been affected.

Why has the shortage been magnified? The semiconductor sector has always had a cyclical trend, but the coronavirus pandemic has exacerbated the magnitude of the fluctuations. During 2021, after having overcome the critical phase of the pandemic, thanks to the arrival of vaccines, semiconductor production was not able to respond to the explosion of demand driven by four main factors. (1) Remote work has increased the demand for new PCs, recording its strongest growth in the last 10 years. (2) The data-center demand has boomed as people have turned to video-calling, video-streaming, and video gaming. (3) The car industry lowered sales forecasts during the initial lockdowns, but then raised them as vaccines were developed. (4) Microsoft and Sony have launched new video-game consoles, making exceptional orders with major chipmakers. However, increasing operational capacity is difficult, and it is practically impossible to do in the short term. The demand for semiconductors has become more sophisticated. Avant-garde plants, used to make cutting-edge chips for smartphones and gaming consoles, cost tens of billions of dollars to build. Even manufacturers using old technologies and producing low-priced semiconductors are struggling to increase production because of a dearth of plant suppliers.

Political tensions between the United States and China have been another source of problems. Only two countries possess the most advanced technologies and they are both in Asia, where around 80% of the world's chip-making capacity is located. When the cost of using new technologies rose sharply, the number of companies able to keep pace quickly dropped, from about 30 at the beginning of the century to only two: Samsung in South Korea and TSMC in Taiwan. Running for cover, American chipmakers have launched a lobbying campaign to induce the government to fund the development of domestic production and reduce dependence on Asia. Twenty European countries have also asked the European Commission to take action to increase semiconductor production on the continent.

Car companies have acted belatedly. The most frequent solution has been to shorten supply chains (reshoring), but this decision requires a long lead time. As a result, the car industry, which is used to working with flexible 'just in time' supply chains, has been hit hard.

References

Dani, S. (2020). *Strategic supply chain management*. Kogan Page.

Dummet, B., & Paris, C. (2021). *Maersk buys Asian warehouse giant LF logistics for $3.6 billion"*. Wall Street Journal. www.wsj.com/articles/maersk-nears-deal-to-buy-lf-logistics-for-about-3-billion-11640141333.

Edgecliffe-Johnson, A. (2022). *Winners and losers emerge from lingering US supply chain crisis*. Financial Times. www.ft.com/content/76791405-3750-4965-a42a-8e0969564de1.

Fraser, J. (June 1, 2020). *Apple Inc: Global supply chain management*. Ivey Publishing. www.iveypublishing.ca/s/product/apple-inc-global-supply-chain-management/01t5c00000CwpgJAAR.

Gilchrist, A. (2018). *Supply chain 4.0. Fueled by Industry 4.0*. Copyright ©Alasdair Gilchrist.

Guernsey, D. (2021). *4 ways procurement is evolving in 2021 and beyond*. Harvard Business Review.

Harrington, L. (2022). *Digitalization business brief: The age of the smart DC, DHL supply chain*. www.dhl.com/content/dam/dhl/global/dhl-supply-chain/documents/pdf/SCI_Warehousing-4-Brief.pdf.

Johnston, I., & Dempsey, H. (2022). *Why supply chain crisis is a 'big' problem for furniture*. Financial Times. www.ft.com/content/10805068-2891-407f-827a-e446485a5d96.

Kraljic, P. (1983). Purchasing must become supply management. *Harvard Business Review*. https://hbr.org/1983/09/purchasing-must-become-supply-management.

Narasimhan, R., & Das, A. (1999). An empirical investigation of the contribution of strategic sourcing to manufacturing flexibilities and performance. *Decision Sciences, 30*(3), 683–718. https://doi.org/10.1111/j.1540-5915.1999.tb00903.x

Nudurupati, S. S., Bhattacharya, A., Lascelles, D., & Caton, N. (2015). Strategic sourcing with multi-stakeholders through value co-creation: An evidence from global health care company. *International Journal of Production Economics, 166*, 248–257. https://doi.org/10.1016/j.ijpe.2015.01.008

Pellicelli, M. (2009a). From outsourcing to offshoring and virtual organizations: How management redefines the boundaries of companies. *The International Journal of Knowledge, Culture, and Change Management: Annual Review, 9*(7), 77–88. https://doi.org/10.18848/1447-9524/CGP/v09i07/59141

Pellicelli, M. (2009b). *L'outsourcing e l'offshoring nell'economia dell'impresa*. Giappichelli.

Pellicelli, M. (2018). Gaining flexibility and innovation through offshore outsourcing. *Sustainability, 10*(5), 1672. https://doi.org/10.3390/su10051672

Pereira, C. R., Christopher, M., & Lago Da Silva, A. (2014). Achieving supply chain resilience: The role of procurement. *Supply Chain Management, 19*, 626–642. https://doi.org/10.1108/SCM-09-2013-0346

Plimmer, G., & Dempsey, H. (2021). *Covid casts light on port infrastructure crisis*. Financial Times.

Shippeo. (September 2, 2021). *Supply chain logistics and real-time visibility*. www.shippeo.com/blog/supply-chain-logistics-and-real-time-visibility.

The Economist. (2022a). *Chain reactions*. The Economist, Special report. http://www.economist.com/special-report/2002/02/02/chain-reaction.

The Economist. (2022b). New robots—smarter and faster—are taking over warehouses. *The Economist, Science & Technology*. www.economist.com/science-and-technology/a-new-generation-of-smarter-and-faster-robots-are-taking-over-distribution-centres/21807595.

Voss, M. (2021). In E. Aktas, M. Bourlakis, I. Minis, & V. Zeimpekis (Eds.), *Collaborative robotics. Transforming warehouse logistics*. Kogan Page.

CHAPTER FIVE

Managing the supply chain: technologies for digitalization solutions

5.1 The irresistible march of technological disruption

In the globalization era, competition, which also affects companies in the supply chain, pushes toward the search for increasingly innovative solutions. The term innovation comes from the Latin word 'innovare', meaning "creating something new". The literature agrees that this consists in the creation of new combinations of ideas. The innovation process is described as a problem of search (how to find opportunities for innovation), selection (what to do and why), implementation, and capture (how to achieve results and benefits) (Aloini & Martini, 2013; Bessant et al., 2005). In a dissimilar perspective. Hamel (2006) asserts that: "There is no sausage crank for innovation, but it's possible to increase the odds of a 'Eureka!' moment by assembling the right ingredients" (Hamel, 2006; Kumar et al., 2021).

The concept of technical innovation, as an economic development driver with an impact on the economy, was introduced by Schumpeter (1912). Schumpeter believed that innovations were "new combinations of knowledge" needed in five main cases (Schumpeter, 1934): (a) developing a new product or introducing products with new properties to the market; (b) introducing a new method of production; (c) opening up a new market; (d) acquiring new sources of raw materials; (e) carrying out a new organization of economic processes. The Schumpeter concept of "Creative destruction", which is continuous destruction of old structures and the constant development of new, more effective ones (Witkowski, 2017), still reverberates in the literature on innovation. According to Schumpeter's thinking, innovation has become imperative for and synonymous with the survival and growth of companies as well as associated with the state of national economies (Dekkers et al., 2014).

In recent years, technology has profoundly impacted strategies as well as their implementation. Modern methods have continued to uproot traditional practices, with many supply chains facing challenging times,

The Digital Transformation of Supply Chain Management
ISBN: 978-0-323-85532-7
https://doi.org/10.1016/B978-0-323-85532-7.00002-5

necessitating in many instances reorganizing the suppliers' network. For example, progress in software technology has shifted the center of gravity in the automobile industry from a mechanical supply chain to a software one. As a consequence, many carmakers and suppliers have lost their power. Being forced to shift from one sector of suppliers (lower demand for mechanical parts) to another (more software and digital products), the main carmakers decided to define their core business in new ways and to change their business models.

There are no obstacles to the disruption of the previous equilibria. Moving further into software brings manufacturers in all sectors up against specialized information technology companies. The Internet of Things is set to transform the supply chain of many industries, from transport to manufacturing. Acquiring digital skills has become a must for those firms that want to be competitive and in the vanguard in the near future. In this challenging and crowded market, new competitors are emerging all the time. As they involve, technologies traditionally embedded in an industry can suddenly make room for new competitors from other industries, competitors who are often cash rich and looking for new investments. This is the case with Apple and Google, which are trying to enter the car industry through the new driverless technologies.

5.1.1 The role of risk and uncertainty

Deciding when and how to react to a negative trend is made difficult by growing uncertainty regarding the economy, technology, and politics. One of the greatest obstacles is that the more the uncertainty increases, the shorter the time is for making efficient decisions and the faster management needs to react. How should management respond? The question has great importance in managing the global supply chain and has led to great attention among researchers and managers.

Koulopoulos and Roloff suggest a set of fundamental principles that can be used "to turn the chaos of uncertainty into opportunity for growth and prosperity" (Koulopoulos & Roloff, 2006).

The most relevant principles for managing a supply chain in the face of uncertainty are the following.

(1) "Uncertainty increases as the volume of information increases". In managing a supply chain, executives gain a lot of information about the details about what suppliers must do and how they must do it, and this provides them with warning signals. However, they need "an equally greater amount of time to reach decisions". Having a lot of information,

and the warning signals this provides, is an advantage, but the more information available, the more time is needed for a decision to be made. Delaying decisions in governing the supply chain means risking setting off a series of negative consequences. The answer to this information overload is above all knowing how to select, skim and identify the key points in order to make quick decisions.

(2) "Uncertainty creates a greater need for radical thought, creativity and innovation". The first reaction to uncertainty is to limit the risk, in this way organizations often become risk-averse. In the fast-paced current environment, taking risks is "ultimately the only avenue to innovation". However, this does not mean abandoning all defenses, but accepting that degree of risk that can lead to new ways of growth and innovation in products and processes.

5.2 Digital technologies are reshaping supply chains

Digital technology, by which everything is going to be connected, is forcing companies across all industries to rethink their operations. The plunging costs of sensors, progress in communications, data storage, and in analytics allow companies to record and process huge amounts of information about physical systems. This information has increased efficiency in various management areas, in particular concerning the supply chain. It can be used to improve performance, prevent failures and organize contingency plans. Acquiring digital skills and technology has become a must for companies that wish to be competitive and remain at the vanguard in the next few years.

The development of the Internet and mobile technologies has involved a fundamental impact of new technologies on economics and business. Every technology has distinctive elements that enable it to operate in specific domains.

Cloud computing, Big Data, Internet of Things (IoT), Blockchain, Robotics, Additive Manufacturing (AM), Autonomous Vehicles (AV), Artificial Intelligence (AI), Co-creation, and Digital Value Chain (DVC) are some of the many innovations that digital technology has made possible and that have forced companies to rethink the organization of their supply chains, thanks to the advantages they offer in terms of simplification, efficiency, security, and timeliness.

According to Kumar et al. the 'new-age technologies' - in particular the Internet of Things (IoT), Artificial Intelligence (AI), Machine Learning

(ML), and Blockchain – are widely considered to be the way of the future (Kumar et al., 2021). Therefore, greater attention will be reserved for them in the following pages.

The origin and the fundamental concepts of these innovative technologies available for managing and increasing the efficiency of supply chains are introduced in the following sections.

5.3 Cloud computing

Cloud computing is a significant technological trend that provides shared processing resources and data with computers and other devices. It is a model for providing ubiquitous, on-demand access to a shared pool of computing resources, and it enables cost savings, high availability, and easy scalability.

Cloud computing is Internet-based computing where users can use a variety of devices including PCs, laptops, smartphones, and PDAs to access programs, storage, and application development platforms over the Internet through services offered by Cloud computing providers (Furht, 2010).

It is widely believed that Cloud computing was introduced in the late 1980s with the diffusion of grid computing concepts and the application of a large number of systems to a single (hard, scientific) problem for the first time.

According to the official NIST definition: "Cloud computing is a model for enabling ubiquitous, convenient, on-demand network access to a shared pool of configurable computing resources (e.g.: networks, servers, storage, applications and services) that can be rapidly provisioned and released with minimal management effort or service provider interaction" (Mell & Grance, 2011).

A broad definition of Cloud computing is the following.

Cloud computing is a network-based or Internet-based storage environment that enables and facilitates sharing of knowledge, information, files or resources.
(Dirican, 2015).

This advanced technology presents many advantages over traditional IT models; for example: faster data transactions, elasticity, resource-sharing, pay-per-use, flexibility, ease of configuration, low IT deployment cost, the need for data centers, and increased IT performance (Novais et al., 2019).

It is structured through the following service models: Software as a Service (SaaS), Platform as a Service (PaaS), Infrastructure as a Service (IaaS), and the following deployment models: Private Cloud, Community Cloud, Public Cloud, and Hybrid Cloud (Mell & Grance, 2011).

Cloud computing provides a series of new characteristics compared to other computing paradigms (Grossman, 2009; Wang et al., 2019). Furht describes the main features of Cloud computing (Furht, 2010), which can be summarized as follows (Table 5.1).

As Shafiq et al. explain, all cloud entities work together to handle the cloud environment (Shafiq et al., 2022): the cloud auditors ensure the control in terms of quality and integrity of services offered by CPSs and the stable connection to carry services to customers (cloud users) is provided by cloud carriers (Fig. 5.1).

Commonly in the Cloud Computing environment, there are two components: the 'frontend side' and the 'backend side'. The 'frontend side' is

Table 5.1 The main features of Cloud computing.

The main features	A brief description
Scalability and on-demand services	Cloud computing provides resources and services for users on demand. The resources are scalable over several data centers.
User-centric interface	Cloud interfaces are location independent and can be accessed by well-established interfaces such as web services and internet browsers.
Guaranteed quality of service (QoS)	Cloud computing can guarantee QoS for users in terms of hardware/CPU performance, bandwidth, and memory capacity.
Autonomous system	Cloud computing systems are autonomous systems managed transparently to users. However, software and data inside clouds can be automatically reconfigured and consolidated to a simple platform depending on user's needs.
Pricing	Cloud computing does not require up-from investment. No capital expenditure is required. Users pay for services and capacity as they need them.

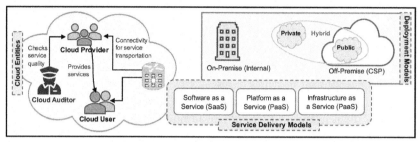

Figure 5.1 *Cloud computing overview.* The figure explains how all cloud entities work together to handle the cloud environment. *From Shafiq, D. A., Jhanjhi, N. Z. & Abdullah, A. (2022). Load balancing techniques in cloud computing environment: A review.* Journal of King Saud University-Computer and Information Sciences, 34(7), 3910–3933. *https:// doi.org/10.1016/j.jksuci.2021.02.007.*

accessible through connections over the Internet. Whereas the 'backend side' is focused on cloud service models and consists of a Data Center where multiple physical machines (known as servers) are stored. As the Authors (Shafiq et al., 2022) detail incoming user requests are received by the dynamically scheduled application, and resources are allocated to clients through virtualization (Fig. 5.2).

In managing the supply chain, companies are forced to continually chase business partners to order materials, components, and modules, control inventory levels, organize logistics, or make deliveries to customers. When a manufacturer receives an order, it has little idea if its partners can provide the materials needed to fulfill it on schedule, the transport capacity required to deliver it, or the shelf space to display it to customers. Cloud technology can provide a place for supply chain partners to collaborate.

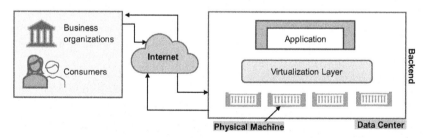

Figure 5.2 *Cloud computing architecture.* The figure illustrates the Cloud computing architecture, based on 'physical machine' and 'data center'. *From Shafiq, D. A., Jhanjhi, N. Z. & Abdullah, A. (2022). Load balancing techniques in cloud computing environment: A review.* Journal of King Saud University-Computer and Information Sciences, 34(7), 3910–3933. *https://doi.org/10.1016/j.jksuci.2021.02.007.*

Globalization has made supply chains longer, more dynamic, more exposed to sudden changes in the environment, and riskier than ever before. Reactions to unexpected events must be rapid to be effective. E-mail, phone calls, and even supply chain traceability have their limits. Cloud computing provides a new platform where partners can get together to exchange information in real-time. Responding by means of a contingency plan becomes more rapid and effective in detecting potential or actual sources of disruption. Cloud services save costs because they are flexible and available on demand and companies do not have to invest to cover peak load.

5.4 Big Data

'Big Data' is used as an umbrella term to cover a range of data, technologies, and applications. It generally describes the collection, processing, analysis, and visualization associated with very large data sets. It is considered a form of data that exceeds the processing capabilities of traditional database infrastructure or engines. Compared to traditional datasets, Big Data typically includes masses of unstructured data intended for real-time analysis, allows new opportunities for value discovery, and enables the effective organization and management of datasets.

The term was introduced for the first time in 2001 by Doug Laney, an analyst at META (today Gartner) who defined in a research report the challenges and opportunities due to the large increase in data using a 3versus model (Laney, 2001). Although the initial definitions were provided a few years later, the 3versus (Volume, Velocity, and Variety) are widely accepted as the basis for the definition of Big Data (Bedi et al., 2014; Chen et al., 2014; Demchenko et al., 2013; Gandomi & Haider, 2015; Khan et al., 2014). In this model, Volume means that the scale of data becomes larger and larger; Velocity means that data collection and analysis, etc., must be conducted quickly and timely; and Variety means various types of data, which include semistructured and unstructured data (such as audio, video, web pages, and text) and traditional structured data.

Recently, the great potential of Big Data has gained interest in the industry, as well as in the public media (such as: The Economist, The New York Times, Nature and Science). Government agencies have also promoted extensive plans to accelerate Big Data research and applications (Chen et al., 2014).

On the basis of the Apache Hadoop[1] definition of Big Data ("datasets which could not be captured, managed, and processed by general computers within an acceptable scope"), in 2011, McKinsey and Company announced that Big Data was the next frontier for innovation, competition, and productivity (Chen et al., 2014), "a key basis of competition, underpinning new waves of productivity growth, innovation, and consumer surplus". McKinsey provided the following definition: "Big data refers to datasets whose size is beyond the ability of typical database software tools to capture, store, manage and analyze" (Manyika et al., 2011).

Other different and broad definitions of Big Data that can be mentioned are the following.

Big Data consists of extensive datasets primarily in the characteristics of volume, variety, velocity, and/or variability that require a scalable architecture for efficient storage, manipulation, and analysis.

(Chang and Grady, 2019).

Big Data technologies describe a new generation of technologies and architectures, designed to economically extract value from very large volumes of a wide variety of data, by enabling the high-velocity capture, discovery, and/or analysis.

(Gantz et al., 2011).

The term Big Data describes a data environment in which scalable architectures support the requirements of analytical and other applications which process, with high velocity, high volume data which may have a variety of data formats and which may include high-velocity data acquisition.

(Emmanuel and Stanier, 2016).

In the literature, other characteristics in terms of the versus have been added in subsequent studies (Dean & Ghemawat, 2008; Gandomi & Haider, 2015; Khan et al., 2014; Schroeck et al., 2012). In their study, Khan et al. describe the characteristics, issues, and challenges of Big Data (Khan et al., 2014), which can be summarized as follows (Table 5.2).

Sundarakani et al. propose a high-level architecture for Big Data-driven supply chain analysis (Fig. 5.3). "The various sources of input data in the supply chain are represented by the entities at the bottommost layer, consisting

---

[1] Cloudera (https://www.cloudera.com/) rapidly became a leader in the big data market after its launch in 2008.

Table 5.2 The main features of Big Data.

The main features	A brief description
(1) Volume	Data scale
(2) Value	Data usefulness in decision making
(3) Velocity	Data processing: batch and stream
(4) Veracity	Data quality and accuracy
(5) Viscosity	Data complexity
(6) Variability	Data flow inconsistency
(7) Volatility	Data durability
(8) Viability	Data activeness
(9) Validity	Data properly understandable
(10) Variety	Data heterogeneity: structured, semistructured, unstructured

of suppliers, manufacturers, warehouses, distributors, retailers, and customers" (Sundarakani et al., 2021).

Big Data has changed the dynamics of the supply chain. Some of the clearest savings come from using Big Data for predictive maintenance and statistical process control. Big Data can improve the efficiency of managerial systems like global supply chains and might also lead to more rational resource allocation among their segments. In addition, applying AI to Big Data can deepen our real-time understanding of how fast the real world is changing.

Suppliers can fit sensors on more bits of machinery, which can report back when anything abnormal is detected; for example, operators learn in real-time when a turbine engine is beginning to consume more oil than usual. Big Data can beget growth in many areas of the supply chain, such as efforts to reduce inventories by observing movements of stock. Companies such as Nestlé and Kraft are linking up to supermarket point of sale data and analyzing this to predict consumption trends. While this kind of stock control exercise is similar to what companies have done in the past, Big Data allows this to be done in a matter of minutes and at a speed heretofore impractical.

5.5 Internet of Things (IoT)

The term 'Internet of Things' (IoT) was introduced by Kevin Ashton, a British entrepreneur, and startup founder, as the title of his presentation to Procter & Gamble in 1999, attributing to it the meaning of a system in

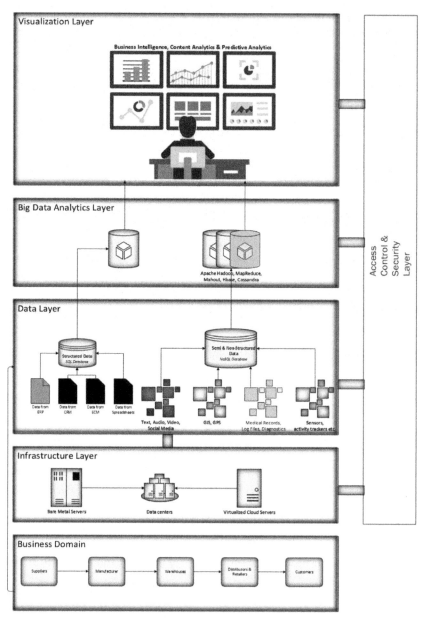

Figure 5.3 *A high-level architecture for Big Data-driven supply chain analysis.* The figure illustrates a high-level architecture for Big Data-driven supply chain analysis from the 'business domain' to the 'visualization layer'. *From Sundarakani, B., Ajaykumar, A. & Ajaykumar, A. (2021). Big data driven supply chain design and applications for blockchain: An action research using case study approach.* Omega, *102, 1—19. https://doi. org/10.1016/j.omega.2021.102452.*

which the material world communicates with computers-exchanging data-through 'omnipresent' sensors. He subsequently used it at the Massachusetts Institute of Technology (where he became co-founder of the Auto-ID Center). Ashton highlighted that what defines the Internet of Things is data capture. His simple and innovative idea was to connect RFID to the Internet in Procter & Gamble's supply chain to allow the chip to communicate information so that machines could share data (with other machines and people), that could be used to monitor their performance and optimize production.

In his book "Making sense of IoT", Ashton identifies the meaning of the Internet of Things with the following statement: "sensors connected to the Internet, behaving in an Internet-like way by making open, ad hoc connections, sharing data freely, and allowing unexpected applications, so computers can understand the world around them and become humanity's nervous system" (Ashton, 2017). Although Ashton's idea, revolutionary at the time, was promising, it remained a concept used only by specialists until 2010, and it took several years before its potential to improve society in different fields could be fully understood.

The founder of the term 'Internet of Things' stated in an interview (Gabbai, 2015): "Tenacity is far more important than talent. Innovators don't do things that have never been tried; they do things that have never been done. The difference between successful innovators and everybody else is that innovators keep failing until they don't. They have to be irrationally passionate. Innovators keep banging their head against the wall until they make a door". According to Ashton (2017), this occurred because sensors work best in networks: "Consider the human nervous system: it's a network that connects sensors to the brain, which matches inputs to memories and interprets - or makes sense of - them. Your eyes cannot see a hot apple pie. They only see a pie. Your nose senses the apple. Your fingers sense the heat. It's the correlation of these inputs with memories of hot apple pies past that tells you what's in front of you. The things we think of as our senses — in the case of the nervous system, our eyes, ears, and so on — have limited value unless they are connected. Or, the network is the sensor".

The great limitation of computers was mainly due to people's dependence on obtaining information (usually via keyboards), which greatly limited early computers as the world was a complex system in constant change. According to the Author, the solution was quite simple: "let computers sense the world by themselves". Sensing systems appeared only in the late twentieth century (including optical character recognition, barcodes, navigation satellites, and radio frequency identification tags), but these systems were isolated and needed local data storage. The first in–car navigation products, for instance, used satellites as their only sensor and stored map data on cassette tapes. In this way, information inevitably became obsolete quickly, mainly as a result of changes in the roads stored in memory.

A good example of IoT concerns the connected vehicles of Ford (Box 5.1).

Box 5.1 Ford's connected vehicles

Ford Motor Company has had great success since 2007 collaborating with Microsoft on SYNC technology, an in-car, voice-controlled system for operating in-car entertainment and cell phones (optional available at the cost of $395). By adding new sensor-enabled features, SYNC has become an Internet of Things platform. Ford cars could automatically contact emergency services if they deployed their airbags or shut off their fuel pumps because of a collision and automatically generate reports about their fluid levels and the condition of their brakes and engines. They also had GPS-based navigation services. Trucks for the construction industry were also equipped with radio frequency identification readers to track tools and GPS-enabled fleet tracking.

Ford immediately had to counter the offensive from Microsoft's competitors, particularly Apple. Aside from the initial difficulties it faced with SYNC technology, Ford was still very successful in creating a new software platform (BlackBerry's QNX, a Unix-like system already used in millions of cars). It succeeded in restoring the SYNC brand and upgraded 911 Assist to provide emergency responders with essential information (e.g.: the speed and nature of a crash). It also expanded its Autonomous Vehicle fleet and worked with Hewlett Packard Enterprise to use Big Data to improve corporate fleet management. Ford formed an entirely new company in 2016, Ford Mobility Services LLC, to bring all these new products to market.

Ashton plainly describes how Ford Motor Company transformed the Internet of Things features into an Internet of Things strategy.

In January 2007, Ford announced SYNC, connecting to entertainment, phone, and SMS text messages. The carmaker added: 911 Assist, which is activated by airbag deployment, and Vehicle Health Report, which connects to in-car sensors (January 2008); GPS navigation and, for businesses, RFID-enabled Tool Tracking, vehicle tracking, and maintenance reports (April 2009). Ford started its predictive parking trial in London, using in-car sensors to locate parking spots (February 2016). Finally, the creation of Ford Smart Mobility LLC to offer Internet of Things services including predictive parking, car sharing, and Autonomous Vehicles (March 2016) made it possible to achieve sales of 10 million

> **Box 5.1 Ford's connected vehicles (*cont'd*)**
> SYNC units by the end of 2016 (Ashton, 2017). The assertions about the new company's purpose by Ford CEO Mark Fields are exhaustive: "As our vehicles become a part of the Internet of Things, and as consumers choose to share their data with us, we want to be able to use that data to help make their lives better" (Ziegler & Patel, 2016).

5.5.1 The Internet of Things: potential areas of use

In order to fully understand the significance of the phenomenon and the number of devices that can be found within the Internet of Things, the main examples of the potential areas of use of IoT solutions, as proposed by Witkowski (2017), can be summarized as follows (Table 5.3).

Table 5.3 The main examples of the potential areas of use of IoT.

The main examples of the potential areas of use	A brief description
(Smart) environment	Urban, industrial areas, and agricultural areas.
(Smart) water management	The impact of water resources on the environment, their use and protection deficits, regulation of rivers and protection against floods, waterways, hydropower, or security.
(Smart) industry	Sectors of the national economy.
(Smart) production as well as intelligent industry within specific sectors of the economy	Agriculture, breeding, and control of production lines as well as control of the rotation of products on store shelves and in warehouses.
(Smart) transport	The location of transported goods, control of the conditions of transport or storage conditions.
(Smart) energy	Management of utilities, including the monitoring of individual consumption, as well as the processes for its production and use, e.g.: solar systems, windmills, and water management.
(Smart) cities	The organization of pedestrians and traffic, the diagnosis of safety threats, noise, lighting, and waste management.

(Continued)

Table 5.3 The main examples of the potential areas of use of IoT.—cont'd

The main examples of the potential areas of use	A brief description
(Smart) buildings	Facilities that can be used both at the individual as well as industrial level: monitoring the property, motion sensors, smart irrigation, learning thermostats.
(Smart) apartments	Individual applications (e.g.: refrigerators, remote machines).
(Smart) health	Applications used in the monitoring of health and physical activity, vitality, and patient safety.
(Smart) life	Consumer solutions aimed at comfort and safety.

5.5.2 Internet of Services

While IoT deals with tangible objects, sensors, and machines, the Internet of Services entails a more intangible perspective, which is to be expected from services. The term 'Internet of Services' originated from the convergence of two other concepts: Web 2.0 and SOA (Service-Oriented Architecture). Web 2.0 is characterized by four aspects: interactivity, social networks, tagging, and web services. The SOA is a method of designing and building a set of computer applications in which application components and Web Services make their functions available on the same access path for mutual consumption. In a cloud manufacturing system, various resources and manufacturing capabilities can be intelligently perceived and connected on a larger Internet (Reis & Gonçalves, 2018).

5.5.3 Definitions and salient features of the Internet of Things

Based on the spread of service platforms and a multitude of services available on the Internet (Internet of Services), the Internet of the future will be the basis for a web-based service economy. The role of the IoT is to bridge the gap between the physical world and its representation in information systems. From this perspective, the 'Internet of Things' is commonly described by definitions such as the following.

A global infrastructure for the information society, enabling advanced services by interconnecting (physical and virtual) things based on existing and evolving interoperable information and communication technologies.

(Initiative, 2012).

A world where physical objects are seamlessly integrated into the information network, and where the physical objects can become active participants in business processes. Services are available to interact with these 'smart object' over the Internet, query their state and any information associated with them, taking into account security and privacy issues.

(Haller et al., 2009).

A dynamic global network infrastructure with self-configuring capabilities based on standard and interoperable communication protocols where physical and virtual 'things' have identities, physical attributes, and virtual personalities and use intelligent interfaces, and are seamlessly integrated into the information network.

(Vermesan et al., 2011).

The Internet of Things consists of objects that connect to the network to interact independently with other objects (e.g.: household appliances, cars, smartphones) or people. As Vermesan et al. highlight: "In the IoT, 'things' are expected to become active participants in business, information and social processes where they are enabled to interact and communicate among themselves and with the environment by exchanging data and information 'sensed' about the environment, while reacting autonomously to the 'real/physical world' events and influencing it by running processes that trigger actions and create services with or without direct human intervention" (Vermesan et al., 2011).

The connection is possible thanks to the internet and the use of software. Its distinctive features are context, omnipresence, and optimization (Witkowski, 2017):

(1) context refers to the ability of objects to interact in an advanced way with the external environment and respond immediately to change, thus enabling objects to provide information such as location, physical condition, or weather conditions;

(2) omnipresence entails the possibility for objects to communicate with each other on a large scale;

(3) optimization is the functionality that each object possesses.

"Nowadays, most of the corporations have a hybrid architecture that is the combination of both centralized and decentralized networking where companies assets are distributed across different countries and cities" (Rathee et al., 2021). According to the Authors the Industrial Internet of Things (IIoT) offers the advantage of monitoring or controlling all illegal or legal actions occurring at any of its branches from a single place. The Figure illustrates different locations of a company, which communicate with each other via the Internet. Even if located in different countries, all companies are connected with IoT devices that can be easily managed and tracked by the owners (Fig. 5.4).

While in the past the information flows related to the technical resources within the supply chain were mainly managed by people, thanks to IoT information today is exchanged directly among the objects without human intervention. For example, the parts of a product to be assembled communicate directly with the machine that transmits the data to the computer; the information flow during this process moves in the opposite direction to the physical flow and includes any exchange of data necessary for the completion of the order. In their study, Kumar et al. analyze the main features of the Internet of Things (Kumar et al., 2021), which can be summarized as follows (Table 5.4).

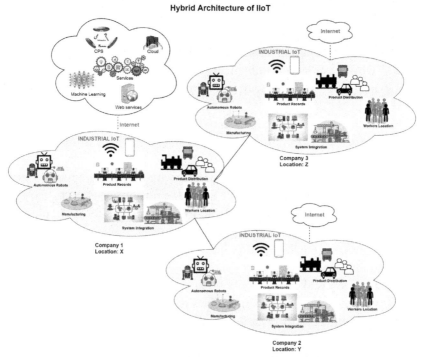

Figure 5.4 *Hybrid architecture of industrial Internet of Things. The figure illustrates the hybrid architecture of industrial Internet of Things in different location of a company.* From Rathee, G., Ahmad, F., Sandhu, R., Kerrache, C. A. & Azad, A. M. (2021). On the design and implementation of a secure blockchain-based hybrid framework for Industrial Internet-of-Things. Information Processing & Management, 58(3), 1–15. https://doi.org/10.1016/j.ipm.2021.102526.

Table 5.4 The main features of the Internet of Things.

The main features	A brief description
(1) Key elements	• Based on sensors that capture device-level data • Record events in the physical world, and communicate them to connected computing systems to trigger responses • Computing systems analyze data in real-time at the device level and across devices • Enable better communication between devices, and between humans and devices
(2) The operative domains	• Functional/utilitarian efficiency
(3) Key benefits to the consumer	• Greater convenience and ease of access • Reduced need for human intervention • Real-time, proactive alerts • Easy to monitor, control and manage interconnected devices
(4) Key benefits to the firm	• Greater data on consumer behaviors, usage patterns, and preferences • Signal alerts in rapid response to unusual behavioral patterns • Improved customer experience through personalized customer service, promotional offers, and products and services • Increased productivity, improved efficiency, and reduced operating costs through the device; monitoring, usage control, the interconnectivity of devices, and demand assessment
(5) Orientation	• Data

The Internet of Things will revolutionize the global supply chain with both operational efficiencies and revenue opportunities. Through IoT sensors and data points ubiquitous in the IoT ecosystem, efficiencies can be developed to leverage operational benefits and differentiation in areas such as asset tracking, last-mile delivery, forecasting and inventory, and scheduled maintenance. IoT is already transforming numerous markets and companies. As Nicolas Windpassinger (2017) observes: "Technologies are evolving laser fast but have not yet established their 'rules of the game'. Indeed, it is an exciting and important time because you have a unique opportunity to change and adapt the game rules to suit your needs – and in so doing, outperform your competitors" (Windpassinger, 2017).

A significant example of IoT and Supply Chain Management concerns the strategies of Xiaomi (Box 5.2).

Box 5.2 Xiaomi: smart home devices and the 'AioT strategy

According to Liang and Kang: "IoT is an intelligent technology and service that connects all things to the Internet to exchange and collect information. Smart home products realize functions such as remote control devices, interconnection between facilities, and self-learning of facilities, and provide personalized living services through collection and analysis of users' behaviors, thereby enhancing the safety, comfort, energy saving, and high efficiency of family life" (Liang and Kang, 2021). Some examples of the application of these new technologies are the development of heating systems in homes where the owner is about to arrive and wants to give a command to the system, the automatic selection of the washing machine program for specific clothing material, or the follow-up of food deliveries that the refrigerator orders after asking the user, who is traveling in his car, what groceries he would like to find when he arrives home (Mehic et al., 2019). The main objective is to exchange data and make decisions on the basis of the information received.

Examples of IoT instruments include refrigerators, thermostats, televisions, washing machines, music systems, lighting systems, health check instrument systems, home automation systems, and surveillance systems.

Xiaomi has adopted two main strategies: (1) the 'cost lead' strategy and (2) the 'differentiation' strategy (Liang & Kang, 2021), which are discussed below.

(1) **'Cost lead' strategy'**. The 'cost lead' (cost advantage) strategy aims at an increasing value to the customer through cost advantages obtained by providing products and services comparable to those of competitors but at lower costs. The 'cost lead' strategy is based on three pillars: the 'product R&D stage', the 'supply chain management stage', and the 'service stage'.

- 'Product R&D stage'. Xiaomi Home Service operates the MIUI system through close collaboration with companies specialized in the development of operating systems. The MIUI system is a platform that connects a series of smart devices such as Xiaomi phones, Xiaomi TVs, and Xiaomi routers. This service has many users, and Xiaomi pays particular attention to updating products and developing cooperation relationships with third parties.

- 'Supply chain management stage'. Xiaomi Smart Home selects suppliers very carefully and with innovative techniques. In particular, the Xiaomi Smart Home service has a supplier evaluation system that verifies the quality of each product and compliance with the assigned

Box 5.2 Xiaomi: smart home devices and the 'AioT strategy (*cont'd*)

production specifications. The indicators used include product costs, production capacity, business conditions, and delivery and testing costs. The contraction of supplies during the postpandemic period because of strong demand threatened the continuity of production lines. Xiaomi outsources most of its electronics products except for those it considers to be its core competencies. The scouting of the best venture companies is an integral part of Xiaomi's strategy of continuous innovation in products and production processes. Particular attention is paid to quality control. The strong development of the company's activities was achieved through a large number of suppliers and production plants. For this reason, it has not always been possible to guarantee the quality provided by suppliers in their factories. Therefore, in the case of Xiaomi Smart Home, it was necessary to develop a system that controlled every product supplied before it was placed in the Xiaomi production chain or placed on the market. As sales volumes have increased, new problems have arisen that suppliers must contribute to solving. They must not only improve their production activities but also classify the related issues and draw up guidelines to constantly improve procedures.

- 'Service stage'. Reducing the cost of customer services is one of Xiaomi's top goals, to achieve which it focuses on logistics and after-sales services. In the early stages of its operations, Xiaomi adopted a distribution strategy based on online sales, creating as a support an online video corner that provides information on product-related problem-solving and technical guidance. Much attention has been paid to customer marketing and customer service.

(2) **'Differentiation' strategy.** In today's business environment, customer needs are increasingly diverse. To respond to this trend, when standardized products (the "cost lead" area) cannot meet customer demands, Xiaomi has also developed a differentiation strategy to take into account the variety of demand. This strategy requires the continual development of new products to keep up with the evolution of demand. The differentiation strategy necessitates continued investments in the development of the design. The supply chain of Xiaomi's Smart Home products must follow innovative production models and meet personalized customer demands. It must focus on building and strengthening competitive advantages by increasing patented technologies and the protection of intellectual property. This is the framework of Xiaomi's Smart Home's 'AioT' strategy. 'AioT' is a combination of AI (Artificial Intelligence) and IoT. AI is a technology that applies human capabilities such as learning and reasoning to computer systems. Therefore, AI can help overcome the difficulties humans have in solving problems.

5.6 Blockchain

Blockchain is considered one of the most disruptive technologies. It is a peer–to–peer (P2P) ledger for transactions. More specifically, it is a set of technologies that relies on a ledger structured as a chain of blocks containing transactions and on a peer-to-peer (P2P) system, which is a network in which each connected device is both client and server, through which you can share with other users the files contained on your computer, thereby preserving the privacy of the users.

It can be described as an ingenious system entailing the chaining of information in consecutive blocks, a sort of distributed database in which everyone operates at the same level, with some specific characteristics and with constant control over the authenticity of the content. The main features of the database are the following: it is immutable in its registry, traceable and verifiable in each transaction, and secure because it uses cryptographic techniques. Blockchain is a storage system that, in combination with any data container (e.g:. IoT-generated data), makes it reliable from a privacy point of view since any data creation, modification, or deletion is recorded in the Blockchain and attributed to a specific identity, which is virtual, verified, and authorized (Morriello, 2019). Each block contains a reference to the previous block, and, after the block storage, the transactions of the block are considered confirmed.

This transaction system uses public key encryption. The user has a private key to sign transactions and a public key that is used as a system address, which allows the user to connect under a pseudonym. Transactions are organized in a data structure (blocks) using system peers (P2P) called miners. Each block contains a hash2 (unique code) as well as the code from the previous block. This creates the link between successive blocks, whose arrangement is defined by hash (Conoscenti et al., 2016).

Rathee et al. analyze an example where a company whose headquarters are located in a country 'A' and the raw material supplying units and factories are situated in a country 'B', as well as their corresponding consumer stores are located at various places across the world keeping in mind the international business associated with the firm (Rathee et al., 2021). The Authors delineate how implementing the Blockchain level-wise could reduce complexity. In this perspective, each level should be separated with a distinct Blockchain that supports the implementation and efficiency of the system (Fig. 5.5).

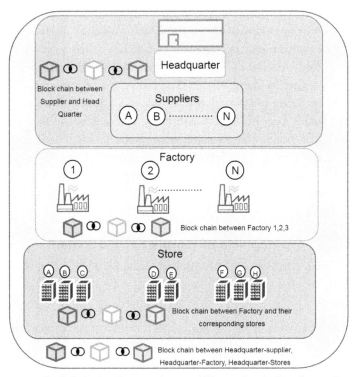

Figure 5.5 *A Blockchain implementation at different levels.* The figure illustrates a Blockchain implementation at different levels: supplier and headquarter, between factories (e.g.: 1, 2, 3) and between factory and their corresponding stores. *From Rathee, G., Ahmad, F., Sandhu, R., Kerrache, C. A. & Azad, A. M. (2021). On the design and implementation of a secure blockchain-based hybrid framework for Industrial Internet-of-Things.* Information Processing & Management, 58(3), 1—15. https://doi.org/10.1016/j.ipm.2021. 102526.

5.6.1 Cryptocurrencies and Bitcoin

This technology is currently used mainly for commercial transactions with cryptocurrencies, especially Bitcoin, an electronic cash transaction system created in 2009. Cryptocurrencies are tools based on the principles of cryptography, which can allow a network of people unknown to each other to generate money and circulate it in the absence of a central authority that validates its transactions.

Nakamoto, the inventor of Bitcoin, whose identity is still unknown, proposed a purely peer-to-peer version of electronic money that would allow payments to be sent directly online from one entity to another without the need to go through a financial institution. Nakamoto (2008) defines the 'electronic coin' as "the chain of digital signatures" (Nakamoto, 2008). The owner transfers the coin to the next owner by digitally signing a hash of the previous transaction and the public key of the next owner, also adding these to the end of the coin. The signatures and the chain of ownership can be verified by the payee. Nakamoto proposed a peer-to-peer and robust network using proof-of-work to record a public history of transactions, that quickly becomes computationally impractical for an attacker to change if honest nodes control a majority of the Central Processing Unit (CPU). This technology is useful to manage financial transactions without the need for trusted intermediaries (such as banks), even though it is also particularly interesting for its use in areas related to business activities, including the supply chain.

5.6.2 Definitions and salient features of Blockchain

The Blockchain concept is mainly applied to the context of use, to describe its properties or how security can be achieved. A few significant definitions are as follows.

> *Blockchain is an open, distributed ledger that can record transactions between two parties efficiently and in a verifiable and permanent way.*
>
> **(Iansiti and Lakhani, 2017).**

> *Blockchain is a type of distributed ledger (data structure) containing information about transactions or events, which is replicated and shared among the participants in the network.*
>
> **(Li et al., 2020).**

> *Blockchain is a distributed ledger and immutable database for transferring data very securely. The name is a combination of two words — the 'block' that contains batched transactions and a 'chain' that represents cryptographically linked blocks.*
>
> **(Maslova et al., 2018).**

In a broader context, to describe its characteristics, Blockchain is defined as: "A technology that enables immutability and integrity of data in which a record of transactions made in a system are maintained across multiple distributed nodes that are connected in a peer-to-peer network" (Viriyasitavat & Hoonsopon, 2019).

There are multiple factors that characterize Blockchain systems. The following represent the important characteristics regarding deployments, implementation, and properties: (1) Private, Public, and Permissioned Blockchain, (2) Centralization and Decentralization, (3) Persistency, (4) Validity, (5) Anonymity and Identity, (6) Auditability, (7) Closedness and Openness.

Regarding the business aspect, the salient characteristics of Blockchain are: (1) Transient and Persistent, (2) Dynamic and Static, (3) Workflow Formation and Enactment, (4) Centralized and Decentralized Management. In their study, Kumar et al. analyze the salient features of Blockchain (Kumar et al., 2021), which can be summarized as follows (Table 5.5).

An important case study concerns the Blockchain in the aviation industry (Box 5.3).

Because a Blockchain allows secure data exchange in a distributed way, it begins to have a significant impact on how supply chain relationships are structured and transactions are conducted. Integrating it with the Internet of Things (IoT), the Blockchain might be used to create a permanent, shareable, and actionable record of every moment of a product's journey through its supply chain, while also possibly enabling product traceability, authenticity, and legitimacy (Wang et al., 2019).

Table 5.5 The main features of Blockchain.

The main features	A brief description
(1) Key elements	• Decentralized electronic records secured by cryptography, implying greater security • Immutability of records and consensus-based system ensure the integrity of records through the Blockchain • Enables disintermediation rendering the middle-men unnecessary through automated execution of contracts
(2) The operative domains	• Process economies
(3) Key benefits to consume	• Greater trust in brands due to higher traceability of products • Transparency in the supply chain logistics, contracts, etc. • Greater data security, allowing consumers to have more control over their personal information
(4) Key benefits to the firm	• Transparency in business operations • Reduced processing time for transactions • Ability to better track the impact of marketing communications on consumers • Automatic execution of contracts, direct compensation of customers • Can help safeguard individual consumers' identities
(5) Orientation	• Security

Box 5.3 The Blockchain in the aviation industry

Blockchain is a digital ledger of transactions taking place in a network in which each computer part's can act as a server for the others, allowing shared access to files without the need for a central server.

Why is Blockchain technology important in the aviation construction industry? The industry has one of the largest and most complex supply chains with global ramifications. Blockchain offers a new and secure solution for the industry to track a myriad of components while deterring counterfeiting and improving the ability to achieve efficient maintenance. Used in conjunction with other digital technologies, such as digital twins and digital threads, Blockchain can be a game-changing innovation for the industry.

In the aerospace industry Blockchain technology can record each time a part is installed or removed from an airplane. It can also capture how long the part being replaced was in service and the identity, location, and credentials of the technician performing the repair. "It's like having a digital 'birth certificate' for every part, updated every time the plane is serviced or inspected" said an expert. These birth certificates provide a real-time picture of the plane's condition from the moment it leaves the assembly line to when it is returned to its lessor by the lessee or retired from the fleet.

Experts have defined the aerospace and aviation industry in general as a perfect match for Blockchain networks that, among other benefits, ensure an incorruptible and digital efficient way of keeping track of materials (Satair, 2019). It has given substantial and durable benefits to the aviation industry (manufacturers and airlines). Some enthusiasts, perhaps with exaggeration, define Blockchain as "the biggest innovation since Internet" (Alkurd, 2020).

Among the companies that have devoted a lot of attention to the real power of Blockchain are Airbus and Rolls-Royce. The first one has created a special unit in its organization responsible for exploring how Blockchain can be used in current and future supply chain management problems. One example of how Blockchain technology has helped to solve problems involves the collaboration between Rolls-Royce (engines) and Boeing (fuselages) to give power to Boeing's Dreamliner with Roll-Royce's Trent 1000 engine (Satair, 2018).

Several airlines have also expressed their interest in Blockchain technology. Lufthansa and British Airways have started collaborative projects in various fields with Blockchain start-ups. For its part, Air France has announced that it has a maintenance system adopting Blockchain technologies.

Advances are also made by companies on the other side of the field, the Blockchain solution providers. For example, some vendors have built platforms to digitize past records easily, ensuring all industry stakeholders have the necessary complete overview of an asset's lifecycle.

In which areas can Blockchain technology make a difference? According to a report by the international management consultant, Deloitte, Blockchain has a long list of potential applications in the aviation industry, some of which are

Box 5.3 The Blockchain in the aviation industry (*cont'd*)

already used extensively while other innovations are on the horizon (Millar et al., 2021).

Some examples of Blockchain applications are currently in use and they can be detailed as follows.

- **Aircraft parts tracking.** Parts tracking is one of many potential applications within the aerospace industry that aligns well with the capabilities of Blockchain technology (Proponent, 2018). Blockchain is really a key to transforming records and parts tracking. It can help to ensure that the parts produced are legitimized, they can live up to the necessary airworthiness requirements, and can ultimately offer a virtually immutable record of every part of an aircraft, as well as all the times those parts have been manipulated and by whom. At the same time, this means that airlines may be able to sell and buy parts with the confidence that the documentation is accurate and meets all maintenance regulations.
- **Supply chain.** An area where Blockchain in aerospace and aviation in general offers benefits in a special way relates to collaboration within the supply chain, which ranges from end-builders to suppliers, 'integrators' in the marketplace, and the airlines themselves. Everybody can benefit from a transparent and accurate approach to the often exorbitant amount of data (Lemasson et al., 2019). In the long term, the use of Blockchain to connect the many parts of the supply chain could be seen as a game-changer. The technology offers a way to track and deliver consistent data configuration along the aircraft construction supply chain. Knowing the actual configuration of an in-service aircraft at any point in its structure is very important, commented one expert, adding that Blockchain allows aerospace companies to securely share, capture and authenticate data from any single source. It also means that distributors in the aftermarket can have a better understanding of the parts needed by aerospace customers, airlines, and others. They could know the status and expectations of the remaining lifecycle of each aircraft part, and aerospace manufacturers could have a clearer view of future demand for parts and components.
- **Redefining engines and parts leasing through smart contracts.** One cost-efficient alternative may be to lease aircraft parts instead of actually purchasing parts. Managing leasing contracts with multiple partners is complex and time-consuming and the risks of making mistakes are high. Blockchain also in this area could be a game-changer according to Deloitte, introducing particular types of contracts (Millar et al., 2021). These contracts could use Blockchain to automate transactions in the supply chain, effectively removing the need for invoicing and payment processes, as Blockchain could operate on a standardized, commonly-agreed micropayment basis.

(Continued)

Box 5.3 The Blockchain in the aviation industry (cont'd)

- **Loyalty programs.** In the aviation industry Blockchain can be used to simplify and automate loyalty program transactions and bookkeeping. This is particularly relevant today, as many airlines have partnered with credit card issuers, rental car companies, hotels, and so forth. By creating a common digital currency, called 'tokens', in the Blockchain, travelers can get instant value on the spot. At the other end of the scene, airline management can have a clear understanding of revenue flows from reward programs.

According to Sundarakani et al. pointed out: "A fully connected digital supply chain will provide companies the capability to exchange business transactions electronically. The absence of a digital backbone will handicap companies from exploiting the benefits of technologies like IoT, artificial intelligence and blockchain" (Sundarakani et al., 2021). In order to solve this challenge, the Authors propose a mechanism of Blockchain—Big Data that would reduce the back-and-forth communication between the distribution center and consignee through a series of hashes, and thus would help to formulate secure smart contracts through encrypted blocks. In this perspective, the integration of Blockchain with the supply chain network eliminates back-and-forth communication between shippers, consignees, and logistics service providers (Fig. 5.6).

5.7 Robotics

Robotics is an interdisciplinary science born as a branch of mechatronic engineering, in which approaches from many disciplines converge, such as: computer science and psychology, linguistics and automation, mechanics, and biology. According to researchers: "Robotic is an intelligent robot or a mechanical creature that can function autonomously" (Murphy, 2000).

The word 'robot' comes from the Czech word 'Robota', which means slave; it was introduced by Czech dramatist Karl Capek's play in 1921, in which mechanical men built to work on factory assembly lines rebel against their human owners. The English derivative term 'Robotics' was first coined by science-fiction writer Isaac Asimov in 1942 in his short story "Runabout", with a decidedly more optimistic view of the role of the robot in human society than Capek had.

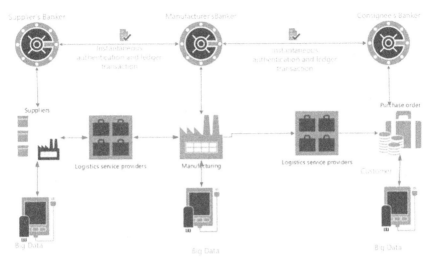

Figure 5.6 *Blockchain integrated streamlined process for instantaneous authentication and fund transactions.* The figure illustrates the integration of Blockchain-Big Data with the supply chain network. *From Sundarakani, B., Ajaykumar, A. & Ajaykumar, A. (2021). Big data driven supply chain design and applications for blockchain: An action research using case study approach. Omega, 102, 1–19. https://doi.org/10.1016/j. omega.2021.102452.*

Some early applications in this area are the following.
- The first industrial robot in history, a mechanical arm, was introduced by General Motors in 1961;
- The first anthropomorphic robot designed by Waseda University in Tokyo was created in Japan in 1970 (Wabot-1);
- The first military drone capable of taking off autonomously was created in the United States.

Robotics has achieved its greatest success in the world of industrial manufacturing. From a broader perspective, human-like robots could replace the human work form in different businesses and company operations. Robots could be implemented in many activities, including at the front end supported by Artificial Intelligence, and drones could be employed, for example, to move documents (Dirican, 2015).

Many functions that were once done solely by human hands are being carried out by robots as advanced automation takes root. Robotics spans a broad spectrum of technologies from software bots to Autonomous Vehicles. In the context of supply chains, robots are used in warehousing, transport, and logistics operations. In a 2016 pan-industry study, 51% of respondents said that Robotics is now a disruptive technology in the supply chain; the report indicates the catalytic role of Robotics and automation in disruptively shaping competitive advantages for supply chains (Deloitte, 2016).

Considerable demand for robots in industrial and personal settings has led to significant developments in Robotics. The area of greatest development involves mobile robots, in which robots are able to navigate an environment and interact with it through sensors and actuators (Köseoğ;lu et al., 2017). Mobile robots can be classified as Automated Guided Vehicles (AGVs) and Autonomous Mobile Robots (AMR), as detailed below.

• Automated Guided Vehicles (AGVs)

Since their introduction in 1955, their use has grown enormously. They are used to move all types of materials related to the manufacturing process, in both indoor and outdoor environments, such as production, distribution, transshipment, and (outdoor) transportation. Automated Guided Vehicles (AGVs) are utilized in a variety of areas of interest, including container terminals, flexible manufacturing systems, warehousing, agriculture, military operations, health management, mining, and many others (Vis, 2006). They range from vehicles with manual controls for human drivers and autonomous support systems to fully autonomous vehicles. "Automated Guided Vehicles (AGVs) is the future drift that provides unmanned transportation - that transports all kinds of products without human intervention in production" (Sankari & Imtiaz, 2016).

Synthesizing its properties: "An Automated Guided Vehicle (AGV) is a driverless transport system used for horizontal movement of materials" (Vis, 2006). An AGV system requires addressing many tactical (e.g.: system design) and operational (e.g.: routing) issues. On the other hand, an AGV system can be used to achieve various objectives, such as: (a) maximizing the throughput of the system; (b) minimizing the time required to complete all jobs; (c) minimizing vehicle travel time; (d) evenly distributing the workload across AGV; (e) minimizing total movement costs; (f) minimizing the time that work is handled after the scheduled time; (g) minimizing maximum or average AGV crossing times to travel to the new job destination; (h) minimizing the expected wait times for loads.

In this regard, these robots could minimize the internal vulnerability of the supply chain and increase organizational agility, particularly in a network economy context (Bechtsis et al., 2017).

• Autonomous Mobile Robots (AMR)

In recent decades, technology has advanced rapidly, and very important development is the transformation of Automated Guided Vehicles (AGVs) into Autonomous Mobile Robots (AMR).

The guidance system that characterizes AGV material handling systems has evolved through various stages of mechanical, optical, inductive, inertial, laser, and even vision-based system guidance. This very innovative vision-based system uses ubiquitous sensors, powerful on-board computers, Artificial Intelligence (AI), and SLAM (Simultaneous Location and Mapping) technology, allowing the device to understand its operating environment and opening it up to a new dimension in navigation flexibility (Fragapane et al., 2021).

• Robotic Process Automation (RPA)

RPA is also constantly evolving. This particular technology amalgamates Robotics, referring to software agents that act like humans in system interactions and process automation. Robotic Process Automation is a relatively new technology comprising software agents called 'bots' that mimic the manual path taken by a human through a range of computer applications when performing certain tasks in a business process (Syed et al., 2020). RPA uses software, called 'software robots', that can automatically perform repetitive tasks by mimicking the behavior of operators and interacting with computer applications like humans. Thanks to the convergence of Artificial Intelligence with this technology, it is moving toward the acquisition of cognitive capabilities that allow the software to implement decision-making processes also in cases of unexpected events.

Progress in robot technology can also trigger reshoring, the restructuring of supplier network organizations, and the definition of what to outsource. As the agility of robots improves, their use has spread from traditional strongholds such as production into other functions. For instance, the advance in robots has shaken up the core of the logistics sector. Many functions that were once done only by human hands are being carried out by robots. Advanced automation has taken root in this segment of the supply chain, and we are going to see a real change in the way the logistics industry is organized.

5.8 Additive Manufacturing and 3D printing

3D printing is actually considered a subset of Additive Manufacturing (AM). The name Additive Manufacturing refers to the addition of raw materials during manufacturing, which includes various assembly and rapid prototyping processes (Khosravani & Reinicke, 2020). AM technology first emerged in 1977 when Swainson suggested a method to create 3D objects directly using two electromagnetic beams and a sensitive polymer

(Swainson, 1977). It was introduced as a rapid prototyping method that can be used for various materials, and in recent decades it has evolved considerably. Researchers have focused on improving old and creating new techniques, as well as on developing new materials.

Additive Manufacturing is defined as the "process of joining materials to make objects from 3D model data, usually layer upon layer" (ISO/ASTM, 2015). It is significantly used in various applications, such as in the automotive, aerospace, electronics, dentistry, and medicine areas. Industrial applications of 3D printing demonstrate that the list of materials involved in this technique is continually growing. Campbell et al. (2011) exhaustively describe the generalized steps of Additive Manufacturing technologies: "The AM process begins with a 3D model of the object, usually created by computer-aided design (CAD) software or a scan of an existing artifact. Specialized software slices this model into cross-sectional layers, creating a computer file that is sent to the AM machine. The AM machine then creates the object by forming each layer via the selective placement (or forming) of material. Think of an inkjet printer that goes back over and over the page, adding layers of material on top of each other until the original works are 3D objects" (Campbell et al., 2011).

If 3D printing continues to develop at the rate it has in the past few years, it could change the dynamics of the supply chain for some industries. Instead of shipping a nut or bolt to a customer, suppliers would sell permission to download a software file with instructions on how to print the component. Transport costs would disappear, and it would become economically viable to produce very small batches of a component. 3D printing has a wide range of possible applications such as printing spare parts on demand, where needed, and 'just in time', manufactured locally through various production cells. A company's investment in warehoused stock would come close to zero.

An example of how digital technology leads to a rethinking of the organization of the global value chain is the introduction of 3D printers, thanks to which small components can be directly produced, thereby avoiding the need to turn to providers. This means reorganizing in part the network of suppliers. The same reasoning can be used for financial advisers replaced by Robo-adviser websites. The progress of 3D printers is destined to revolutionize the supply chain in many sectors. Companies can print much of what they need rather than outsource this function. For example, Bosch Rexroth (the electronics arm of the German supplier) predicts that by 2025 up to 40% of the manufacturing equipment it produces could be printed instead of purchased. Many companies send digital files to produce goods in remote locations. The progress of 3D printing technologies could lead many companies to rethink their location of production.

5.9 Autonomous Vehicles (AV) and Intelligent Transport Systems (ITS)

'ITS' stands for Intelligent Transport System(s). Intelligent comes from the Latin interlego, which means "I link together" or "I link with or through"; another meaning of inter-lego is "I read through", which signifies being able to read between the lines, in other words being intelligent (Dalla Chiara, 2021).

A deep comprehension of 'intelligent' implies a wide and long-lasting path for ITS, here intended as 'inter-connected' transport systems, which are able to include both humans (i.e.: travelers, drivers or supervisors of a control room, who contribute with their personal intelligence) and goods. This interconnection also allows motionless communication to be achieved, even during traveling (i.e.: remote working, remote courses, teleconferences, teleseminars, and telediagnostics), as the person involved is devoted to communication and not necessarily to driving, when needed.

This interconnection, and the presence of humans within the connected subsystems, should have at least one purpose: to improve the safety, security, quality, or efficiency of transport systems for passengers and freight, by optimizing the use of natural resources-including energy sources for the traction and propulsion of vehicles - and respecting the environment.

Among ITS, a great expectance is related to assisted driving, addressed toward Autonomous Vehicles in the medium-long period and integrated mobility, which is much synthesized in the concept of MaaS[2] (Dalla Chiara, 2022).

The transitory toward assisted driving, in the form of Advanced Driver Assistance Systems (ADAS), and - in the long period, though with already existing applications in protected contexts - road Autonomous Vehicles (AV) are gaining significant adoption in both research and industry,

---

[2] MaaS (Mobility as a Service) represents the concept of integrated transport services, that can include both public and private transport, through a single travel ticket and a single payment interface: MaaS "makes it possible to find out about the offer of rail services, public transport services, parking, the availability of recharging for plug-in or plug-in cars (including both plug-in hybrids and pure electric vehicles), bicycles or motorbikes or car sharing through a single networked interface" (Dalla Chiara, 2022).

including both private cars commercial vehicles. In the future, thanks to these technological evolutions, it could be possible to reduce the amount and severity of accidents, increase the quality of mobility for people with disabilities and the elderly, reduce local emissions, possibly even the global ones, and use infrastructure more efficiently (Fagnant & Kockelman, 2015).

The Figure illustrates the transmitting information onboard through broadcasting, infrastructure-to-vehicle, or vehicle-to-vehicle information (Fig. 5.7).

The progress realized in recent years can be explained in terms of three successive waves of development (Anderson et al., 2014).

In the first phase, from the '80s' to indicatively 2003, basic studies on autonomous transport operating on roads have been undertaken by university centers often in collaboration with transport agencies and research centers of carmakers (the Lancia Nea, 2000) was already operating on roads of Turin-Italy in 2003 with the first application of assisted driving that was still up to date in 2019. In particular, two relevant areas of research were developed: (1) automated highway systems in which vehicle guidance is significantly dependent on highway infrastructure, and (2) semiautonomous and Autonomous Vehicles that depended little or entirely, on infrastructure.

In the second phase, from 2003 to 2007, Grand Challenges were initiated, first among all those by the U.S. Defense Advanced Research Projects Agency (DARPA) through which significant advances in AV technology were undertaken. The first experiences made in Europe, as those of Fiat-Lancia and a few others, e.g.: the famous Autonomous Vehicle by Prof. Broggi (VisLAb, 2003-2018, University of Parma), which traveled from Europe to Asia.

In the third phase, called Commercial Development, the DARPA Challenges solidified partnerships between car manufacturers and university centers, mobilizing a range of automotive industry efforts to advance AVs.

Figure 5.7 *Transmitting information on board.* The figure illustrates the transmitting information on board through broadcasting, infrastructure-to-vehicle, or vehicle-to-vehicle information. From Dalla Chiara, B. (2021). *ITS for Transport Planning and Policy (By R. Vickerman; Elsevier, Ed.; Vol. 6, pp. 298–308). https://doi.org/10.1016/B978-0-08-102671-7. 10699-2; https://www.sciencedirect.com/referencework/9780081026724/international-encycl opedia-of-transportation#book-info.*

Some well-known examples of collaborations have been the following.

- GM and Carnegie Mellon University;
- Volkswagen and Stanford University;
- Google's Driverless Car initiative has built autonomous cars from the university lab.

In this field it can be interesting to specify the development of two connected vehicle technologies (Van Brummelen et al., 2018), as: (1) Vehicle-to-Infrastructure communication and (2) Vehicle-to-Vehicle communication, generally recognized as 'V2X'.

(1) Vehicle-to-Infrastructure (V2I) communication can provide a network for intersections, traffic, and construction signs to transfer important infrastructure information such as road layout changes, speed limits, and traffic light information to AVs (Barrachina et al., 2013; Guler et al., 2014).

(2) Vehicle-to-Vehicle (V2V) communication could allow vehicles to share data, such as vehicle status, positioning, and interaction with other vehicles (Dalla Chiara et al., 2009; Dang et al., 2014; Dey et al., 2016).

The advances in technologies have made possible the realization of Autonomous Vehicles defined as: "a vehicle in which a computerized system, consisting of hardware and software, partially or fully replaces or totally replaces human input" (Automobile Club Italia - ACI et al., 2017).

In the future, assisted driving, self-driving, and connected vehicle technologies could radically change the world of road transportation. The use of these technologies could greatly increase traffic safety (especially ADAS), and reduce energy consumption, emissions, and the cost of traffic congestion. The possible interaction between road infrastructure with new technologies and the new vehicles could increase overall efficiency. As well as new models of sharing or public transport and different mobility schemes could help change the face of our cities. In this context, strategic and political choices will be crucial to guide the process.

In order to comprehend the different levels of possible autonomy of vehicles, it is possible to observe the classification defined by the Society of Automobile Engineers (SAE), in 2013.

The SAE classification proposes five levels with increasing automation: the system has full control of at least one of the driving phases only from level 2 (partial automation); in the following levels the vehicle "progressively takes command". The passage to the fourth and fifth levels defines the passage from high to total automation of the vehicle (Automobile Club Italia - ACI et al., 2017).

The development of these technologies could improve significant impetus to many businesses, particularly the automotive industry.

5.10 Artificial Intelligence (AI)

The Artificial Intelligence (AI) is the broad science of mimicking human abilities. It is described as a technology that is capable of imitating humans and carrying out tasks in a way that is considered 'intelligent'.

The term was coined in the mid-1950s by McCarthy, who defined it as "the science and engineering of making intelligent machines". AI was inspired by research in various fields on the concept of 'intelligence', adding an engineering aspect to this: it aims to build intelligence and create real intelligent artifacts (Sartor, 1996).

AI consists of the application of software programmed to learn how to react to the occurrence of events through an experiential process, thus enabling the software to respond to requests through a simple cognitive process. "Artificial intelligence (AI) brings with it a promise of genuine human-to-machine interaction. When machines become intelligent, they can understand requests, connect data points and draw conclusions. They can reason, observe and plan" (Thompson et al., 2021).

Considering its objectives, AI can be summarized using two opposing perspectives: (1) AI as science, where the goal is to understand the mind by means of computational models; (2) AI as engineering, where the goal is to solve real-world problems (examples: robotics, vision, speech recognition, etc.). The main areas of AI application are the following: financial analysis, office automation, industrial automation, databases, medical diagnosis, games, robotics, design systems, and machine translation.

A significant example of Artificial Intelligence concerns Mc Donald (Box 5.4).

5.10.1 The bases of Artificial Intelligence

AI is based on ideas and results obtained in other fields: philosophy, psychology, linguistics, mathematics, computer science, computer engineering, signal processing, image recognition, and systems and control theory.

In philosophy, the thought of some philosophers has introduced some concepts that are the basis of AI (for example, in addition to some general ideas already inherent in the thought of Socrates and Aristotle, Descartes' thesis on the dualism of the human mind, Liebniz's thesis of materialism, Hume's induction principle, and Russell's logical positivism).

Box 5.4 McDonald's: 'Accelerating the arches'

Starting from the goal of increasing the efficiency of both the customer ordering process and supply chain management, McDonald's decided in 2019 to make further use of Artificial Intelligence (AI). This plan, named 'Accelerating the arches' (alluding to the two arches in the company's logo) has been additionally accelerated with the spread of the coronavirus pandemic. Three areas of operations management have made significant progress with AI: (1) the customer ordering process; (2) customization of supply in order to increase demand; and (3) the increased efficiency of the supply chain.

(1) Before the pandemic, McDonald's had made advances to improve the 'customer experience' throughout the ordering process at drive-thru locations. It developed new technologies to modernize the process by adopting technologies from two acquired start-ups. The first one is used for ordering by voice and the second one is for customizing the order on a digital menu, both with extensive use of AI, and enticing customers to order more. For example, to reduce order and product delivery times in certain geographic areas of the U.S., McDonald's had experimented with AI tools that are able to scan license plates (with driver permission) to predict what they might order and prepare kitchens for their possible order. In 2019, the average order time in U.S. McDonald's was 6 min and 18 s. In the following year, it dropped to 5 minutes and 49 s. According to data from the market research firm SeeLevel HX, the 29-s reduction in time was achieved principally due to the decision to offer simpler menus and predominantly through the use of AI. During the pandemic, while restaurants were closed in many parts of the United States, McDonald's and the other fast food restaurant chains relied extensively on drive-thru sales. The demand from the usual customers through their car windows was enriched by the demand from those who, because of social distancing guidelines, could not attend restaurants. Long lines of waiting cars and inaccurate orders have always been a threat to managing the order process, but they have become even more important in a phase of the sector where overall sales have declined due to the pandemic. As the drive-thru represents more than 70% of sales in the U.S., all major chains have increased their efforts to reduce order times. For McDonald's, this was a bigger challenge than for the industry average because as many as 94% of its locations in the U.S. have a drive-thru. Covid-19 made critical advances in the speed of ordering. In order to address this need, McDonald's has invested in new technologies. It has accelerated experimentation with Alexa-style forms of assistance and increased automation in ordering and payment processes by also experiencing facial recognition payments (Metz, 2021).

(2) Personalizing the offer with the use of AI has been a second goal. Lucy Brady, McDonald's chief digital customer engagement officer has very clear ideas about what AI technology can do to improve offerings and customer

(Continued)

Box 5.4 McDonald's: 'Accelerating the arches' (*cont'd*)

satisfaction. "Humans sometimes forget to greet people, they forget, they make mistakes, they don't hear as well. A machine can actually have a consistent greeting and remain calm under pressure". The program of application of AI technology has a name: 'Accelerating the arches'. In the experimental phase, it was developed in the United States. It will then be extended to other countries starting with Mexico and Canada. The program involves systematic observation of the customer experience from navigating McDonald's website to talking to its customer service and which products customers bought from the fast-food company (Metz, 2021). Lucy Brady explains: "We're really looking systematically at that customer experience and thinking. 'Where can technology make this better and easier and faster'?". For example, the technology automatically changes the offerings (menus) according to environmental conditions and indicates to customers, which items were already showing popularity at that particular location that day. "Welcome to McDonald's, what can I get for you?" asks the system in a welcoming and unmistakably feminine tone. The system (computerized voice) is connected to a digital menu board. In addition to taking orders, it can provide suggestions depending on environmental factors such as time of day, traffic levels, and weather conditions. It allows the menu to change dynamically when a customer takes an order. Lucy Brady clarifies: "Order any type of product and the system will suggest a meal update. Order a healthy option like a salad, and it will pair it with a related product like a bottle of water. One menu will be able to promote different options".

(3) McDonald has always placed great importance on the supply chain and quickly realized the importance of moving AI advances through the supply chain to improve operations. Digital technologies capture large amounts of data. Thanks to AI, these data can be analyzed with a high degree of accuracy. The decision to acquire Dynamic Yield, an Israel-based tech company specializing in personalization software, has been crucial to progress in this direction. The objective is to deploy AI's best solutions at all levels of its supply chain from suppliers to customers (Lucas, 2019).

The variety of customized offerings mentioned earlier has severe implications for the supply chain. For example, consider the final stage of the supply chain: the menus (Cooper, 2021; Future Supply Chain, 2021). Using an AI platform for both menu management (offer) and inventory management, McDonald's can promote or withdraw items based on inventory availability. For example, if the restaurant is running low on type A meat while it has an abundance of type B meat, the menus can give products prepared with type B cards greater prominence and reduce demand for type A products. This improves inventory management by preventing the restaurant from being out of stock.

> **Box 5.4 McDonald's: 'Accelerating the arches' (*cont'd*)**
> With the acquisition of Dynamic Yield, McDonald's can bring together the two sides of supply and demand very effectively. Being able to influence demand at the restaurant level it is possible to reduce waste to a minimum and optimize choices throughout the organization. This is an example of the transition from mass marketing to mass personalization based on tying the data collected by the ecosystem in a way that is useful to a customer and therefore useful for profitability. In practice, supply chain management (based on the availability of raw materials) acts on demand because it suggests offers to the customer and also acts on what happens in the kitchens and therefore in production.
> An expert in the restaurant industry commented on the progress with AI technology as follows: "If the 1950s were the golden age of fast food - a decade during which the drive-thru rose to popularity - then the 2020s could be the golden age of drive-thru tech" (Metz, 2021).

Other important concepts have been introduced in the field of mathematics, such as Boole's formal language to make a logical inference, Frege's first-order logic used in most modern-day systems for the representation of knowledge, Tarski's theory, which allows real-world objects to be related to objects of a logical representation, Gödel's incompleteness theorem, Turing's machine, and the Church-Turing thesis (which states that machines are capable of representing any computable function).

Psychology has also made some important contributions, such as Helmholz-Wundt's scientific method to study human vision and the behavioral theories of Watson and Thorndike, as well as the linguistic foundations attributable to Chomsky's theory of syntactic models. Undoubtedly of fundamental importance in this panorama are the contributions of computer engineering, such as the first modern computer (Heath Robinson) built by Alan Turing's group in 1940, followed a few years later by the first programmable computer (Z-3), with a high-level programming language, and the first electronic computer (ABC).

If its foundations, as we have seen, have distant roots in certain areas, Artificial Intelligence is nevertheless a young field of research. McCulloch and Pitts proposed an early model of an artificial neuron in 1943; Hebb, a learning mechanism in the human brain, still of great interest, in 1949; Shannon and Turing worked (independently) on chess programs (1950–53);

Minsky and Edmonds developed the first 'neural' computer in 1951, and Newell and Simon developed the Logic Theorist in 1956.

John McCarthy was the first to call these types of research 'Artificial Intelligence', the year span can be detailed as follows.

- Newell and Simon develop the General Problem Solver - GPS (1961)
- Samuel develop a program that learned to place checkers (1952)
- First attempts at automatic translations (1957)
- McCarthy invents LISP (1958)
- Minsky and his students study problems related to microworlds (e.g.: ANALOGY, SHRDLU) (1963)
- Rosenblatt develops Perceptron, a neural network that learns from examples (1962)
- Feigenbaum et al. (Stanford) develop DENDRAL, an expert system for the inference of molecular structures (1969)
- MYCIN, an expert system of around 450 rules to diagnose infectious diseases (1976)
- PROSPECTOR, an expert system providing advice on mining exploration (1979)
- R1, an expert system (marketed) for the configuration of DEC VAX systems (1982).

5.10.2 The Turing Test: the imitation game

Alan Turing (1950) proposed an 'operational' definition of intelligence, called the Turing Test (Turing, 1950). To better understand the Author's proposal, below is a description of the test.

"I PROPOSE to consider the question, 'Can machines think?' This should begin with definitions of the meaning of the terms 'machine' and 'think'. The definitions might be framed so as to reflect as far as possible the normal use of the words, but this attitude is dangerous. If the meaning of the words 'machine' and 'think' are to be found by examining how they are commonly used it is difficult to escape the conclusion that the meaning and the answer to the question, 'Can machines think?' is to be sought in a statistical survey such as a Gallup poll. But this is absurd. Instead of attempting such a definition, I shall replace the question with another, which is closely related to it and is expressed in relatively unambiguous words. The new form of the problem can be described in terms of a game that we call the 'imitation game'. It is played with three people, a man (A), a woman (B), and an interrogator (C) who may be of either sex. The interrogator stays in a room apart from the other two. The object of the game for the interrogator is to determine, which of the other two is the man and which is the woman. He knows them by labels X and Y, and at the end of the game he says either 'X is A and Y is B' or 'X is B and Y is A'. The interrogator is allowed to put questions to A and B thus: C: Will X please tell me the length of his or her hair?

Now suppose X is actually A, then A must answer. It is A's object in the game to try and cause C to make the wrong identification. His answer might therefore be 'My hair is shingled, and the longest strands are about nine inches long'. In order that tones of voice may not help the interrogator, the answers should be written, or better still, typewritten. The ideal arrangement is to have a teleprinter communicating between the two rooms. Alternatively, the question and answers can be repeated by an intermediary. The object of the game for the third player (B) is to help the interrogator. The best strategy for her is probably to give truthful answers. She can add such things as 'I am the woman, don't listen to him!' to her answers, but it will avail nothing as the man can make similar remarks. We now ask the question, 'What will happen when a machine takes part of A in this game?' Will the interrogator decide wrongly as often when the game is played like this as he does when the game is played between a man and a woman? These questions replace our original, 'Can machines think?'" (Turing, 1950).

"Some other advantages of the proposed criterion may be shown up by specimen questions and answers. Thus:

Q: Please write me a sonnet on the subject of the Forth Bridge.

A: Count me out on this one. I never could write poetry.

Q: Add 34,957 to 70,764.

A: (Pause about 30 s and then give an answer) 105,621.

Q: Do you play chess?

A: Yes.

Q: I have K at my K1, and no other pieces. You have only K at K6 and R at R1. It is your move. What do you play?

A: (After a pause of 15 s) R–R8 mate" (Turing, 1950).

In this sense, the Turing Test can be passed if the machine has the following capabilities: (1) natural language processing (to interact with the interrogator); (2) representation of knowledge (to store information before and during dialogue); (3) automatic reasoning (to use the acquired knowledge to answer questions or draw conclusions); (4) learning (to adapt to new circumstances).

In an attempt to develop a stronger 'benchmark' of intelligence, Harnad (1991) proposed a variant of the test, called the Total Turing Test, which requires a machine to be able to perceive and interact with its environment.

"The candidate must be able to do, in the real world of objects and people, everything that real people can do" (Harnad, 1991)

5.10.3 Definitions and salient features of Artificial Intelligence

There has been considerable confusion regarding a precise definition of Artificial Intelligence. The definitions have also changed over the years. Starting from the definition provided by its founding father, some significant definitions of Artificial Intelligence are the following.

AI is the science and engineering of making intelligent machines, especially intelligent computer programs.

(Turing, 1950).

Artificial Intelligence is the science of making machines do things that would require intelligence if done by man.

(Raphael, 1976).

Artificial intelligence (A.I.) is the study of how to make computers do things that people are better at or would be better at if they could extend what they do to a worldwide web-sized amount of data and not make mistakes.

(Rich, 1985).

A recent and much stronger definition refers to the capacity to "imitating intelligent human behavior" (Kok et al., 2009). In this context, it is appropriate to note that Artificial Intelligence (AI) means different things to different people. "Some believe that AI is synonymous with any form of intelligence achieved by nonliving systems; they maintain that it is not important if this intelligent behavior is not arrived at via the same mechanisms on which humans rely" (Lucci & Kopec, 2015). In line with this meaning, a current definition could be the following: "Artificial intelligence is a computerized system that exhibits behavior that is commonly thought of as requiring intelligence" (National Science and Technology Council - NSTC, 2016).

In AI, a computer system can perform tasks that normally require human intelligence, such as: visual perception, speech recognition, decision making, and translation between languages. In their study, Kumar et al. analyze the salient features of Artificial Intelligence (Kumar et al., 2021), which can be summarized as follows (Table 5.6).

Artificial Intelligence is expected to dominate production research in manufacturing for the foreseeable future (Rauch, 2020; Walsh, 2017). The application of AI in the context of digital transformation will allow companies

Table 5.6 The main features of Artificial Intelligence.

The main features	A brief description
(1) Key elements	• Capable of imitating human behavior in an intelligent way • Interacts with other machines to control and communicate with them, can also communicate with humans • Enables automation of routine business processes • Applies various methods such as Machine Learning, Deep Learning, natural language programming, etc. to train machines to conduct tasks in human-like ways
(2) The operative domains	• Automation and learning
(3) Key benefits to consumer	• Personalized communication, products, and services, with increasing personal relevance • Enhanced machine-to-machine and machine-to-human interactions • Better customer experiences with products and services
(4) Key benefits to firm	• Gaining insights from patterns in consumer behaviors, usage, and preferences to predict future behaviors • Perform highly frequent, large-scale, computerized tasks accurately and reliably, without human fatigue • Improved customer experience through personalized recommendations and communications to customers, and automation of interactions • Improved efficiency on account of automation, human employees can focus on more complex tasks
(5) Orientation	• Analytics

to make supply chains largely autonomous and capable of regulating and deciding for themselves how to operate in the face of events and changes.

The application of AI allows for: (1) any critical issues to be highlighted through the transfer of data and information; (2) the development of proactive skills to solve complex business problems throughout the chain; (3) the supply chain to become smarter and more agile. The ability to optimize stocks by increasing the accuracy of reordering policies, predictive distribution to improve demand planning for production, automation of daily operations decisions, and cost reduction are important benefits this technology offers to improve the management of production processes (Grasso & Grasso, 2019).

5.10.4 Machine Learning (ML) and Deep Learning (DL)

AI makes it possible to differentiate the following three terms: Artificial Intelligence, Machine Learning (ML), and Deep Learning (DL).

Machine Learning (ML) is considered a specific and fundamental subset of AI that trains a machine how to learn. It is based on the idea that machines should be able to learn and adapt through experience. ML aims at enabling machines to learn for themselves using the data provided and at making accurate predictions. Machine Learning utilizes methods taken from neural networks, statistics, operations research, and physics to find hidden intuitions in data without being explicitly programmed (Thompson et al., 2021). In their study, Kumar et al. analyze the salient features of Machine Learning (Kumar et al., 2021), which can be summarized as follows (Table 5.7).

Artificial Intelligence is already embedded in many products and services. Amazon's book recommendations, Apple's Siri assistant, Facebook's news

Table 5.7 The main features of Machine Learning.

The main features	A brief description
(1) key elements	• A specific subset of AI that trains a machine to learn by developing automated, self-training • Algorithms can perform highly frequent, large-scale, computerized analysis on huge datasets accurately and reliably, with increasing accuracy • Automates the process of learning to help machines integrate data, identify patterns in data, and apply the model to new data to make predictions
(2) The operative domains	• Learning and integration
(3) key benefits to the consumer	• Personalized communication, products, and services • Better experiences with products and services.
(4) key benefits to the firm	• Identification of patterns in consumer behaviors, usage, and preferences • Ability to build models to predict future behaviors, usage, and preferences of customers

Table 5.7 The main features of Machine Learning.—cont'd

The main features	A brief description
	• Can perform large-scale analyses iteratively and accurately, without fatigue, and being adaptable and adjust to new data • Improved customer experience by providing personalized recommendations and communications to customers • By handling routine analyses, allows human employees to manage more complex analyses and customer interaction
(5) Orientation	• Analytics

feed are all examples of services driven by Machine Learning algorithms. As they move toward fully self-driving vehicles, carmakers are now introducing AI, which relies on high-definition maps as well as hardware such as remote-sensing technology and ultrasonic cameras.

Some of the most important changes at work in the new connected devices are used by AI to make decisions in complex systems. Global supply chains are extremely complex systems. The spread of AI to outsourcers is more likely to increase the reshoring tendency. For example, not all of the increased use of AI in voice recognition is falling to suppliers. Huawei, the world's third best-selling smartphone maker, has brought more components in-house, having decided to make wide use of AI.

AI can also be deployed to build predictive models that, based on data from the past, generate forecasts about the future evolution of supply cost structure. How might a change in one or more elements of the supply chain influence profitability or risk levels?

There is increasing recognition of the importance of understanding and rigorously evaluating the digital impact on business. Walsh (2017) argues that AI will eventually have an impact on our economy and society as profound as the Industrial Revolution. The only uncertainty concerns when this might occur, he says. What is clear is that its effects on the management of supply chains have already become deeply evident (Walsh, 2017).

Deep Learning is a subset of machine learning and is considered the evolution of ML. DL algorithms are approximately inspired by the information processing schemes found in the human brain (Rauch, 2020). Deep Learning utilizes massive neural networks with many layers of processing units, leveraging advances in computing power and improved training techniques to learn complex models for large amounts of data (Thompson et al., 2021).

"Deep learning with a stack of Convolution Neural Networks (CNN) is a widely used technique at present due to the enhancement of computer power and this is used extensively in the domains of visual object recognition, speech recognition, image synthesis, speech synthesis, and machine translation" (Baduge et al., 2022). The Figure illustrates the domains of AI, ML, DL, and widely used algorithms: where MLP is Multi-Layer Perceptron, GAN is Generative Adversarial Network, CNN is Convolutional Neural Networks, RNN is Recurrent Neural Network, LSTM is Long Short-Term Memory Network and RBFN is Radial Basis Function Network (Fig. 5.8).

Artificial Intelligence, Machine Learning, and Deep Learning have the potential to increase the productivity of science, encourage new forms of the invention, and increase reproducibility (Organisation for Economic Cooperation and Development - OECD, 2018). To this end, the Organization for Economic Cooperation and Development (OECD) has produced several documents that address the need for governments to take charge of

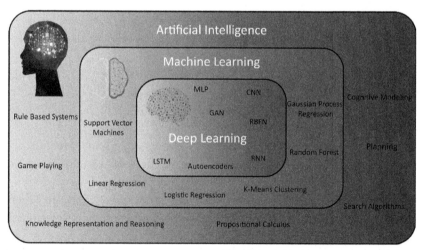

Figure 5.8 *Domains of AI, ML, DL.* The figure illustrates the domains of AI, ML, DL, and widely used algorithms. *From Baduge, S. K., Thilakarathna, S., Perera, J. S., Arashpour, M., Sharafi, P., Teodosio, B., Shiringi, A. & Mendis, P. (2022). Artificial intelligence and smart vision for building and construction 4.0: Machine and deep learning methods and applications.* Automation in Construction, 141, 1—26. https://doi.org/10.1016/j.autcon.2022. 104440.

directing the development of Artificial Intelligence toward the public good and to promote education, public safety, and health.

5.11 Co-creation

Recently, companies have been able to achieve and sustain innovation using a wide range of external actors and sources, and a central part of the innovation process involves the search for new ideas that have commercial potential. This process redefines the boundary between the firm and the environment, making the firm more porous. Laursen and Salter (2006) argue that "the network of relationships between the firm and its external environment can play an important role in shaping performance" (Laursen & Salter, 2006). There is a value-generating effect from integrating the external parties in the innovation process, such as: suppliers, customers, competitors, consultants, research institutes, and universities (Bahemia & Squire, 2010; Giannopoulou et al., 2011).

Co-creation is considered as 'a value generator' for companies operating in the Industry 4.0 revolution age (Adamik et al., 2018; Adamik & Nowicki, 2018). Value Co-creation is a collaborative practice for developing systems, products, or services involving customers, suppliers, and other stakeholders (Ramaswamy, 2011). The Co-creation strategy is evaluated along the dimensions of real-time learning, interoperability and integration, interconnection, collaboration, quality, and economic outcomes, and at the same time, customer experience is considered as being in a positive relationship with Co-creation development (Ramaswamy, 2011; Wasono Mihardjo et al., 2019).

5.11.1 Power to customers in designing a product

Local Motors is an American motor vehicle company that manufactures through a network of microfactories. The company develops vehicles using 3D printing. The cars' features are created by the potential users themselves, who discuss design, engineering, and construction, focusing on vehicle innovation. Local Motors has an online 'community' made up of its product enthusiasts, previous customers, and designers that help to come up with new ideas.

Local Motors manufactures Strati, the world's first 3D printed electric car and uses other innovations in its production technology. The car consists of 50 individual parts, far less than a traditional vehicle (which is manufactured with roughly 30,000 parts). The Local Motors website is a digital community whose members contribute with their own ideas and projects.

The idea of Co-creation (between manufacturer and user) along with that of microfactories has attracted large companies as well. In partnership with Local Motors, General Electric opened its first microfactory in Kentucky, involving the local community and a global network of innovators in cocreating the next generation of consumer appliances more rapidly and cost-effectively. The partners use new technologies such as 3D printing and digital prototyping and have rediscovered the principles of small-batch production.

Even if the spread of Co-creation has been limited, its potential is considered relevant for experts in that it responds to the tendency of demand to break up into many segments as a consequence of the growing desire of consumers from high-income countries to stand out and to differentiate the products they purchase.

The disruptive effects to the global value chain from these tendencies in certain industries are explosive. Consider, for example, that Local Motors can reach the break-even point for a new car when the volume of production exceeds 100 units and is sold at an average price of $120,000, an unattainable objective for most manufacturers. The secret is in the very low costs of Co-creation. Normally, the development of a new vehicle starting from a 'blank page' is estimated at around one million dollars. Co-creation brought clients into the product development process and realized the dream of many manufacturers to succeed in true mass customization.

For all these reasons, many firms are reevaluating the advantages and disadvantages of extended, complex supply chains and the inherent risks of managing them. In the past, minimizing labor costs was the primary offshoring objective; now, since what matters more in a digital world is speed to market and faster execution times, firms are considering other costs of doing business, such as logistics costs, lead times, productivity, and proximity to company organizations in other areas or to countries where the final products are consumed.

While we believe that disruption is the main factor of change, it must also be remembered that there is another interpretation for the present economic phase, known as 'decay storytelling'; this interpretation holds that the problem is the lack of innovation. According to research by the Economic Innovation Groups, dynamism is in retreat, as evidenced by the decline in the number of new enterprises in developed countries. After the financial crisis in 2008–09, more companies in the U.S. closed down than were started up. The consequent lower intensity of competition benefitted the incumbents rather than the new competitors. This would also explain why average profits increased in some industries.

5.12 Digital Value Chain (DVC)

Value results from any activity that makes the final product worth more to the final customer. In a supply chain, this can entail the rapid and precise delivery of components, the production of a tangible product or the physical positioning of a product to be available as needed. The value chain was first developed as a business idea by Michael Porter. Each link in a value chain consists of a collection of activities fastened together, and this collection is put together by a firm to "design, produce, market, deliver and support its product" (Porter, 1985). "Value activities are the discrete building blocks of competitive advantage" wrote the Author. In the decades after the book was published, the idea "became one of the most discussed and most misunderstood in the whole of the management arena" (Hindle, 2008).

Koulopoulos and Roloff (2006) observed that the modern value chain is far more complex than even those of the recent past. New levels of connectivity, relentless pressure to run efficient and lean operations and to focus on core competencies, and market demand for innovation have created strong complexity in connections among players. For all that, they argue that business today needs a new notion of the value chain, one that considers the impact of tighter integration of information, what the two Authors call 'Digital Value Chain' (DVC) (Koulopoulos & Roloff, 2006).

The ultimate goal of a DVC is to facilitate the connection among partners. A Digital Value Chain gathers and integrates all the information that accompanies a product, from the generation of new ideas to its delivery and use, including not only the traditional sources of information and systems, such as purchasing, manufacturing, sales, and marketing, but also a connection to the information system of suppliers, customers, and partners.

References

Adamik, A., & Nowicki, M. (2018). Co-Creating value in the era of industry 4.0. *Entrepreneurship Manage, 19*(6), 23—39.

Adamik, A., Nowicki, M., & Szymańska, K. (2018). Openness to co-creation as a method of reducing the complexity of the environment and dynamizing companies' competitive advantages. *Management & Marketing, 13*(2), 880—896. https://doi.org/10.2478/mmcks-2018-0011

Alkurd, I. (2020). What is the blockchain and why does it matter? *Forbes*, 1—4. Forbes, May, 18 www.forbes.com/sites/theyec/2020/05/18/what-is-the-blockchain-and-why-does-it-matter/?sh=30753e2748a1.

Aloini, D., & Martini, A. (2013). Exploring the exploratory search for innovation: A structural equation modelling test for practices and performance. *International Journal of Technology Management, 61*(1), 23—46. https://doi.org/10.1504/IJTM.2013.050242

Anderson, J. M., Nidhi, K., Stanley, K. D., Sorensen, P., Samaras, C., & Oluwatola, O. A. (2014). *Autonomous vehicle technology: A guide for policymakers*. Rand Corporation.

Ashton, K. (2017). Making sense of IoT. *Hewlett Packard Enterprise*, 1−41. http://book.itep. ru/depository//iot/HPE_Aruba_IoT_eBook_English.pdf.

Mauro, V., Dalla Chiara, B., Deflorio, F., Carboni, A., Cossu, F., & Automobile Club Italia - ACI, Fondazione Filippo Caracciolo. (2017). Auto-matica. Il futuro prossimo dell'auto: Connettività e automazione. *Panorama Assicurativo, June*, 1−84. Ania www. panoramassicurativo.ania.it/articoli/68423.

Baduge, S. K., Thilakarathna, S., Perera, J. S., Arashpour, M., Sharafi, P., Teodosio, B., Shiringi, A., & Mendis, P. (2022). Artificial intelligence and smart vision for building and construction 4.0: Machine and deep learning methods and applications. *Automation in Construction, 141*, 1−26. https://doi.org/10.1016/j.autcon.2022.104440

Bahemia, H., & Squire, B. (2010). A contingent perspective of open innovation in new product development projects. *International Journal of Innovation Management, 14*(4), 603−627. https://doi.org/10.1142/S1363919610002799

Barrachina, J., Sanguesa, J. A., Fogue, M., Garrido, P., Martinez, F. J., Cano, J. C., Calafate, C. T., & Manzoni, P. (2013). V2X-d: A vehicular density estimation system that combines V2V and V2I communications. *IFIP Wireless Days*, 1−6. https://doi.org/10.1109/WD.2013.6686518

Bechtsis, D., Tsolakis, N., Vlachos, D., & Iakovou, E. (2017). Sustainable supply chain management in the digitalisation era: The impact of Automated Guided Vehicles. *Journal of Cleaner Production, 142*, 3970−3984. https://doi.org/10.1016/j.jclepro.2016.10.057

Bedi, P., Jindal, V., & Gautam, A. (2014). Beginning with big data simplified. International conference on data mining and intelligent computing. *ICDMIC, 2014*, 1−7. https://doi.org/10.1109/ICDMIC.2014.6954229

Bessant, J., Lamming, R., Noke, H., & Phillips, W. (2005). Managing innovation beyond the steady state. *Technovation, 25*(12), 1366−1376. https://doi.org/10.1016/j.technovation.2005.04.007

Campbell, T., Williams, C., Ivanova, O., & Garrett, B. (2011). *Could 3D printing change the world? Technologies, potential, and implications of additive manufacturing.* www.atlanticcouncil.org/in-depth-research-reports/report/could-3d-printing-change-the-world/.

Chang, W. L., & Grady, N. (2019). Big data interoperability framework. *NIST*, 1. www.nist.gov/publications/nist-big-data-interoperability-framework-volume-1-definitions.

Chen, M., Mao, S., & Liu, Y. (2014). Big data: A survey. *Mobile Networks and Applications, 19*(2), 171−209. https://doi.org/10.1007/s11036-013-0489-0

Conoscenti, M., Vetro, A., & De Martin, J. C. (2016). Blockchain for the internet of things: A systematic literature review. In *Proceedings of IEEE/ACS international conference on computer systems and applications, AICCSA*, 1−6. https://doi.org/10.1109/AICCSA.2016.7945805

Cooper, B. (2021). *McDonald's delivers AI at the drive-thru.* www.digitalsignagetoday.com/articles/mcdonalds-delivers-ai-at-the-drive-thru/.

Dalla Chiara, B., Deflorio, F., & Diwan, S. (2009). Assessing the effects of inter-vehicle communication systems on road safety. *IET Intelligent Transport Systems, 3*(2), 225−235. https://doi.org/10.1049/iet-its:20080059

Dalla Chiara, B. (2021). In R. Vickerman (Ed.), *ITS for transport planning and policy* (Vol. 6, pp. 298−308). Elsevier. https://doi.org/10.1016/B978-0-08-102671-7.10699-2

Dalla Chiara, B. (2022). La mobilità come servizio: Ecco come funzionerà il MAAS. *Mondo Economico, May*, 1−7. https://mondoeconomico.eu/infrastrutture/la-mobilita-come-servizio-ecco-come-funziona-il-maas.

Dang, R., Ding, J., Su, B., Yao, Q., Tian, Y., & Li, K. (2014). A lane change warning system based on V2V communication. In *17th IEEE international conference on intelligent transportation systems* (pp. 1923−1928). ITSC. https://doi.org/10.1109/ITSC.2014.6957987, 2014.

Dean, J., & Ghemawat, S. (2008). MapReduce: Simplified data processing on large clusters. *Communications of the ACM, 51*(1), 107−113. https://doi.org/10.1145/1327452.1327492

Dekkers, R., Talbot, S., Thomson, J., & Whittam, G. (2014). Does Schumpeter still rule? Reflections on the current epoch. *Journal of Innovation Economics*, 7. https://doi.org/ 10.3917/jie.013.0007

Deloitte. (2016). MHI Annual Industry Report Accelerating change: How innovation is driving digital. *always-on Supply Chains*, 1—52. http://cpbucket.fiu.edu/1168-geb6368x81168_emba-97075%2F2016-industry-report-2016-(1).pdf

Demchenko, Y., Grosso, P., De Laat, C., & Membrey, P. (2013). Addressing big data issues in scientific data infrastructure. In *Proceedings of the 2013 international conference on collaboration technologies and systems* (pp. 48—55). CTS. https://doi.org/10.1109/CTS.2013.6567203, 2013.

Dey, K. C., Rayamajhi, A., Chowdhury, M., Bhavsar, P., & Martin, J. (2016). Vehicle-to-vehicle (V2V) and vehicle-to-infrastructure (V2I) communication in a heterogeneous wireless network - performance evaluation. *Transportation Research C: Emerging Technologies, 68*, 168—184. https://doi.org/10.1016/j.trc.2016.03.008

Dirican, C. (2015). The impacts of robotics, artificial intelligence on business and economics. *Procedia - Social and Behavioral Sciences*, 564—573. https://doi.org/10.1016/ j.sbspro.2015.06.134

Emmanuel, I., & Stanier, C. (2016). *Defining big data*. ACM International Conference Proceeding Series. https://doi.org/10.1145/3010089.3010090

Fagnant, D. J., & Kockelman, K. (2015). Preparing a nation for autonomous vehicles: Opportunities, barriers and policy recommendations. *Transportation Research A: Policy and Practice, 77*, 167—181. https://doi.org/10.1016/j.tra.2015.04.003

Fragapane, G., de Koster, R., Sgarbossa, F., & Strandhagen, J. O. (2021). Planning and control of autonomous mobile robots for intralogistics: Literature review and research agenda. *European Journal of Operational Research*. https://doi.org/10.1016/j.ejor.2021.01.019

Furht, B. (2010). Cloud computing fundamentals. In B. Furth, & A. Escalante (Eds.), *Handbook of cloud computing* (pp. 3—19). Springer. https://doi.org/10.1007/978-1-4419-6524-0_1

Future Supply Chain. (2021). *McDonald's is using AI and data to optimize its supply chain*. https:// supplychainnext.wbresearch.com/blog/mcdonalds-ai-data-optimize-supply-chain

Gabbai, A. (2015). *Kevin Ashton describes \the internet of things\: The innovator weighs in on what human life will be like a century from now*. Smithsonian: Smithsonian Institution. http:// www.smithsonianmag.com/innovation/kevin-ashton-describes-the-internet-of-things-180953749/.

Gandomi, A., & Haider, M. (2015). Beyond the hype: Big data concepts, methods, and analytics. *International Journal of Information Management, 35*(2), 137—144. https:// doi.org/10.1016/j.ijinfomgt.2014.10.007

Gantz, J., Reinsel, D., & EMC Corporation. (2011). Extracting value from chaos. *IDC Iview, June*, 1—12. https://pdf4pro.com/view/idc-i-v-i-e-w-extracting-value-from-chaos-dell-emc-5a42d1.html.

Giannopoulou, E., Yström, A., & Ollila, S. (2011). Turning open innovation into practice: Open innovation research through the lens of managers. *International Journal of Innovation Management, 15*(3), 505—524. https://doi.org/10.1142/S1363919611003465

Grasso, A., & Grasso, L. (2019). Ruolo ed impatto sull'economia delle tecnologie emergenti nel paradigma della globalizzazione 4.0. *Economistas*, 129—136.

Grossman, R. L. (2009). The case for cloud computing. *IT Professional, 11*(2), 23—27. https://doi.org/10.1109/MITP.2009.40

Guler, S. I., Menendez, M., & Meier, L. (2014). Using connected vehicle technology to improve the efficiency of intersections. *Transportation Research Part C: Emerging Technologies, 46*, 121—131. https://doi.org/10.1016/j.trc.2014.05.008

Haller, S., Karnouskos, S., & Schroth, C. (2009). The internet of things in an enterprise context. In J. Dominigue, D. Fensel, & P. Traverso (Eds.), *Vol. 5468. Future internet — FIS 2008. FIS 2008. Lecture notes in computer science* (pp. 14—28). Springer. https:// doi.org/10.1007/978-3-642-00985-3_2

Hamel, G. (2006). The why, what, and how of management innovation. *Harvard Business Review, 84*(2). https://hbr.org/2006/02/the-why-what-and-how-of-management-innovation.

Harnad, S. (1991). Other bodies, other minds: A machine incarnation of an old philosophical problem. *Minds and Machines, 1*(1), 43−54. https://doi.org/10.1007/BF00360578

Hindle, T. (2008). *Guide to management ideas and gurus* (Vol. 42). John Wiley & Sons.

Iansiti, M., & Lakhani, K. R. (2017). The Truth about blockchain. *Harvard Business Review, 95*(1), 118−127.

Initiative, I. (2012). *Overview of the internet of things.* www.itu.int/en/ITU-T/gsi/iot/Pages/default.aspx.

ISO/ASTM 52900. (2015). *Standard Terminology for additive manufacturing—general principles—Terminology.* ISO/ASTM 52900; American Society for Testing Materials. https://web.mit.edu/2.810/www/files/readings/AdditiveManufacturingTerminology.pdf.

Khan, M. A. U. D., Uddin, M. F., & Gupta, N. (2014). Seven V's of big data understanding big data to extract value. In *Proceedings of the 2014 Zone 1 conference of the American society for engineering education - \engineering education: Industry Involvement and interdisciplinary trends\.* https://doi.org/10.1109/ASEEZone1.2014.6820689. ASEE Zone 1 2014.

Khosravani, M. R., & Reinicke, T. (2020). On the environmental impacts of 3D printing technology. *Applied Materials Today, 20*, 1−11. https://doi.org/10.1016/j.apmt.2020.100689

Kok, J. N., Boers, E. J., Kosters, W. A., Putten, & Poel, M. (2009). Artificial intelligence: Definition, trends, techniques, and cases. *Artificial Intelligence, 1*, 270−299.

Köseoğlu, M., Çelik, O. M., & Pektaş, Ö. (2017). *Design of an autonomous mobile robot based on ROS. IDAP 2017 - international artificial intelligence and data processing Symposium.* https://doi.org/10.1109/IDAP.2017.8090199

Koulopoulos, T. M., & Roloff, T. (2006). *Smartsourcing: Driving innovation and growth through outsourcing.* Simon and Schuster.

Kumar, V., Ramachandran, D., & Kumar, B. (2021). Influence of new-age technologies on marketing: A research agenda. *Journal of Business Research, 125*, 864−877. https://doi.org/10.1016/j.jbusres.2020.01.007

Laney, D. (2001). *3D data management: Controlling data volume, velocity and variety.* META Group Research Note.

Laursen, K., & Salter, A. (2006). Open for innovation: The role of openness in explaining innovation performance among U.K. manufacturing firms. *Strategic Management Journal, 27*(2), 131−150. https://doi.org/10.1002/smj.507

Lemasson, M., Marx, C., Parker Sealy, R., Thompson, S., & Watkins, A. (2019). *Data for the life of the aircraft. How the adoption of blockchain can provide a boost of power and efficiency to the aerospace industry.* www.pwc.com/gx/en/aerospace-defence/assets/data-for-the-life-of-the-aircraft.pdf.

Li, X., Jiang, P., Chen, T., Luo, X., & Wen, Q. (2020). A survey on the security of blockchain systems. *Future Generation Computer Systems, 107*, 841−853. https://doi.org/10.1016/j.future.2017.08.020

Liang, J., & Kang, M. (2021). A study on the marketing strategy of IoT (internet of Things)-based smart home service companies focusing on the case of Xiaomi. *International Journal of Internet, Broadcasting and Communication, 13*(1), 20−25.

Lucas, A. (2019). *McDonald's acquires A.I. company to help automate the drive-thru, its third tech deal this year.* www.cnbc.com/2019/09/10/mcdonalds-acquires-ai-company-trying-to-automate-the-drive-thru.html.

Lucci, S., & Kopec, D. (2015). *Artificial intelligence in the 21st century.* Stylus Publishing.

Manyika, J., Chui, M., Brown, B., Bughin, J., Dobbs, R., Roxburgh, C., & Byers, A. H. (May 2011). *Big data: The next frontier for innovation, competition, and productivity.* www.mckinsey.com/~/media/mckinsey/business functions/mckinsey digital/our insights/big data the next frontier for innovation/mgi_big_data_exec_summary.pdf.

Maslova, N., CMA, C. T. P., & PMP. (2018). Blockchain: Disruption and opportunity. *Strategic Finance, 100*, 24−29. McKinsey Global Institute.

Mehic, M., Selimovic, N., & Komosny, D. (2019). About the connectivity of Xiaomi internet-of-things smart home devices. *IEEE*, 1−6.

Mell, P. M., & Grance, T. (2011). *The NIST definition of cloud computing, national institution of standards and technology* (pp. 800−945). Department of Commerce, Special Publication.

Metz, R. (2021). *McDonald's and other chains are giving their drive-thrus the Jetsons treatment.* https://edition.cnn.com/2021/02/26/tech/mcdonalds-drive-thru-artificial-intelligenc e/index.html.

Millar, K., Schneider, J., & Brooks, B. (2021). *Blockchain in aerospace and defense.* https://www2. deloitte.com/us/en/pages/energy-and-resources/articles/blockchain-in-aerospace-and-de-fense.html.

Morriello, R. (2019). Blockchain, intelligenza artificiale e internet delle cose in biblioteca. *AIB Studi, 59*(2), 45−68. https://doi.org/10.2426/aibstudi-11927

Murphy, R. (2000). *Introduction to AI robotics.* MIT press.

Nakamoto, S. (2008). Bitcoin: A peer-to-peer electronic cash system. White Paper https:// bitcoin.org/en/.

National Science and Technology Council - NSTC. (2016). *Preparing for the future of artificial intelligence.* https://obamawhitehouse.archives.gov/sites/default/files/whitehouse_files/ microsites/ostp/NSTC/preparing_for_the_future_of_ai.pdf.

Novais, L., Maqueira, J. M., & Ortiz-Bas, Á. (2019). A systematic literature review of cloud computing use in supply chain integration. *Computers and Industrial Engineering, 129*, 296−314. https://doi.org/10.1016/j.cie.2019.01.056

Organisation for Economic Co-operation and Development - OECD. (2018). *OECD science, technology and innovation outlook 2018: Adapting to technological and societal disruption.* https://doi.org/10.1787/sti_in_outlook-2018-en

Porter, M. E. (1985). Technology and competitive advantage. *Journal of Business Strategy, 5*(3), 60−78.

Proponent. (2018). *How Blockchain Technology could completely change aerospace.* www. proponent.com/how-blockchain-technology-change-aerospace/.

Ramaswamy, V. (2011). It's about human experiences...and beyond, to co-creation. *Industrial Marketing Management, 40*(2), 195−196. https://doi.org/10.1016/j.indmarman.2010. 06.030

Raphael, B. (1976). *The thinking computer.* W.H. Freeman.

Rathee, G., Ahmad, F., Sandhu, R., Kerrache, C. A., & Azad, A. M. (2021). On the design and implementation of a secure blockchain-based hybrid framework for Industrial Internet-of-Things. *Information Processing & Management, 58*(3), 1−15. https://doi.org/ 10.1016/j.ipm.2021.102526

Rauch, E. (2020). Industry 4.0+: The next level of intelligent and self-optimizing factories. *Lecture Notes in Mechanical Engineering*, 176−186. https://doi.org/10.1007/978-3-030-50794-7_18

Reis, J. Z., & Gonçalves, R. F. (2018). The role of internet of services (IoS) on industry 4.0 through the service oriented architecture (SOA). *IFIP Advances in Information and Communication Technology, 536*, 20−26. https://doi.org/10.1007/978-3-319-99707-0_3

Rich, E. (1985). Artificial intelligence and the humanities. *Computers and the Humanities, 19*(2), 117−122. https://doi.org/10.1007/BF02259633

Sankari, J., & Imtiaz, R. (2016). Automated guided vehicle (AGV) for industrial sector. *10th International Conference on Intelligent Systems and Control (ISCO), IEEE*, 1−5.

Sartor, G. (1996). *Intelligenza artificiale e diritto: un'introduzione.* Giuffrè Editore.

Satair. (2018). *A new frontier: OEMs on next-generation engines and future challenges.* https://blog. satair.com/next-generation-aircraft-engines.

Satair. (2019). *Blockchain in the aviation industry − why it's not just a buzz word.* https://blog. satair.com/blockchain-in-aviation.

Schroeck, M., Shockley, R., Smart, J., Romero-Morales, D., & Tufano, P. (2012). Analytics: The real-world use of big data. *IBM Global Business Services, 12*, 1−20.

Schumpeter, J. (1912). *Theorie der Wirtschaftlichen Entwicklung [The theory of economic development]*. Dunker & Humblot.

Schumpeter, J. (1934). *The theory of economic development*. Harvard University Press.

Shafiq, D. A., Jhanjhi, N. Z., & Abdullah, A. (2022). Load balancing techniques in cloud computing environment: A review. *Journal of King Saud University-Computer and Information Sciences, 34*(7), 3910−3933. https://doi.org/10.1016/j.jksuci.2021.02.007

Sundarakani, B., Ajaykumar, A., & Ajaykumar, A. (2021). Big data driven supply chain design and applications for blockchain: An action research using case study approach. *Omega, 102*, 1−19. https://doi.org/10.1016/j.omega.2021.102452

Swainson, W. K. (1977). *U.S. Patent No. 4,041*. U.S. Patent and Trademark Office.

Syed, R., Suriadi, S., Adams, M., Bandara, W., Leemans, S. J. J., Ouyang, C., ter Hofstede, A. H. M., van de Weerd, I., Wynn, M. T., & Reijers, H. A. (2020). Robotic process automation: Contemporary themes and challenges. *Computers in Industry, 115*, 1−15. https://doi.org/10.1016/j.compind.2019.103162

Thompson, W., Li, H., & Bolen, A. (2021). *Artificial intelligence, machine learning, deep learning and beyond*. SAS Insight www.sas.com/it_it/insights/articles/big-data/artificial-intelligence-machine-learning-deep-learning-and-beyond.html.

Turing, A. M. (1950). Computing machinery and intelligence. *Mind, 59*(236), 433−460. https://doi.org/10.1093/mind/LIX.236.433

Van Brummelen, J., O'Brien, M., Gruyer, D., & Najjaran, H. (2018). Autonomous vehicle perception: The technology of today and tomorrow. *Transportation Research Part C: Emerging Technologies, 89*, 384−406. https://doi.org/10.1016/j.trc.2018.02.012

Vermesan, O., Friess, P., Guillemin, P., Gusmeroli, S., Sundmaeker, H., Bassi, A., & Doody. (2011). Internet of things strategic research roadmap. Internet of things-global technological and societal trends. *Internet of Things-Global Technological and Societal Trends, 1*, 9−52.

Viriyasitavat, W., & Hoonsopon, D. (2019). Blockchain characteristics and consensus in modern business processes. *Journal of Industrial Information Integration, 13*, 32−39. https://doi.org/10.1016/j.jii.2018.07.004

Vis, I. F. A. (2006). Survey of research in the design and control of automated guided vehicle systems. *European Journal of Operational Research, 170*(3), 677−709. https://doi.org/10.1016/j.ejor.2004.09.020

Walsh, T. (2017). *Android Dreams: The past, present and future of artificial intelligence*. Oxford University Press.

Wang, Y., Han, J. H., & Beynon-Davies, P. (2019). Understanding blockchain technology for future supply chains: A systematic literature review and research agenda. *Supply Chain Management: An International Journal, 24*(1), 62−84. https://doi.org/10.1108/scm-03-2018-0148

Wasono Mihardjo, L. W., Sasmoko, Alamsjah, F., & Elidjen. (2019). Digital transformation: A transformational performance-based conceptual model through co-creation strategy and business model innovation in the industry 4.0 in Indonesia. *International Journal of Economics and Business Research, 18*(3), 369−386. https://doi.org/10.1504/IJEBR.2019.102736

Windpassinger. (2017). *Digitize or Die: Transform your organization. Embrace the digital evolution*. Lowe: Rise above the competition.

Witkowski, K. (2017). Internet of things, big data, industry 4.0 - innovative solutions in logistics and supply chains management. *Procedia Engineering, 182*, 763−769. https://doi.org/10.1016/j.proeng.2017.03.197

Ziegler, C., & Patel, N. (2016). *Meet the new Ford, a Silicon valley software company, the Verge*. www.theverge.com/2016/4/7/11333288/ford-ceo-mark-fields-interview-electric-self-driving-car-software.

PART THREE

Global supply chain and global strategies

CHAPTER SIX

Waves of disruption have undermined but not defeated globalization

6.1 The first waves of globalization: 1980's and 1990's

The word globalization came to the fore in management literature with the writings of Theodore Levitt, whose article "The Globalization of Markets" was published by the *Harvard Business Review* in 1983. The Author noted, "the emergence of global markets for standardized products on a previously unimagined scale of magnitude" (Levitt, 1983, pp. 92—102). One measure that reflects the growth of globalization is the value of cross-border world trade expressed as a percentage of world GDP, which was around 27% in 1970 and grew to around 58% in 2019 (Macrotrends, 2022).

Since its inception, globalization has spurred economic progress both in emerging countries and in developed ones; however, due to its inherent nature, it has created instability. We define "the new waves of globalization" as an abrupt change in the degree of internalization of production and in the scope of offshore transactions that have occurred in the recent past.

The structure of international trade and investment changed dramatically beginning in the second half of the 1980s (Bartlett & Goshal, 2000; Friedman, 2006; Ghemawat, 2007; Levitt, 1983, pp. 92—102; Milberg & Winkler, 2013). In the following decades, political and economic changes have brought new actors to the international economic stage, helped bring down the barriers to trade, and set off new waves of globalization. Three main consequences of outsourcing and offshoring have resulted from these changes: (1) an increase in the number of 'participants' in international trade, and thus in the demand for products and services and in their supply; (2) a revival of protectionism in Western countries, and (3) an 'unbeatable' uncertainty that is forcing outsourcers to frequently revise their strategies.

The main events that have disrupted the outsourcing strategies can be examined as follows.

The Digital Transformation of Supply Chain Management
ISBN: 978-0-323-85532-7
https://doi.org/10.1016/B978-0-323-85532-7.00001-3

6.1.1 The tide of changes

The new direction in the policies of some countries and the fast pace of technological innovation has changed the structure of international trade, providing a new relationship between imports and exports, on the one hand, and international investment on the other. A growing number of firms in high-income countries have looked beyond their own borders, for the most part to low-income countries, for suppliers to produce parts, components, or services to integrate into their final products.

At the same time, these firms have concentrated their resources on the activities they consider to be 'core' for their main functions: from design to R&D, finance to marketing. They have gradually developed what we understand as outsourcing and offshoring, substituting onshore production with nearshore or offshore production to increase, other things equal, the amount of international trade. However, Foreign Direct Investment (FDI) has not increased to the same extent.

Several changes in the political environment have led to this new situation. The breakup of the Soviet Union has introduced into international trade increased demand for products and caused a chain reaction in countries that previously were part of Russia's sphere of influence. Two giants such as China and India have abandoned (in part) their protectionist policies, gradually accepted market rules, focused on aggressive export policies and offered protection to foreign investments.

Never before in history have so many countries signed so many trade agreements. The number of members in the World Trade Organization (WTO) has increased, tariff barriers have been lowered on average, and there was less recourse to nontariff barriers. Many countries have gradually emerged from poverty and begun to develop their economies.

The changes brought about by emerging countries from their entry into the international economy have been formidable and contributed to the development of offshoring. Agtmael identified four factors that have led to a profound change in the globalization of production (Agtmael, 2007): (1) no longer is a technology under the exclusive control of Western firms; (2) the fastest growing markets are no longer in the West; (3) 'The power of unconventional thinking'; that is, the ability to go against the tide. Many innovations from firms in emerging countries are the result of breaking the rules (diverging from accepted standards or models, not limited or bound by convention); and (4) middle-class purchasing power has been eroded in Western countries while it has increased rapidly in size in emerging ones.

In addition, the supply of skilled labor has increased, as many people seeking employment in emerging countries have received good professional training. Education skills have been increasing in provider countries and, as a consequence, workers are able to carry out new business tasks requiring high levels of knowledge. This has encouraged outsourcers to shift product development and other functions offshore as opposed to just looking for low-cost activities. Clusters have specialized in offshoring activities mainly in India, with few rivals emerging in Western countries in terms of costs and technological progress.

Since the 1980s, offshoring has contributed to changing corporate strategies (Lazonick & O'Sullivan, 2000). From a business model based on retained earnings and the reinvestment of profits to sustain the autonomous development of the firm, there has been a shift toward a business model based on downsizing and profit distribution to shareholders (Davis, 2009; Pine, 1993; Prahalad & Hamel, 1990).

Offshoring (which means transferring production to other firms) has allowed firms to cut costs (thus increasing the outsourcer's profits) and reduce the need for investments, thereby allowing the outsourcer to distribute a higher proportion of profits to its shareholders. This has played a part in pushing forward the 1980s trend of 'financialization', which is mainly characterized by the buyback by firms of their own stocks, the rise of dividends paid to stockholders, and mergers and acquisitions paid for mainly in cash.

Waters analyzes the main factors that encouraged global operations during the 1980 and 1990s (Waters, 2007), which can be summarized as follows (Table 6.1).

6.1.2 New and old reinforced drivers

Since the first decade 2000s, old and new reinforced drivers have led to the development of outsourcing and offshoring, offering ways to new business models.

- **Intense competition**

  More than in the past, the increased competition in developed markets has forced many firms to look for lower costs by investing part of their activities abroad in production facilities or in offshoring activities.

- **Technological progress**

  Progress in transportation (lower costs per unit, faster transportation times) and in communication have made it easier and more convenient to

Table 6.1 Reasons for outsourcing and offshoring: the old glory days of stable growth.

Factors	Descriptions
Cost differences	The increasing competition induces firms to look for new ways to reduce costs. One of these is to move one or more functions or processes to countries where labor costs are low.
Growing demand in new markets	Progress in economic development in emerging countries creates new demand and new opportunities for firms in developed countries, especially for industrial products.
Economies of scale	The provider who is able to sell the same component or the same module in several markets and to several customers can build economies of scale that a single firm can rarely reach.
Greater demand from customers	Progress in communications has given consumers greater knowledge of the products and services from other, even distant regions. Not being able to find them from local suppliers, they look outside their borders.
Convergence of market demands	More national markets accept the same product or one that is only slightly different. Firms can thus sell the same product in different markets, thereby increasing the chance of building economies of scale.
Economic liberalization. Removal of trade barriers	Economic liberalization was an important factor in the increasing globalization of production. Free trade areas such as the European Union (EU) or the North America free trade agreement (NAFTA) stimulated international trade. The growing liberalization of markets gave western firms access to new customers.
Upgrading logistics	The relentless shift of logistics to higher standards simplified international trade. For example, the use of container and intermodal transport made the movement of goods easier, cheaper, and faster.
Specialized support services	Many companies transferred part of their activities to others that often operated in other countries (outsourcing and offshoring).
Improved communications in business	Progress in information technology made it easier to get information about other markets and to do business in them.

turn to suppliers from other countries. Also decisive is the progress in information technology and the management of logistics in mass production and in distribution. The Internet has signaled a turning point in the organization of the global supply chain that winds its way across countries and continents, making it easier to communicate with foreign suppliers. It has made the world smaller, drastically lowering the costs of managing far-reaching supply chains and of interactions among technologies. New management techniques have simplified and lowered the coordination costs of scattered innovation activities.

- **Changes in customer behavior**

Several profound economic and social changes account for the need to rethink global supply chains. In the developed world, the incomes and purchasing power of the middle class have stagnated or been eroded. Consumer values are shifting more toward quality than toward quantity. More and more people are becoming worried about getting value for their money. Both trends are leading to a far-reaching revision of the global supply chain. Western companies are turning to low-cost or emerging countries to develop their entire production of frugal products. In this way, they can raise local demand and at the same time sell to cost-conscious consumers in advanced economies.

The car industry is once again showing evidence of this trend. Renault's Dacia brand has built a new segment of low-cost vehicles, becoming the cash cow of the French company. Renault planned to sell the Logan brand to cost-conscious consumers in Eastern countries and the Middle East. The engineers were asked to design a 'no-frills' car that could be sold for no more than 5000 euros. Surprisingly, Logan has also been successful in affluent Western Europe. Research has revealed that in Europe, 30% of consumers on average were willing to buy affordable cars at a low price and that an increasing number of young European consumers were more interested in buying a low-cost than a premium car.

To take advantage of this trend, Renault introduced a new range of products under the brand name Dacia, thereby modifying its entire supply chain. Rather than build the new vehicles in France, Renault decided to invest in a Romanian factory it had bought in 1999. In addition to the original Logan saloon, Renault offered the Logan van, the Logan pickup, the Sandero hatchback, the Duster sports utility vehicle, and the Lodgy minivan.

6.1.3 New economic models

This extraordinary, unprecedented change in history was also aided by the fact that outsourcing and offshoring became an integral part of the strategies of many companies in developing countries. The model of the multinational company organized with wholly-owned subsidiaries or joint ventures in several countries (with the objective of adapting to and exploiting the opportunities offered by the local market) was in part replaced by companies capable of building a global supply chain that crossed several countries and continents and whose objective was to enter the largest number of markets possible. The greatest advantage of global supply chains is that they require less investment and thus provide greater flexibility.

Decades later Apple, with more than 450 suppliers in multiple countries, is light years away from the models adopted by General Motors and Ford, which entered the UK and Germany in the 1920s, the former with a model based on buying existing firms (Vaxhall and Opel) and the latter starting from the 'green field' (at Dabenham in the UK and in Cologne in Germany).

Those firms, which were successful in their first attempts at extending their global networks of production invested even more in this direction; others soon followed. Lazonick described this as the transition from the 'old economic model' to the 'new economic model' (Lazonick, 2009).

The financial crisis in 2008–09 interrupted a long period of expanding economic growth. International trade collapsed, imports to the U.S. and Europe declined, and consequently, the demand for intermediate products declined as well. However, there was no decline in offshoring. The crisis led to lower profits for the largest companies, which responded by trying to further reduce costs by turning to offshore more than they had in the past. Regarding exports from the most advanced countries and sales in their home markets, there was a rise in the content of parts and components imported from offshoring, and thus the value added in these countries fell.

The recovery from the 2008–09 crises was slow in the U.S. and the European Union; however, it was fast-paced in India, China, and other emerging countries. A new trend appeared: the largest companies sought sales outlets to compensate for what they had lost in the traditional markets to competition from the growing markets in the emerging countries. They sold (and sell today) in these countries products that incorporate locally manufactured parts and components, which had become part of the global supply chain but which at times ended up as finished products in other countries, only to be imported into the country that occupies the first link in the chain.

6.1.4 The doctrine of 'comparative advantage' revisited

These new tendencies have also affected the theoretical approach in this area. Several scholars maintain that the traditional theory of international trade can no longer explain what has occurred and is occurring, the reasons trade is developing as it is, and the new relationship between the pace of economic development and the pace of growth in international trade.

Two other concepts have been revisited to interpret the effects of the new waves of globalization: 'comparative advantage' and 'competitive advantage'. In simple words, the question is: what orients the direction of the trade (of which offshoring is a relevant component): the 'comparative advantage' (which means the search for different benefits from a presence in different countries) or the 'competitive advantage' (also termed absolute advantage) that management gains through its strategies?

In order to build a strategy of global sourcing, management compares, by searching for the best combination, its 'competitive advantage' with the 'comparative advantage' of the countries in which it can operate.

The search for sustainable 'competitive advantage' indicates in what direction — functions, processes, management areas — it pays to invest financial and management resources to gain a 'competitive advantage' over rivals. In fact, 'competitive advantage' derives from the possibility of reducing the cost of each activity in the value chain, which means carrying out these activities at the lowest cost; it can also derive from the ability to differentiate products and services with respect to competitors.

'Comparative advantage' depends on the one hand, on sourcing decisions, and thus which countries to acquire intermediate products and services from based on differences between labor costs and the costs of other factors of production; and, on the other, on which countries to sell the finished products, taking into account production costs (including logistics) and the selling prices.

The analysis of the global supply chain and the distribution of value within it (global value chain) represents the logical basis for identifying which activities to invest in the various markets and countries since this indicates the contribution of value from the activities the company carries out to plan, produce, sell and deliver its products.

Going to the root of the concept of offshoring, Milberg and Winkler have written "the story of the refusal and then the revival of the theory of comparative advantage" (Milberg & Winkler, 2013). After having observed that (1) in the past 30 years there has been a great debate over the role that 'comparative advantage' has had in orienting the direction of international trade, the two Authors conclude that (2) several factors "have combined to greatly diminish the relevance of the principle of comparative advantages in the determination of trade flows". Those factors, Milberg and Winkler argued, are the increased international flows of portfolio and direct capital, the increasing vertical disintegration of production, the high level of global excess capacity, and the importance of technological competition (as opposed to price competition. (3) "In this context, absolute advantage matters along with comparative advantage in determining the direction of trade" (Milberg & Winkler, 2013).

In other words, outsourcing and offshoring can be analyzed as two arms of the global disaggregation of the value chain and as attempts by firms to combine the 'comparative advantages' of geographic locations, on the one hand, and their competencies on the other, in order to maximize their 'competitive advantage' (Mudambi & Venzin, 2010). The reciprocal interaction of 'comparative' and 'competitive advantages' can result in the optimal location of the value chain components (offshoring decisions) as well as of the boundaries of the firm's core competencies (outsourcing decisions).

6.1.5 Win-win or lose-win?

In the first part of the 2010s, a revival of protectionism, as well as a wave of 'disruptors', have dramatically changed the context in which offshoring decisions are made. Offshoring was never without its critics. Companies that adopted it always had to defend themselves from accusations of moving jobs offshore. Outsourcing does not necessarily lead to a loss of jobs in certain countries or territories. The activities can simply be transferred to other organizations in the same country or territory that can carry them out more efficiently. When jobs are transferred through offshoring, they are shifted to another country. There are contrasting views regarding the advantages and disadvantages in this case. There has been a very heated debate in the U.S. given the country's role in promoting free trade and thus encouraging offshoring. "For years — even decades — firms in response to intensifying competition decided to outsource their manufacturing operations in order to reduce costs. But we are now seeing the alarming long-term effect of those choices" (Pisano & Shih, 2012). The two Authors:

(a) documented the effects on the contemporary American economy of years of "poor sourcing decisions" and low investment in manufacturing at home;

(b) illustrated that manufacturing activities, undervalued by many, often contain the seeds of innovative products and processes;

(c) argued that firms must return to investing in developing new products and new processes in the industrial sectors in the U.S. Only by reviving these 'industrial commons' can the U.S. economy gain the experience and strength to regain its lost 'competitive advantage'. "America needs a manufacturing renaissance.

For his part, Liveris strongly criticized policies such as the one illustrated by the words on an iPad model: "Designed by Apple in California", with the additional words, printed in smaller characters on the same model: 'Assembled in China' (Liveris, 2012). A new production plant creates the demand for raw materials, constructions, energy, services, maintenance, and other products and services. It becomes an engine for the economy in which it is located. If the plant is opened in China or another country, all these jobs and opportunities disappear, destined never to return. More than any other sector, manufacturing creates jobs outside its own industrial territory. Liveris defines this as 'the multiplier effect', estimating that "indeed for every Apple worker in America, there are 10 Apple workers in China".

Manufacturing is also the main driver of research and development, innovation, and intellectual property, which carries the weight of long-term growth. The U.S. government writes Liveris, has spent huge amounts of money to finance R&D at home, but other countries have gotten most of the advantages from that. He gives the example of the vast investment in R&D in renewable energy, which, however, Japan was the first to commercialize solar panels and China the first to take advantage of in order to achieve dominance in the global renewable resources industry.

There is no foundation to the 'conventional wisdom' that the Western/advanced economies could continue to prosper and grow even though the manufacturing sector is in decline, given that the service sector and other knowledge-based ones could not occupy the space left by manufacturing and sustain economic expansion and employment. Simply said: deindustrialization is not rewarded. Milberg and Winkler observed that: "There is already ample econometric evidence that offshoring has had an adverse impact on low skilled workers in industrialized countries, in terms of pay and employment, in both absolute and relative terms" (Milberg & Winkler, 2013). Other recent studies confirm the negative impact of offshoring on high-skill workers as well (Geishecker, 2008; Winkler, 1995).

On the contrary, those in favor say that offshoring is a win–win game, claiming that both developed countries and providers in developing/ emerging countries gain from offshoring. Let us examine their reasoning.

It is true that countries that are outsourced can capture low-value-added, low-wage, and low-skill sectors and that these countries will become increasingly competitive in global markets; but thanks to their flexibility and capabilities, the Western countries will maintain their supremacy and, above all, their capacity to dominate the new innovative sectors, as occurred for those sectors requiring advanced know-how, such as the semiconductor, computer, aircraft, and automobile sectors.

However, those opposed to this view say it is not true. Countries such as India and China, which for decades received production from countries seeking to gain from their low production costs, now have cutting-edge companies or ones that are fighting to enter the top ranks in sectors such as flat-panel displays, advanced batteries, solar energy, and wind turbines. After acquiring the Swedish car maker Volvo, the Chinese company Geely transformed Volvo into a serious competitor in several segments of the automobile market. Volvo announced that by 2030 it would produce only electric or hybrid vehicles and no longer internal combustion engines. Sectors that up until a few years ago seemed to be exclusively in the hands of the Western economies are now under threat: optoelectronics, space satellites, and aircraft, to name but a few.

A recent McKinsey research report gives an example of very different ideas on the subject. "The impact of outsourcing on labor markets in the economy of origin are neither significant nor lasting. With few exceptions, the research agrees that any negative consequences are nil or negligible" (Ricart & Agnese, 2015).

6.2 Offshoring has become a vital part of global strategies

Rapidly shifting conditions in the marketplace have made offshoring a vital part of any search for sustainable 'competitive advantage' and consequently for global strategies to lead the way to new business models, on the one hand by reducing costs, and therefore improving profitability, and on the other by reducing the investment needs of outsourcers, thereby increasing shareholder value.

In the last 25 years, the intensity of price competition in Western national markets has increased, prompting more and more companies to look for any way to lower costs. Many firms have looked offshore for their manufacturing and service needs, often keeping at the center of their organization only design, R&D, and marketing. For this reason, and under the pressure of technological and political change and global excess capacities, offshoring has gradually become an integral part of a broader business strategy.

Both outsourcers and providers acknowledge the importance of cost reduction, but they no longer see this as the fundamental objective. Lowering costs and having access to new skills is the first motive for offshoring; however, a policy of giving priority to strategic factors such as increased flexibility, finding an engine for innovation, gaining access to global markets, and inducing changes in the organization has gained hold. In many industries, only companies that are globally competitive can aspire to attain sustainable 'competitive advantages' over their rivals.

6.2.1 The need for a constant review of core competences

The growing popularity of outsourcing, which has moved companies to transfer more and more activities, processes, and entire functions abroad, has presented management with the problem of determining the unique 'core' competencies that distinguish a company from the competition and which therefore cannot be handed over to third parties without running the risk of being imitated and succumbing to competition.

Identifying the core competencies means drawing a line between these and the non-core competencies, which is the first step in defending companies against erosion from the competition and, above all, from changes in the economic, technological, and legal environment. It is rare for the boundaries of the core competencies to remain stable for a long. Every important change in the outsourcing environment and market prompts outsourcers to ask what to outsource and how to do this with providers. The needs of customers are changing, there are more generic products, and more services have become factors for market differentiation. Most providers upgrade their products continuously and extend their range of services, becoming strong competitors not only in their market of origin.

The problem of defining the 'core' activities and their boundaries has caught the attention of researchers and academics. Various theories and analyses have been put forward regarding the concept of core competencies and how to define their boundaries. Many of these contradict each another.

The concept of core competence was introduced into the economic literature by Prahalad and Hamel in 1990 (Prahalad & Hamel, 1990), giving rise to many definitions with only slight variations. A firm's core competence is "a competitively valuable activity that a company performs better than its rivals" (Thompson & Strickland, 2005). Core competencies drive the enterprise. The concept defines activities a firm should retain for 'competitive advantage'. Core and outsourcing are complementary concepts. While the core deals with sources of 'competitive advantage', outsourcing transfers activities that do not add value to other organizations.

One of the main characteristics of core competence was noted by Prahalad and Hamel: "... core competence does not diminish with use. Unlike physical assets, which do deteriorate over time, competencies are enhanced as they are applied and shared".

From the beginning, the concept of core competence was useful to management for identifying those activities that were not 'at the core'; therefore, it was useful in making decisions about what to outsource. Management cannot allow 'non-core' activities to consume valuable resources.

Two of the most studied approaches are Resource-Based Theory and Transaction Cost Theory, which suggest contrasting views on how to identify 'core' competencies and are thus relevant in the outsourcing and offshoring literature.

(1) The Resource-Based Theory (RBT) places efficiency in the use of the internal resources of a company as the main determinant of the success of strategic choices. After having described the firm as a collection of productive resources, (Penrose, 1959) stated that the firm can achieve a position of advantage over its rivals not because it has better resources but by having distinctive competencies that involve making better use of its resources.

Similarly, regarding some attributes, Hamel and Prahalad believe that distinctive core competencies internal to the organization are what will deliver winning strategies regarding competitors: "Core competencies are the collective learning in an organization, especially how to coordinate diverse production skills and integrate multiple streams of technologies". In short, they are activities that a firm does exceptionally well. This concept fits together with the process of making outsourcing decisions. Core competence allows the firm to transfer to a third party the processes and functions that are not 'core' to its business.

Prahalad and Hamel suggest three tests to decide whether an activity is 'core': (1) a core competence has the potential to give access to a wide variety of markets; (2) it must help customers perceive the benefits of the end product, and (3) it must be difficult for competitors to imitate by containing a harmonious complex of technologies and skills. Rumelt argued that to sustain the 'competitive advantages' through the RBT, a firm must protect its market position by avoiding imitation (Rumelt, 1997). He thus suggests using an 'isolating mechanism', such as building buyer switching costs, reputation, branding, and economies of scale (Coase, 1937). Valuable resources should also be retained within the firm. To this end, some researchers argue that management should invest in competencies that are 'firm specific' and unique.

(2) The Transaction Cost Theory is not based on resources but on costs incurred during transactions. Introduced by Coase in the 1930s, in his famous "The Nature of the Firm", and later developed by Williamson in the mid-1970s (Williamson, 1985), the theory states that the success of a firm depends on managing a trade-off between transaction costs and internal production costs. Transactions are exchanges of goods and services between separate economic units or actors, inside or outside the boundaries of an organization. Transaction costs include all disadvantages that arise when two parties exchange goods or services. "In recent years transaction costs have dropped sharply". As a result of changes in technology and markets, business models and supply chains can be configured and staffed differently as compared to the past (Magretta, 2002).

Coase, who won the Nobel Prize in economics in 1991 for his work (dating to the late 1930s) on how transaction costs define the limits of organizations, developed a simple principle to explain the size of a firm. When it is cheaper to make a transaction internally (that is, within the limits of a firm), firms grow larger. When it is cheaper to make transactions externally, in the open market, firms stay small or shrink. That is why vertical integration has lost much of its appeal as markets have become more efficient and competitive and transaction costs have fallen.

Magretta observes that Coase's ideas are particularly relevant today since they explain how new technologies and new markets lead management to outsource non-core activities and create organizations whose scope is more narrowly focused (Magretta, 2002). In other words, a firm exists because of its efficiency compared to market relations. Williamson extended Coase's approach in many ways, making a significant contribution to the analysis of globalized production and supply chains (Williamson, 1985, 2002).

Researchers have identified a variety of outsourcing core activities that could generate 'competitive advantages' over rivals (Baden-Fuller et al., 2000). These are determined by four categories of circumstances: (1) 'catch up', when, despite a slow-moving environment, the firm has fallen behind its rivals (in this case the key issue is to build new competencies); (2) 'changing value chain economics', when a change in customer needs and behavior requires a response by the firm (the key issue becomes reducing costs); (3) 'technology shifts', when new technology makes the firm obsolete (key issue: having access to new competencies); and (4) 'new markets emerge', when rapid changes in consumer needs and new technologies open new markets for the firm (key issue: fast track innovations to allow the firm a rapid entrance into new markets).

One of the most complex problems in defining core competence boundaries is whether and to what extent we should consider outsourcing innovation in its various aspects, from the most current technologies to management methods.

Regarding whether to outsource or not, Quinn has no doubts: "Innovate or die. Strategic outsourcing innovation can put a company in a leadership position ... innovation is its frontier" (Quinn, 2000). A single company can rarely sustain the host of external enterprise innovations required by its value chain.

There are many reasons for this. Resources are limited. An external provider can tap many more upstream technological sources and can match many customer problems downstream, managing to build economies of scale and enhance the learning curve. To update the knowledge of how innovation is developing, far-sighted specialists are needed in many fields. In a few instances, a firm can cover a wide spectrum. In addition, monitoring and evaluating the constant change in innovation requires huge investments, which entail risks. While a supplier can divide those risks among several projects and clients, this is not the case for a single firm. Finally, turning to a supplier can speed up the introduction of a product or a service in the market.

As far as the extent of outsourcing is concerned, depending on their needs and capabilities "many companies can profitably outsource almost any element in the innovation chain" (Quinn, 2000), from basic research to advanced development, from outsourcing business processes to outsourcing the introduction of new products.

To define the core competence boundaries, we need to consider what customers are actually expecting. Although augmenting the technological content of a product might create unique, inimitable competencies, we cannot ignore the fact that most customers are attracted by those solutions that solve their specific problems rather than by mere technological ability. If this principle is ignored, the firm might risk launching products or services that customers neither want nor need.

The main conclusion of all the research we have mentioned is that management must be able to clearly identify the 'core' competencies and the 'non-core' competencies, by "[focusing] not only on what is core today but also on what will be core to the company in the future" (Landsdale & Cox, 1998). Defining and rethinking in a timely manner the core competencies in the face of the relentless change in the environment is crucial for successfully governing the global value chain.

6.3 The great variety of models

The 'lead' firm controls the global value chain and is the one that usually sells the final product. Gereffi distinguishes between 'buyer driven' and 'producer driven' value chains (Gereffi, 1994). The 'buyer driven' chain is mainly found in retail apparel, footwear, and toys. Here the lead firm is the large retail chain, which does not directly produce goods but is responsible for the design and marketing functions, outsourcing production through subcontracting. The 'producer-driven' supply chain is found in the medium and high technology sectors, where the lead firm builds significant economies of scale, outsourcing part of its production while maintaining the R&D and marketing functions and the final assembly. A typical example, in this case, is the automobile industry.

The relations between the lead firms and their suppliers may take a variety of forms.

As the number of companies outsourcing at least some functions to offshore vendors has increased and as the complexity of business functions being moved offshore has increased as well, the range of possible relations between the lead firms and their suppliers has grown dramatically. Consequently, organizations using the offshore approach have developed a variety of models to manage the relationships with their providers and to build international networks of production. Because of increasing competition and complexity, choosing the right model of outsourcing and offshoring is a highly critical phase. The increase in the variety of models suggests it can no longer be seen as a passing phenomenon.

At one end of the spectrum are firms that sell products they have not manufactured. This is the traditional model used by retailers, but today it is also adopted in other industries, from clothing (The Gap) to toys (Mattel), electronics, and computers (Apple and Dell). The Austrian company Magna Styer manufactures new vehicles for carmakers such as BMW and Mercedes Benz.

Using a variety of models brings two main advantages: it reduces costs by encouraging competition among suppliers and increases flexibility by varying the type of relations with suppliers. As will be discussed below, the resulting asymmetry of power determined by those two advantages can strengthen the position of outsourcers in managing their global supply chain. On the other hand, too many models may mean more risk of serious shortcomings or failures or too many potential conflicts.

Many solutions have been brought to an end. We distinguish between the type of outsourcing agreement and the way in which the firm manages the supply chain by means of value-added and the sharing of technology.

6.3.1 Types of the outsourcing agreement

As for the type of agreement, variations spring from the disaggregation of the firm's value chain into individually distinct fragments — some to be performed in-house, others to be outsourced — having the objective of reducing costs and risks while also getting in return the advantage from innovations developed by other organizations.

After deciding to disaggregate the value chain, the firm decides whether to allocate one or more fragments to other organizations (outsourcing) and to different countries or geographical areas (offshoring).

Outsourcing involves restructuring the firm's organization and selecting some activities that can be allocated to an organization that operates in the home nation of the firm (inshore) as well as abroad (offshore). On the other hand, offshoring involves restructuring the firm along both organizational and geographical lines. The activities relocated from the home nation to a foreign location are performed by the own subsidiary of a multinational company (MNC), by a foreign contract vendor, or by an allied partner. While models adopted by MNCs to delegate responsibility to their own units, even in different nations, can be homogeneous, this does not hold for the agreement with foreign vendors or with allied partners. Operating in different countries means different tax rules, different laws, and different cultures. Also at play is the type of provider/vendor, in terms of its size, experience, skills, financial resources, and organization.

As for the outsourcing agreement, researchers identify four models (Dreischmeier et al., 2005): (1) offshoring to a vendor in a low-cost country; (2) offshoring to a captive center, or wholly owned subsidiary, in a low-cost country; (3) outsourcing to a local (onshore) vendor; (4) doing the work in-house. Choosing the right model requires an analysis along five dimensions: strategic impact, financial impact, business impact, business risk, and feasibility. For each dimension, the objective of the analysis and some key questions (Dreischmeier et al., 2005) can be detailed as follows (Table 6.2).

Managing the supply chain by means of value-added and the sharing of technology results in an asymmetry of power along the global supply chain.

6.3.2 Asymmetry of power in the global supply chain

The evolution of offshoring within the global supply chain has strengthened the power asymmetry between outsourcers and providers. On the one hand, the concentration (reduction in the number of competing firms) in many industrial sectors has increased, and on the other, the number of countries (sometimes called 'emergents') engaging in international trade and offering low-cost labor has grown significantly (Milberg & Winkler, 2013).

The result is an increasing disequilibrium in negotiating power between outsourcers and providers, to the disadvantage of the latter. This asymmetry of power is the factor that builds and maintains the oligopolistic position of lead firms, thereby allowing them to reduce costs and gain greater flexibility, for instance, by drawing up more agreements or contracts with more providers.

Milberg and Winkler remark that the asymmetry gives the outsourcers the opportunity to pursue different strategies in their relationships with providers along the global supply chain (Milberg & Winkler, 2013). By managing the mark-up (what they pay) over costs (those incurred by the providers) and managing the share of the value added at different points of the vertical sequence in the supply chain (first tier, second tier, third tier, and so on), they can choose among four main strategies:

(1) 'vertical competition' (uniform mark-up and value added at each point of the supply chain);

(2) 'pressure on subcontractors' (reduction tier by tier of mark-up and of value added from offshoring);

Table 6.2 How to choose the right model in the management of the supply chain.

Dimensions	The objective of the analysis	Key questions
Strategic impact	Strategic relevance. The potential to gain 'competitive advantages'.	Will the outsourced process be critical to our business in the future? Does the process help differentiate us from competitors?
Financial impact	The impact on revenue, costs, and the balance sheet.	Will outsourcing translate into significantly lower labor costs? Will it help us penetrate new markets?
Business impact	Service levels, access to skills and technologies; the potential for greater flexibility, and reduced complexity.	Will outsourcing and offshoring increase our ability to deliver services? Will a vendor have greater access to the tools, technologies, and skills necessary for this process?
Business risk	Strategic issues; branding; vendor, country, and operational risks.	Will outsourcing hurt our brand? Is the vendor operating in a region with high geopolitical risk?
Feasibility	The vendor's market, legal constraints, location logistics, and process maturity.	Do vendors have the necessary experience and scale? Will they need ongoing capital to maintain the required knowledge and skills in-house?

(3) 'strong first-tier supplier' (the outsourcers buy only from one or a few first-tier providers, who control the rest of the supply chain); and

(4) 'strong middleman' (a trader gets into the supply chain and is able to squeeze the suppliers below it in the chain and resist the power of its buyers).

Four factors account for asymmetry in the strategy known as 'pressure on subcontractors' sustainable over time: (1) the nature of entry barriers; (2) capital mobility; (3) political interventions (i.e., a government may manage tariffs); and (4) the persistence and growth of excess capacity in many industries.

Milberg and Winkler (2013) point out that to turn the asymmetry to their advantage, outsourcers adopt four strategies: (a) inducing competition among suppliers (diversifying their suppliers to foster competition among them); (b) offloading risks to suppliers (the outsourcer carefully controls the transfer of technology to suppliers to reduce their negotiating power); (c) raising entry barriers (through branding); and (d) minimizing technology sharing among suppliers.

A prevalent habit in the car industry is to have a supply chain organized in 'tiered' suppliers to fit out complete systems such as air conditioning modules or braking-system modules. In this way, a first-tier supplier takes full responsibility for coordinating and managing second- and third-tier suppliers for the final assembly and for delivering the completed module to the customer. Both the first-tier supplier (Tier 1) and the carmaker draw benefits. The first-tier supplier can increase productivity and build greater economies of scale, while the carmaker can concentrate resources on core competencies as well as launch new products more quickly by simplifying the supply chain, thereby obtaining better timing on the assembly line and reducing inventories.

6.4 'Old' providers emerging as new competitors

Global competition brings about intense changes in which innovative, versatile competitors who are well-disposed to attacking others rapidly move into the market and, often without resistance, gradually erode the advantages of the established players, especially the providers. More and more frequently those competitors are the 'old' providers of outsourcers.

Over the last 2 decades, some 'old' providers have emerged and gained a dominant position in their original industry. This phenomenon has been clearly described by Van Agtmael, who observed that the evolution of commercial relationships among the First and Third World countries over the past century was characterized by three waves (Agtmael, 2007): (1) foreign direct investment in overseas plants by Western firms; (2) outsourcing and offshoring; and (3) peer-to-peer, emerging world-class competitors. He then goes on to portray the dynamics of this third wave as follows.

While multinational firms maintained control over the marketing of offshored products and most of them earned high margins, some emergent countries gradually became independent regarding all management functions while strengthening their abilities and negotiating power. 'A role reversal' spurred the third wave. Samsung in consumer electronics, Modelo in beer, Embraer in aviation, Infosys in IT, and Cemex in building material are a few among a group of firms from emerging countries that have reached the top position in their industry and are able now to compete 'peer-to-peer' with traditional multinational companies while preserving the advantage of producing in low-cost countries. As Van Agtmael argued: "Some of them have even reversed, turned the outsourcing model upside down becoming an outsourcer of products or services in the West and no longer an outsourcee (i.e., Embraer and Haier)" (Agtmael, 2007).

Haier is a significant example of a successful strategy (Box 6.1).

Box 6.1 Haier

The Chinese company began as a producer of components for household appliances for Whirlpool, Electrolux, and other European and U.S. multinationals. It subsequently supplied these same clients with complete appliances. At the same time, it adapted its products to the different needs of China's geographic regions, building distribution and service networks to cover the main urban areas as well as the remotest ones. When it decided to expand abroad, it did so gradually, starting with nearby emerging countries: Indonesia, Malaysia, and the Philippines. It first entered Europe in the former Yugoslavia, then the German market, and, 2 years later, the U.S., in both cases presenting its own brand, initially choosing the low-cost segments and selling through large chains such as Walmart and Home Depot. Haier then challenged the high-price segments. For example, the Chinese home appliance manufacturer is now a leading supplier to the U.S. of wine coolers, once a premium product for the affluent.

6.4.1 Performance evolution

The increase in the performance standards of many firms in emerging countries has simplified the selection of suppliers. Decades of evolution have deeply affected the performance of providers. Some have had excellent results while many others have entirely or partly disappointing results.

There is no agreement on how to measure such performances; however, there is a clear difference between a small group of 'world-class performance organizations' and all the others. In any event, it is clear that the performance of outsourcing companies is now quite different from what it was in the past, and there are three main reasons for this (some of which have already been touched on): (1) the number of outsourcers and providers has significantly increased over the years, with strong differences emerging in their ability to manage the global supply chain; (2) an increase in the variety of agreements between outsourcers and providers, which makes it difficult to assess the difference in performance; and (3) a continual influx of firms from new countries. Global competition today occurs in an environment of intense change in which flexible, aggressive and innovative competitors move into markets easily and rapidly, eroding the advantages of the large and established players.

A consolidation characterized by a reduction in the number of competitors in the market is underway among suppliers as well, allowing some of them to have greater contractual power over their outsourcers. Consolidation occurs not only through internal growth, often characterized by great speed but by mergers or acquisitions, i.e., Intel's acquisition of Mobileye (Box 6.2).

Box 6.2 Intel

Intel, like other semiconductor makers, is trying to supply the automotive industry in the hope that the increasing use of electronics in cars will compensate for a slowdown in smartphones and PCs. Founded in Israel in 1999, Mobileye has pioneered computer-vision systems that can "see" cars, pedestrians, and other objects on the road and then help vehicles avoid them. Together, Intel and Mobileye hope to offer car manufacturers a one-stop shop for autonomous-driving technology that allows drivers to take their eyes off the road and their hands off the wheel. The Intel move is combined with a shift toward a strategy based on the objective of occupying positions in an entire industry and not just in one or a few segments. "We have to think in terms of complete industry, not just a product - and that is the reason why we merged" (with Mobileye).

6.4.2 The advantages of the 'new champions'

What are the strategies that allow some companies in emerging countries to successfully deal with rivals in economically more developed ones? What role do outsourcing and offshoring play in their strategies? Why do they represent a serious threat to firms in the West? The main characteristics of these strategies and the consequences of outsourcing and offshoring (Khanna & Palepu, 2004; Kvint, 2010; Sauvant, 2008; Zeng & Williamson, 2003) can be summarized as follows (Table 6.3).

6.5 The main technological disruptors

In recent years, as previously observed, technology has profoundly impacted global strategies as well as their implementation. Modern methods have continued to disrupt traditional practices, necessitating in many cases the restructuring of supplier networks.

The advances in technologies are transforming the supply chain of many industries, from transport to manufacturing. Acquiring digital skills has become a fundamental prerequisite for those firms that want to be competitive and in the vanguard in the near future.

In this difficult and crowded market, new competitors are constantly emerging. As they get involved, technologies traditionally embedded in one sector can suddenly give way to new competitors from other sectors, competitors who are often cash rich and looking for new investments.

The global supply chain allows leading companies greater flexibility by providing rapid adjustments to changes in market demand and, to a greater extent, shifting the risk for supplying companies from possible drops in demand and excess inventory.

The transition from the 'old' to the 'new' outsourcing and offshoring models can be described as follows (Table 6.4).

The consequence of all this is the revival of reshoring and the frequent disequilibrium of power among players in the supply chain, but above all, there is an 'unbeatable' uncertainty that can be faced only by more flexibility in designing and managing the supply chain.

The effects of the main technological disruptors on global supply chain management are examined as follows.

Table 6.3 The characteristics of the strategies of companies in emerging countries and the consequences for outsourcing and offshoring.

Strategies	Key points/Characteristics
Strong export propensity	They have gained by outsourcing western firms. They have quickly gotten out from under state protection. When they enter a developed market, they are smart enough to set attainable goals. They are quick to exploit opportunities. Infosys (India) gained fame by offering protection to firms that were worried about the collapse of their information systems due to the millennium bug.
Aiming at being 'world class'	Their objective is to constantly improve quality and efficiency. They give great importance to technology and design. They want their own R&D program. They rarely resort to 'reversal design'. If they are successful, they build a solid financial base that can sustain them during international expansion. They first develop distinct capacities in the domestic market and then succeed in transferring this capacity to other markets. The Korean company samsung provides a good example.
Inventing new business models. Sometimes they reverse the outsourcing process	They soon learned that entrusting their development to a low-cost strategy does not guarantee long-term growth and success. Low-cost can be easily imitated, and not always is it possible to defend themselves through economies of scale and scope. Information technology is the function most used to create new business models. At times they reverse the outsourcing process. From being suppliers for other firms they become outsourcers for them. To control the supply chain, they sometimes embrace vertical integration, a strategy many western firms have abandoned.
Adopting conglomerate strategies	While for western firms the growth objective is pursued by concentrating on the 'core' activities, emerging countries prefer to share the inherent risk in growth by entering into

(*Continued*)

Table 6.3 The characteristics of the strategies of companies in emerging countries and the consequences for outsourcing and offshoring.—cont'd

Strategies	Key points/Characteristics
	several sectors, even when these are not linked by the same industrial logic. The principal aim is often to learn about management methods, and not, as is the rule in western countries, to acquire, reorganize and sell for the purpose of capital gains.
Acquiring global brands. Maintaining a large part of the supply chain in the original market	After gaining an important share of the domestic market, they enter foreign markets first in emerging countries and then in economically more advanced ones. Thanks to economies of scale and low costs in the markets of origin, they can easily enter low-cost segments and gain positions that serve as a base for reaching more profitable segments. To be successful they prefer to acquire global brands. Lenovo (China) has acquired IBM's personal computer division, Tata motor (India) land Rover and Jaguar from Ford, and Geely (China) Volvo from Ford as well.
Choosing neglected niches	In almost every market in developed countries, there are niches that are neglected by local companies because they are considered unprofitable. They try to dominate these and then extend their presence to other niches or segments, often by acquiring other companies.
Possessing a great innovative capacity	They have the advantage of being able to obtain at zero cost the transfer of technology and management methods through outsourcing and offshoring. They then develop their own R&D. They refuse to overengineer their products. They resort to 'just in time' design. They begin with good enough products and add features incrementally by following the dictates of the market. They pay great attention to innovation in their supply of offshoring services.

Table 6.4 Transition from the 'old' to the 'new' outsourcing model.

Main issues	The 'old' outsourcing model	The 'new' outsourcing model
Key priorities	Cost reductions. Total supply chain costs at the lowest possible levels.	Business and strategic benefits beyond cost efficiencies. In a digital world, speed to market matters even more. The ability to change the supply chain quickly, efficiently, and effectively is essential.
Main focus/Main rewards	Price competition. Working capital and fixed capital efficiency. Tax minimization.	Higher returns to shareholders/higher enterprise value. Digital technologies are reshaping supply chains.
The objective of outsourcing and offshoring	Simple tasks and functions. Low-valued items. Mass production.	More business functions and processes. Simplify the global supply chain. Getting lean, emphasizing simplicity and speed. Gain flexibility and responsiveness for higher performance and better asset management. Mass customization.
Main threats/Risks	Hurdles in logistics and communication.	Protectionism revival. Negotiating power asymmetry. More power shifted to some providers. Inroads by disruptors.
Key criteria for deciding whether or not to outsource	Low cost, access to skills. Efficiency and scale.	Clear and never-ending up-to-date definition of sustainable core competencies. Having advanced capabilities has become a major source of 'competitive advantage'.
Main drivers	Information technology to manage flows end-to-end.	Political and economic factors. Modularity. The relentless march of tech disruption. Artificial intelligence.

(*Continued*)

Table 6.4 Transition from the 'old' to the 'new' outsourcing model.—cont'd

Main issues	The 'old' outsourcing model	The 'new' outsourcing model
The main change over time in nature of contracts	Straightforward, arms-length agreements between a buyer and a supplier. Numerous transactional relations.	Partnership agreements. Strategic partners. Need for more flexibility.
Range of possible approaches	A few, are limited by logistics hurdles.	Many. Great variety of approaches.

6.5.1 The experience in car industry

Understanding what has happened in the car industry in the two first decades of 2000s shows the profound effects of technological change on outsourcing and offshoring in recent times, as follows: (1) a shift of the center of gravity; (2) a change in the business model of carmakers and in the supply chain (from the mechanical age to the software age, and subsequently to the digital age); (3) inroads from unexpected competitors that management has had to face; (4) product modularity has big implications (5) modularity in the supply chain gives suppliers a great advantage. (6) the embattled uncertainty: where is the tipping point?

6.5.1.1 The shift of the center of gravity

From the mid-1990s, cars began to incorporate autonomous features linked by software. The progress in software technology shifted the center of gravity in the automobile sector from the mechanical supply chain to a software one. As a result, many carmakers lost their power. For more than a century, the balance of power in the auto industry was in favor of original equipment manufacturers (OEM). Those firms assembled parts, components, and modules produced by hundreds of suppliers. So long as the core content of a car was mechanical, the companies that assembled and sold cars had more power than their suppliers and had command of the supply chain. As cars have moved toward the electronic and the software age, the main suppliers have gained in power (i.e., Bosch, the pioneer of ABS brakes and anticollision system). In the mid-2010s, the cost of electronic components had risen to 40%–45% of the total cost of components, and even more for premium brand cars.

6.5.1.2 Need to change the business model

Being forced to shift from one sector of suppliers (lower demand for mechanical parts) to another (more software and digital products), the lead carmakers decided to define their core business in new ways, and as a consequence, they changed their business models. Moreover, they were looking at technological advances in driverless and shared vehicle technology. Some carmakers decided to fully embrace the new technologies, while others decided to get ready for the time when their core business would no longer be selling vehicles. They became well aware of having to face a future in which most of their profits would be from technology and services and not from the mechanical products they had assembled for years. They wanted to avoid the fate of PC makers, who were forced out of business as the center of gravity shifted to cloud-based services.

6.5.1.3 Inroads from unexpected competitors

Driverless technology, for a long time in an embryonic phase, promises even greater changes in the network of the outsourcing and offshoring supply chain. The inroads from Apple and Google have sent a shock wave to the industry. The two giants have a huge amount of cash and are looking to diversify their business, and both are experimenting with driverless cars. In the event of success, they will probably not build their own cars. Apple is said to have explored the possibility of subcontracting the manufacture of its driverless cars to the Austrian company Magna Steyr. Google has adopted a somewhat different approach. If it is successful in building a new driverless vehicle and if it decides to enter the mobility industry, it would license the technology to car companies and suppliers. The obvious parallel is Android being licensed to phone manufacturers. New competitors driven by new technology means a new supply chain.

6.5.1.4 Product modularity has big implications

Increasing the variety of brands and models is a strategy pursued in many industries such as automobiles and electrical appliances. The desired effect is to sell more by satisfying the expectations of customers in more than one segment of the market. The undesired effect is that this strategy usually entails a vast number of variants in parts and components, where the relatively low volume does not allow for economies of scale and increases warehousing costs and the risk of obsolescence. When added to the presence of the company in more and more foreign countries where local tastes and different product regulations require adaptation, the results may be skyrocketing costs so high as to exceed any acceptable level of profitability. Introduced by the Swedish truck manufacturer Scania several decades ago in the automotive sector, modularity has spread to other fields, such as consumer electronics and white goods, as manufacturers try to reduce the global supply chain complexity, which is especially strong when producing for global markets. Manufacturing a product by putting together common parts or subsystems with standardized interfaces gives outsourcers the opportunity to pursue flexibility and at the same time to manufacture differentiated products. Modularization has big implications for the supply chain. Modularity gives suppliers a great advantage.

6.5.1.5 Modularity gives suppliers a great advantage

Standardized, homogenized products do not satisfy the expectations of customers, who are more and more demanding and have different habits. For example, refrigerators used by U.S. consumers are bigger than those used by Europeans. For suppliers that can gain the appropriate economies of scale to serve more buyers at a lower cost, modularity allows outsourcers to save time and reduce costs. Great savings in assembly costs are potentially available to the manufacturers when they can reduce the time and simplify the work by using modules and systems. Modular production allows carmakers with a vast portfolio of brands and models to produce vehicles of differing length, width, and wheelbase on the same platform and different models from different brands at one plant. In the white goods industry, common parts or components, such as electric motors and compressors, can be used across a range of products such as air conditioning units, ovens, and fridges. When modularity was first adopted, the costs and risks were transferred to small and medium-sized suppliers, who were in a weak position. However, the evolution of modularity has favored a group of first-tier suppliers, who have emerged and "almost reverse[d] the power ratio" with respect to the outsourcers. Examples of such suppliers are Bosch, TWR, and Continental in the automotive industry. Giving suppliers the task of developing complex modules means a risk for the outsourcer, as illustrated by the experience of Takata. The Japanese automotive supplier, at the center of a global recall of exploding airbags, has filed for bankruptcy protection in Japan and the U.S., which has left carmakers across the world facing huge bills for complex and costly recalls affecting tens of millions of vehicles. The huge recall affects 100 vehicle types sold by at least 13 carmakers around the world. The carmakers are unlikely to fully recover the recall cost. According to industry analysts, Honda, Nissan and Toyota have set aside funds, as they do not expect to recoup the cost from Takata. Carmakers are legally responsible for their customers. At least 17 deaths and more than 100 injuries have been linked to Takata air-bag inflator explosions.

6.5.1.6 The embattled uncertainty: where is the tipping point?

Here is an example of how uncertainty about the future of technology harms outsourcing and offshoring decisions. If a long-term trend can be considered certain and unstoppable, then the direction of a company's decisions must be changed. However, when should today's strategy be abandoned? Lead firms in the automobile sector are prepared for the decline of the Internal Combustion Engine (ICE), but when and how will the tipping point be reached? When should the new technology be embraced? An industrial transformation has been under way in the car industry starting from the second half of 2010. Volvo cars have announced that every car model it would have launched from 2019 on will be pure electric or hybrid, making it the first major carmaker to actively abandon the ICE. Jaguar Land Rover made publicly known that every vehicle in its range would have the option of some form of electric motor technology by the start of the 2020s. Many other carmakers are preparing for the eventual rapid decline of the traditional ICE and planning to shift toward electric vehicles (EV). Their suppliers of catalysts-such as Unicore, Johnson Mattey, and BASF, referred to as the Big Three - were also looking attentively at switching their focus. Platinum is the key component in automobile catalytic converters, which cut exhaust-pipe emissions. Under pressure from the predicted change in the car industry, the Big Three were considering riding the growth in demand for components used in rechargeable lithium-ion cells manufactured by the likes of Samsung and LG and expanding the production of cathode materials critical for increasing the power of a battery. But when to abandon platinum and turn to lithium? How far and how fast can the changes occur? A tipping point may come when the cost of EV ownership falls to the same level as an ICE-propelled car. Some expected this could happen in two-three years, although most analysts predicted not before 2025. An EV might look like another car from the outside, but the interior looks like a computer on wheels. The shift from one technology to another requires changing part of the supply chain, which means a new selection of suppliers, a new method of managing the relationship with them, and new forms of contracting. Not to mention the problem of terminating the contracts with the old suppliers.

What was written above is the history of the continual struggle against uncertainty.

The choice of when to start investing in new technologies and building a new supply chain is particularly difficult in cyclical industries. Companies in those industries are prone to repeating the same mistakes. They invest heavily near the peak of the cycle, trying to beat competitors and take advantage of soaring demand. Then a downturn arrives, just when they are reaching maximum capacity. Prices descend abruptly and steeply and the weakest must leave the market. Choosing and building a new supply chain in those industries, without memories of past experiences, requires perfect timing.

6.6 Managing a supply chain under uncertainty

The fundamental principles for managing a supply chain dealing with uncertainty and which can be used "to transform the chaos of uncertainty into opportunities for growth and prosperity" (Koulopoulos & Roloff, 2006), as previously described, relate to two concepts: (1) "Uncertainty increases as the volume of information increases"; (2) "Uncertainty creates a greater need for radical thinking, creativity and innovation".

To fully understand these two principles, we must recall some basic definitions: (1) risk as opposed to uncertainty and (2) closed systems as opposed to open systems. The roots of both are embedded in the economic and physical world.

(1) Risk is predictable, measurable, and probabilistic. Think of a game played with dice. The probability of any one of the six sides coming up is the same. If you play dice, the risk is calculable. On the other hand, uncertainty is the absolute absence of future knowledge. In 1914, Frank Knight wrote a doctoral thesis at Cornell University that later became the cornerstone of the Chicago School of economics. In "Risk, Uncertainty, and

Profit" (Knight, 2012), the Author argued that knowledge about uncertainty can be gained only by experiencing the event, while risk can be evaluated through either knowledge of past events of the same nature (which Knight called statistical probability) or of the known probabilities of possible future events (which Knight termed a priori probability).

(2) Another useful distinction is between closed and open systems, which differ in terms of risk and uncertainty as well. Closed systems are those in which alternatives and risks are measurable and mostly determinable in advance. This is not the case of a supply chain. Managing a supply chain equates to managing open systems, which are essentially uncertain, as these are influenced by factors that are both unknown and unknowable.

6.6.1 Identifying risks and estimating the probability that an event takes place

The risk inherent in managing a global supply chain has been studied in detail by experts in logistics. The risk management process includes four main steps: (1) identifying all actual and future sources of risks to the company; (2) assessing the risks by quantifying the probabilities of occurrence; (3) analyzing the risk exposure, leading to a differentiation of risks into different categories (based on the extent of the potential damage or gain); (4) taking appropriate measures to control risks on the basis of these analyses. Practical experience shows that identifying risks and estimating the probability that an event takes place and the monetary level of its impact pose considerable problems to management. The most difficult problems emerge in facing: (1) the constant disequilibrium that needs flexibility more than ever; (2) the industries' fear of disruption. (3) the 'value gap'.

6.6.1.1 Flexibility needed for fast times

The more stable the technological, economic, and legal environment, the easier it is to successfully manage a global supply chain. But today, stable equilibria are impossible. As D'Aveni stated decades ago, constantly evolving technology, new waves of globalization, and relentless strategic positioning by lead firms will result in frequent or almost constant disequilibrium in which new entrants and established competitors disrupt the balance of power and gain temporary superiority (D'Aveni, 1995).

For companies, flexibility is more important than ever, as relationships with suppliers are managed through networked organizations and multinational global supply chains. An important reason for leading firms to establish a global supply chain is the flexibility it provides, allowing as it does for rapid adjustments to changes in market demand and, to a greater extent, a shift in the risk to supplier firms from possible declines in demand and excessive inventory. The supply chain must be flexible to respond to change faster than competitors can. Flexibility is the key to competitiveness, regardless of whether the company is asset-intensive, has a high material cost content, or is distribution-dependent.

Many Authors hold that the difficulty for many companies in giving the global value chain the necessary flexibility in a short period of time depends on the desire to solve new, largely unexplored problems using old instruments. Managers need more practical tools to understand the challenges ahead. Many of the instruments used by companies in the 1980s and '90s to build and sustain their strategies — e.g., Porter's Five Forces, Hamel and Prahalad's core competencies concept — have become weakened, worn out, and rendered incapable of adapting to the relentlessly changing environment (Hamel & Prahalad, 1994; Porter, 1980, 1985, 2008; Prahalad & Hamel, 1990).

More than 2 decades ago, D'Aveni argued that existing models of strategy are nearly obsolete in "the intensity of today's fast paced competition". D'Aveni's idea of 'hypercompetition' is relevant in analyzing the reasons for the difficulties in giving the global value chain the needed flexibility (D'Aveni, 1995).

What can be done? In suggesting how to react to the effects of 'hypercompetition', D'Aveni examined four traditional sources of 'competitive advantages' — cost-quality, timing, and know-how, erecting entry barriers, deep pockets advantages (large firms' capability to sustain losses for a long period of time) - and explained how each had been eroded by "the unrelenting maneuvering of companies". He described how this maneuvering had produced a new type of competition that he called 'hypercompetition'. Then he suggested that managers examine a system of seven strategies for competing in this environment: the New7-S's (the title was derived from McKinsey's original 7-S's).

Unlike the original 7-S's, D'Aveni's were designed to cope with 'hyper-competition' using methods based on: (1) approaches useful for changing the company's position in the competitive arena and (2) intentionally disrupting the status quo (the balance of power) by restarting the cycle within each competitive arena or shifting to a new arena (D'Aveni, 1995).

6.6.1.2 Industries' fear of disruption

Digitalization is a threat to many industries and companies. An industry that has to face strong adjustments in managing its outsourcing and offshoring because of digitalization is the premium car industry. Germany is one of the countries most exposed to change in this sector.

As the pillars of Germany's success, its car and machine industries have increasingly been disrupted by software and digital technologies. The fear is that the traditional industries that have dominated Germany's economy - such as the car, mechanical engineering, and logistics industries - could face the same kind of disruption seen in the music, media, and travel sectors.

Experts predict that in the future, 50—60% of the value of a car will consist of digital tools and 20% of batteries. Therefore, traditional carmakers will be responsible only for assembling mechanical parts (the remaining 30% for value). A huge shift is looming inside the industry, and suppliers will be affected as much as will the car manufacturers. Due to uncertainty about the industry's future evolution, few people want to invest in suppliers of mechanical components and are wary of investing massively in those companies that produce software, waiting instead for definite signs that software will become the most valuable component of a car.

In his book *The Attacker's Advantage*, Foster explained the limitations of long-term corporate performance, based on the inevitability of profound changes in the way business is conducted (which the Author calls 'discontinuities' (Foster, 1986). The conclusion reached was that during technological discontinuities, attackers, rather than defenders, have an economic advantage. There are some exceptions to this rule, though not in the case of a new technology that has been making inroads in the car industry.

An important example in the car industry concerns Tesla (Box 6.3).

Box 6.3 Tesla's advantages

Starting in late 2010's, German carmakers are confronted with a new competitor selling products based on new technology (it is more accurate to say a renewed technology): the new competitor is the American company Tesla and the technology is the electric vehicle. Just as the iPhone disrupted Blackberry and Nokia, Tesla might turn out carmakers that make their fortune by selling Internal Combustion Engine (ICE). Tesla has a strong advantage over them. An EV has many fewer parts than one built around an ICE. A report by UBS financial analysts, who tore apart 1 GM Chevrolet Bolt electric car "to see what it cost to make", said that Bolt had just 24 moving parts compared with 149 in a VW Golf, mainly because electric motors are much simpler than ICEs. The report concludes that EVs would probably disrupt the industry faster than is commonly thought. German carmakers would have to turn to other types of engines: plug-in, hybrid, and electric engines, which means a disruption in the supply chain: fewer suppliers and fewer components.

- **Facing the 'value gap'**

No matter how well organized it is, the supply chain is always limited in terms of efficiency and flexibility due to the (often) long distances between the production and product consumption sites, as well as delays in the exchange of information. By 'value gap' we mean the obstacles that make it difficult for firms to "[meet] demand faster, better and cheaper". The problem has gained importance as manufacturers shift from mass production to mass customization. Some firms have been able to bridge the 'value gap' in the following ways (Radjou & Prabhu, 2015):

(a) Reshoring or onshoring

Transferring a production that was moved overseas back to the country from which it was originally developed is convenient "as long as cheap labor and economies of scale (built by providers) exceed the shipping costs", which occurs less and less frequently. Wages are rising in emerging countries along with shipping. 'Made in China' is not as cheap as it once was. Labor costs in this country have risen. Many Chinese businesses have transferred production to Vietnam and Bangladesh and are looking elsewhere. In China, customers love things not made in China, and many firms are moving production toward sales points. Locating production close to the final market reduces carbon emissions and allows for a quicker response to variations in demand. As a result, reshoring or onshoring is gaining strength.

• Local sourcing. Sourcing from local suppliers helps respond to local needs in emerging countries and thus creates more affordable products. However, it also helps in mature economies, where buying smaller quantities from small suppliers located near the outsourcer's factories can reduce costs and risk.

• Sharing resources. Distribution and manufacturing assets may be partially idle. It could be useful/profitable to share their use with other companies even if they are rivals. Such types of agreements share the use of mobile-phone infrastructure, warehousing and transportation assets.

• Distributing to the last mile. It is costly to deploy physical distribution in places with few users, especially at a great distance in remote areas. In both emerging and Western countries, companies may outsource the last-mile distribution to local networks.

• Integrating manufacturing and logistics. Also called postponement or delayed differentiation, this is a supply strategy that defers the customization of a product to a later time when consumer demand is clearly distinguishable. The last step of production is brought closer to the customer when actual orders are known, with the advantage of reducing the risk of unpredictable demand.

• Sharing data with partners. To reduce costs and respond in a timely manner to changes in demand, collecting real-time demand signals becomes a vital part of efficiently managing a supply chain. In multi-tiered supply chains, in particular, it is important to share data on demand signals with suppliers, distributors, and even customers.

(b) More attention needed

The strong potential impact of digital technologies on the management of the supply chain and the need to pay more attention to its evolution has been confirmed by the following findings from numerous empirical studies. (1) The impact of digitization has only begun to penetrate many industries. On average, industries are less than 40% digitized. But as digitization continues its advance, "the implications for revenues, profits, and opportunities will be dramatic" (Dawson et al., 2016). (2) By lowering barriers to competition, digitization gives way to more intense rivalries that exert pressure on revenue and profit growth as measured by earnings before interest and taxes (EBIT). As digital penetration advances, more pressure is expected in the future. (3) Digital technologies have widely expanded the range of available investment options among internal functions and processes. The biggest future impact on revenue and EBIT growth is expected from the digitization of supply chains (Bughin et al., 2017).

6.7 Has COVID-19 and Russia's invasion of Ukraine brought down globalization?

In the last 2 decades, globalization has had its 'center of gravity' in the supply chain, the process by which raw materials, parts, and components are exchanged across the borders of multiple nations before being incorporated into finished goods and sold everywhere by logistical processes.

- **The first blow**

On the threshold of the 2020s, globalization was weakened by the arrival of the COVID-19 pandemic, the slowdown in the growth of the world economy and uncertainties about its future, and the trade war between the U.S. and China.

Globalization had already been weakened before the arrival of the pandemic. In previous years, there had been many threatening events, such as the '9/11' terrorist attack, the SARS-CoV-1 virus, and the tsunami in Japan. However, the consequences of these events affected limited geographical areas and in a short time exhausted their most obvious effects. The supply chains were disrupted but soon restored. Even the strong rise in oil prices in 2008, which approached $150 per barrel and forced many companies to reconsider the globalization of their supply chains, has been subsequently absorbed.

In the past, there were other threatening events, such as the wave of protectionism brought on by Trump's election as U.S. president with his 'America First' slogan and the United Kingdom's exit from the European Union due to the makeover of its many ties with other European nations. However, with the coronavirus the consequences were different: the shock affected the entire global supply chain. In a few months, the major economies have entered recession, and it is a widespread belief that the effects will remain in the economy and society for a long time to come.

The pandemic has caused the largest and fastest decline in international flows — including trade, foreign direct investment, and international travel — in modern history (Altman, 2020).

According to a current of thought among academics, the impact of the COVID-19 pandemic on business globalization strategies entails four mechanisms: the politics of national governments, the attitudes of consumers, the way of thinking of management in multinational companies, and the economics of business globalization (Yip, 2021).

Some governments have used the pandemic as a pretext to withdraw from multilateral and free trade agreements. Consumers, with rare exceptions, have continued to prioritize 'price and value' in their choices, without much regard to the origin of products. Although the first outbreak of the pandemic exploded in Wuhan, consumers continued to buy 'Made in China'. Instead, the management strategies of companies with extensive geographic networks of supply chains have been very complex and debated.

Resolving the conflicts between low-cost, quality levels, and short-term profits in supply chain management have been a difficult task, especially "in the face of Black Swan disruptions such as COVID-19" (Yip, 2021). The need to provide flexibility and resilience to supply chains has forced companies to sacrifice short-term profit margins while the pandemic has reduced demand for many products in end markets.

According to the Author, the complexity of choices and solutions has highlighted the differences between the 'Anglo-Saxon' model of corporate governance adopted by American and British companies, on the one hand, and that of other European and Asian companies on the other. The former gives priority to the short-term interests of current shareholders, and the latter to the long-term interests of the company.

In conclusion, it should also be remembered that globalization can also be a powerful contributor to growth. Countries with higher scores on the DHL Global Connectedness Index tend to enjoy faster economic growth.[1]

6.8 Russia's invasion: a tipping point in globalization

In recent decades, globalization has helped to foster global prosperity. From the start of the 1990s to the present day, the number of people living in extreme poverty has fallen by 60%. Average living standards have gone up considerably, but within many countries inequality has grown. Capital transferred to countries with low labor costs to finance local production has had the effect of curbing wage growth and creating unemployment in the economically more advanced countries, affecting especially the lower middle classes. Most of the increase in profits generated by globalization has gone to China and other Asian countries, as well as to the major Western multinationals.

---

[1]The DHL Global Connectedness Index measures globalization based on international trade, capital, information, and people flows. It is unique in that it tracks both the size of countries' international flows relative to their domestic activity ('depth') and their geographic reach around the world ('breadth').

For decades, new investment projects have been based on the fact that cheap offshore manufacturing and lean supply chains could lower costs for businesses and keep inflation low. Many companies have taken production offshore, exploiting low labor costs and the advantage of keeping both components and finished product prices and interest rates low. They were also able to deal with high-risk investments, given the prospects of a high ROI.

The last 2 decades have seen no shortage of strains on globalization: the financial crisis of 2007—09, Brexit, trade wars between the U.S and China, and more recently the pandemic have highlighted the perils of relying on a handful of countries, which has led to severe supply chain disruptions. Between 2008 and 2020, world trade relative to global GDP fell by 5%, the levels of tariffs and other barriers to trade have risen, and global flows of long-term investment plunged. Even before 2020 (after the Covid-19 outbreak), the major companies had shown less interest in true globalization. Noneconomic factors such as pressure from activists against sourcing from countries known for human-rights abuses had also contributed to this trend. And at the end of February 2022, Russia's invasion of Ukraine began disrupting supply chains and the export of critical commodities, from food and mining to car and aircraft production.

Even before the invasion, the Western governments were grappling with rising energy prices that threatened to slow economic recovery after 2 years of the pandemic. The invasion turned fears into reality. Energy prices have risen sharply along with inflationary pressures. "From crude oil to diesel to natural gas, the fossil fuels that power the global economy are trading at or toward record levels, threatening to redraw geopolitical relations between producers and consumers, drive up inflation and potentially even disrupt the fight against climate change" (Brower et al., 2022).

The past decade has witnessed an increase in risks in world politics, from the contrasts between China and the United States to the tensions in the Middle East, but the world economy and financial markets, through ups and downs, have mitigated and overcome them. Russia's invasion of Ukraine seems to have broken this ability of the economy to overcome difficulties and regain its equilibrium toward development. The clash between the world's largest economies, on the one hand, and their largest supplier of raw materials on the other has weakened the globalization of supply chains and the integration of financial markets, in the short term pushing inflation further upwards and slowing development.

It is widely believed that the long-term impact will be to accelerate the division of the world into economic blocs. Russia will be pushed to look East by focusing more on trade and financial links with China. "The invasion of Ukraine might not cause a global economic crisis today but it will change how the world economy operates for decades to come" (The Economist, 2022).

References

Agtmael. (2007). *The emerging markets economies*. The Free Press.

Altman, S. (2020). Will Covid-19 have a lasting impact on globalization? *Harvard Business Review*. https://hbr.org/2020/05/will-covid-19-have-a-lasting-impact-on-globalization.

Baden-Fuller, C., Targett, D., & Hunt, B. (2000). Outsourcing to outmanoeuvre: Outsourcing Re-defines competitive strategy and structure. *European Management Journal, 18*(3), 285–295. https://doi.org/10.1016/S0263-2373(00)00010-4

Bartlett, C., & Goshal, S. (2000). Going global: Lessons from late movers. *Harvard Business Review, March-April*, 1–20. https://hbr.org/2000/03/going-global-lessons-from-late-movers.

Brower, D., Wilson, Giles, C. (2022). The new energy shock: Putin, Ukraine and the global economy. *Financial Times*. www.ft.com/content/5a7ea3b8-c446-46a9-a836-fce811a97069.

Bughin, J., LaBerge, L., & Mellbye, A. (2017). The case for digital reinvention. *McKinsey Quarterly, January*, 1–15.

Coase, R. H. (1937). The nature of the firm. *Economica, 4*(16), 386–405. https://doi.org/10.1111/j.1468-0335.1937.tb00002.x

D'Aveni, R. A. (1995). *Coping with hypercompetition: Utilizing the new 7S's framework* (pp. 45–57). Academy of Management Perspectives. https://doi.org/10.5465/AME.1995.9509210281

Davis, G. (2009). *Managed by the market: How finance reshaped America*. Oxford University Press.

Dawson, A., Hirt, M., & Scanlan, J. (March 15, 2016). *The economic essentials of digital strategy*. McKinsey & Company. www.mckinsey.com/business-functions/strategy-and-corporate-finance/our-insights/the-economic-essentials-of-digital-strategy.

Dreischmeier, R., Colsman, T., Minz, R., & Sirkin, H. (2005). *Achieving success in business process outsourcing and offshoring* (Vols. 1–4). The Boston Consulting Group.

Foster, R. (1986). *Innovation: The Attacker's advantage*. Summit Books.

Friedman, T. (2006). *The world is flat. A brief history of the globalized world in the twenty-first century*. Penguin.

Geishecker, I. (2008). The impact of international outsourcing on individual employment security: A micro-level analysis. *Labour Economics, 15*(3), 291–314. https://doi.org/10.1016/j.labeco.2007.06.015

Gereffi, G. (1994). The organization of buyer-driven global commodity chain: How US retailers shape overseas production networks. In G. Gereffi, & M. Korzeniewicz (Eds.), *Commodity chains and global capitalism* (pp. 95–122). Greenwood Press.

Ghemawat, P. (2007). *Redefining global strategy: Crossing borders in a world where differences still matter*. Harvard Business School Press.

Hamel, G., & Prahalad, C. K. (1994). *Competing for the future*. Harvard Business School Press.

Khanna, T., & Palepu, K. (2004). Emerging giants: Building world class companies from emerging markets. *Harvard Business School Working Paper*, 1–41.

Knight, F. H. (2012). *Risk, uncertainty and profit*. Courier Corporation.

Koulopoulos, T., & Roloff, T. (2006). *Smartsourcing. Driving innovation and growth through outsourcing*. Routledge.

Kvint, V. (2010). *The Global Emerging Market*, 107–142. https://doi.org/10.4324/9780203882917-12

Landsdale, C., & Cox, A. (1998). *Outsourcing: A business guide to risk management tools and tecniques*. Earlsgate.

Lazonick, W. (2009). *Sustainable prosperity in the new economy? Business organization and high-tech employmrnt in the*. The Upjoin Institute.

Lazonick, W., & O'Sullivan, M. (2000). Maximizing shareholder value: A new ideology for corporate governance. *Economy and Society, 29*(1), 13–35. https://doi.org/10.1080/030851400360541

Levitt, T. (1983). The globalization of markets. *Harvard business Review*. May-June.

Liveris, A. (2012). *Make it in America. The case for reinventing the economy*. John Wiley & Sons.

Macrotrends. (2022). *World trade to GDP ratio* (pp. 1970–2022). www.macrotrends.net/countries/WLD/world/trade-gdp-ratio#:~:text=Trade%20is%20the%20sum%20of,a%201.65%25%20increase%20from%202017.

Magretta, J. (2002). *What management is*. Profile Books.

Milberg, W., & Winkler, D. (2013). *Outsourcing economics: Global value chains in capitalist development*. Cambridge University Press.

Mudambi, R., & Venzin, M. (2010). The strategic nexus of offshoring and outsourcing decisions. *Journal of Management Studies, 47*(8), 1510–1533. https://doi.org/10.1111/j.1467-6486.2010.00947.x

Penrose, E. (1959). *The theory of the firm*. John Wiley & Sons.

Pine, B. (1993). *Mass customization*. Harvard Business School Press.

Pisano, G., & Shih, W. (2012). *Producing prosperity*. Harvard Business School Press.

Porter, M. E. (1980). *Competitive strategy: Techniques for analyzing industries and competitors*. Free Press.

Porter, M. E. (1985). *Competitive advantage: Creating and sustaining superior performance*. Free Press.

Porter, M. E. (2008). The five competitive forces that shape strategy. *Harvard Business Review, 86*(1), 25–40.

Prahalad, C. K., & Hamel, G. (1990). The core competence of the corporation. *Harvard Business Review, 3*(68), 79–91.

Quinn, J. B. (2000). Outsourcing innovation: The new engine of growth. *Sloan Management, 41*(4), 1–13.

Radjou, N., & Prabhu, J. (2015). Frugal Innovation: How to do more with less. *The Economist*. The Economist.

Ricart, J., & Agnese, P. (2015). *Adding value through offshoring. More than cost cutting*. McKinsey Quarterly.

Rumelt. (1997). Towards a strategic theory of the firm. In R. Lamb (Ed.), *Competitive strategic management* (pp. 556–571). Prentice-Hall.

Sauvant, K. (2008). *The rise of transnational corporation from emerging countries*. Edward Elgar.

The Economist. (2022). *The economic consequences of the war in Ukraine*. www.economist.com/finance-and-economics/2022/02/26/the-economic-consequences-of-the-war-in-ukraine.

Thompson, A., & Strickland, A. (2005). *Strategic management*. John Wiley & Sons.

Waters, D. (2007). *Global logistics*. Kogan Page.

Williamson, O. E. (1985). *The economic institution of capitalism: Firms, markets, relational contracting*. The Free Press.

Williamson, O. E. (2002). The theory of the firm as governance structure: From choice to contract. *Journal of Economic Perspectives, 16*(3), 171−195. https://doi.org/10.1257/089533002760278776

Winkler, D. (1995). Services offshoring and its impact on productivity and employment: Evidence from Germany. *World Economy, 33*(12), 1672−1691.

Yip, G. (2021). *Does COVID-19 mean the end for globalization?*. www.forbes.com/sites/imperialinsights/2021/01/08/does-covid-19-mean-the-end-for-globalization/?sh=76841444671e.

Zeng, M., & Williamson, P. (2003). The hidden dragons. *Harvard Business Review, 81*(5), 92−99. https://hbr.org/2003/10/the-hidden-dragons.

PART FOUR

The Effects on the Supply Chains of COVID-19 and the Russia's Invasion of Ukraine

CHAPTER SEVEN

Never so much attention to the digital transformation of supply chains

7.1 Unexpected speed

The supply chain effects of the COVID-19 crisis have impacted the global economy. A lot of companies have been pushed to rethink their business models, with digital transformation playing a decisive role in supply chain management. Never in recent history has a crisis been so rapid and so widespread around world as that brought on by the coronavirus pandemic.

An important example concerns the Cirque du Soleil (Box 7.1).

After the initial and hardest phase of the pandemic, which took place in 2020 and in the first part of 2021, demand began to grow ahead of and faster than supply.

The consequence of this great difference, which in part reflects the successes of government action in stimulating demand (easy money and government spending), have been the many bottlenecks, shortages of materials, delays to deliveries, and the sharp increase in shipping costs that have emerged in supply chains, which have slowed down production in factories and the economic recovery, all of which has fed into higher prices for many manufactured goods.

Central banks could do little to avert this slowdown as they simultaneously had to curb inflation and initiate tighten monetary policy. Making it less easy for businesses to have credit means curbing the recovery in demand and limiting the development of the economy and employment.

- **February–March 2022, the storm is coming.** In a short time, forecasts for the future of the economy have worsened. "The IMF warned that the world economy was confronting lower growth and higher inflation and that a global recovery from the pandemic was moving away". The IMF's first deputy director confirmed that: "the crisis and the ongoing recovery is like no other".

As inflation started to bite, the EU has cut growth forecasts. The revisions highlighted the drag of supply chain bottlenecks, rising energy prices, and

The Digital Transformation of Supply Chain Management
ISBN: 978-0-323-85532-7
https://doi.org/10.1016/B978-0-323-85532-7.00004-9

Box 7.1 Cirque du Soleil. From $1 billion to zero revenues in 48 h

"I never thought in my life, that within 48 h. I would go from a billion dollars of revenue to zero revenue, and there were people saying that the debt was too high and this and that" (Hill, 2022), said Daniel Lamarre, executive vice-chair of Cirque du Soleil. On March 13, 2020, in various parts of the world, governments, in trying to stop the spread of the pandemic, banned circus shows, leading to 75 Cirque du Soleil performances being canceled. Lamarre defines that day as "Black Friday".[1]

Cirque du Soleil had to repatriate the cast and the support staff of most of the touring shows, while air flights between countries were blocked. Less than a week after "Black Friday", Lamarre was forced to lay off, by video, 95% of its employees: 4679 people. In June 2020, he asked the authorities to admit the company into bankruptcy protection, and with a small group of employees he continued to manage the few remaining activities. Two months later, the chief executive of one of the former investors in Cirque du Soleil said that "Cirque had been one of the first businesses to close and would be the last to reopen" (Hill, 2022). Lamarre and his team have confounded that forecast. Coronavirus was still a threat, but two shows reopened in June 2021 and there was a rebirth in touring production.

[1] Black Friday: expression that in the U.S. indicates the Friday following the national Thanksgiving Day holiday, which occurs on the Thursday of the fourth week of November. The name black Friday would be linked to the traffic jams that hit many of the major American cities in 1975, in particular Philadelphia (Treccani, 2022).

the outbreak of the Omicron variant on the region's economic recovery. Although there were already signs of possible conflicts in Ukraine on the horizon, Brussels remained broadly optimistic, predicting the EU would remain in a "prolonged and robust expansionary phase" thanks to a strong labor market and rising household spending (Financial Times, 2022a).

To secure supplies of the chips that drive the global economy, Europe has followed the US in setting out plans for a massive increase in semiconductor manufacturing. The reason was that the coronavirus pandemic had "painfully exposed the vulnerability of Europe's supply chains" as Ursula von der Leyen, the Commission president, said. Unveiling a €43bn investment plan, the European Commission said that "it wanted to use state aid to promote research and production of higher technology chips used in computers, smart-phones, vehicles and other products" (Financial Times, 2022b).

7.2 COVID-19 rolls the dice again

What happened in the hardest phase of the coronavirus pandemic (2019−21) has left lasting wounds in supply chains. Several factors have contributed to the situation, two in particular: the suppliers' slow pace in adapting to the growing demand and the action of governments in support of the economy.

7.2.1 The supply-demand mismatch

When the pandemic gripped the world, consumer demand patterns had a sharp and sudden change due to remote work, closed schools, and heavy reliance on online shopping. The demand for some products soared dramatically, while that of others languished.

The rapid adjustment between supply and demand has been prevented by the pandemic, which has caused factory closures, material shortages, and shipping delays. In normal times, the adjustment would have been quickly achieved through price increases, which would have stimulated supply and at the same time reduced part of the demand, thereby pushing the market toward equilibrium. However, during the pandemic prices, after rising, remained high and shortages in supply chains proliferated.

A case in point concerns the implications for sea transport (Box 7.2).

The imbalance between supply and demand got worse beyond all measure as the months went by because consumers, fearing they would no longer find what they normally sought on store shelves, ran to make purchases beyond what was strictly necessary. For their part, many

---

Box 7.2 Sea transport

Staff restrictions and quarantines have reduced supply. When economic activity resumed, the ports with the most traffic failed to meet the normal times for loading and unloading operations. The consequences were long lines of ships waiting for weeks, large numbers of containers stuck on ships without being able to be reloaded and shipped, and a sharp increase in the cost of transportation. To transport a container from Asia to the East Coast of the United States, the cost rose from around $1400 per container before the pandemic to around $20,000 on the threshold of 2022 (Sheffi, 2021).

manufacturers have increased their demand for parts and materials fearing they would run out of stock. This hoarding created additional shortages, partly because most parts manufacturers were reluctant to invest in new operational capacity fearing that the increase in demand could be temporary (see below on the bike industry).

7.2.2 The disruptive influence of governments

Governments played a role in the imbalance between supply and demand. By injecting a considerable amount of liquidity into the economy they have driven demand in all sectors, though not equally, leading at times to a huge increase in demand in some sectors while in others there has been a modest increase or none at all.

As governments discovered last century, subsidies lead to overcapacity and gluts, and eventually to more calls for public money to prop up uncompetitive businesses, which is why many have suggested letting market forces act. "The chip shortage is mostly a self-solving problem. Governments should resist the temptation to see themselves as saviors" (The Economist, 2021b).

Beginning in midi-2021, in many countries, the producers in various sectors have had to face the consequences of a succession of events that have destroyed the structure of many pivotal supply chains, causing a weakness in the ongoing economic recovery and fueling the revival of inflation.

A significant example in the furniture industry is Ikea (Box 7.3).

Box 7.3 Ikea

The furniture industry was one of the last to experience supply chain disruption. Not even a giant like Ikea could avoid being harmed. In September 2021, Henrik Elm, Ikea's global supply manager, told the *Financial Times* that he "cannot predict" when normal supplies will resume because of a "perfect storm of issues" that includes a shortage of truck drivers. "We're not naive to think that it's over in the next weeks or even months" (Romei et al., 2021). According to a report by the European Commission, one in three EU furniture makers has suffered a cessation of activity due to supply shortages. Another consequence has been the increase in the cost of sea transport. To bypass that problem, Ikea diverted part of its transport to railway lines.

7.3 Unprecedented in history

When extraordinary events arise in economics, it is natural to wonder if they have had precedents in the past from which lessons can be drawn to deal with them in the present. With the coronavirus pandemic, consideration has turned to the financial crisis of 10 years ago.

For a decade after the financial crisis (2008—2009) the world economy's problem was a lack of spending. Worried households paid down their debts, governments imposed austerity and wary firms held back investment, especially in physical capacity, while hiring from a seemingly infinite pool of workers.

(The Economist, 2021c)

During the coronavirus pandemic, contrary to what had happened 10 years earlier, governments have decided to stimulate the economic recovery through the injection of capital (some \$10.4 trillion of global stimulus in easy money and government spending). This has caused demand to grow faster than supply as consumers responded by spending more than normal for certain products, straightening many global supply chains. Meanwhile, the spread of the Delta variant has shut down factories in many parts of the world, thereby creating shortages.

All this could take us back to the early 1970s, when the embargo on oil supplies decided by the producing countries created long waiting lines at the gas pumps and inflation began to gallop, but even this comparison is not valid. "Half a century ago politicians got economic policy badly wrong, fighting inflation with futile measures like price controls. But in the face of the spread of Covid-19 there was a consensus that central banks had to inject liquidity in the system" (The Economist, 2021c).

The recession caused by the pandemic is not like the others, and even the exit from the recession is not like the the others previous. Recession usually means a drop in output and a fall in incomes. But government aid to the economy (cash infusion for people and business) has given rise to effects that are different from those expected in a recession, in which people have less money to spend.

Moreover, some experts warned that in the event the variants (Delta and Omicron in particular) drastically weakened the economic recovery, governments could hardly repurpose financial support to people and businesses since the governments themselves had already greatly indebted their countries.

In the spring of 2022, Europe was emerging from the coronavirus crisis, growing faster than the U.S. and China; investments were floating and unemployment decreasing. But some signs indicated that the recovery would not be as smooth as many had thought. The most worrying alarm was coming from bottlenecks in global supply chains that have generated shortages and raised prices from semiconductors to steel, from plastic to pasta (see below and in Chapter 9).

7.4 Running out of steam

Before examining the response of companies, let us examine the effects the pandemic has had on the management of supply chains. Four interconnected tendencies are at play: (1) factory closures, (2) bottlenecks, (3) shortages, and (4) shipping cost increases.

7.4.1 Factory closures

In the face of growing concerns about the coronavirus, many governments ordered the closure of factories in nonessential industry. Moreover, some manufacturers in industries not subject to this ban have opted to go idle rather than risk spreading infection among employees and their families. The closure was everywhere and very sudden, triggering serious social and economic outcomes. A few companies were able to quickly respond with a medium-long term recovery plan. The experience of Cirque du Soleil discusses above and Nike portray the drama of an unwanted shutdown in a service industry (the former) and the ability to quickly react and plan in personal goods (the latter) (Box 7.4).

7.4.2 Bottlenecks

There are many sources of interruption in the normal course of many activities and processes. But over the course of the pandemic, shipping bottlenecks have been one of the most serious threats to the world economy, rapidly increasing freight costs, causing transport delays that have spread to production and retail distribution, triggering and fueling inflation, resulting in the concentration of companies in the shipping industry (eight companies account for 85% of the world's tonnage) and a change the structure of world trade.

Bottlenecks and shortages have been at the origin of strong difficulties for many manufacturers during the pandemic. For a small minority, which seeks to provide continuity to production and cohesion to supply chains, these

Box 7.4 Nike's four-phase COVID-19 response strategy

For months, the demand for Nike products has outpaced supply. Over half of Nike footwear and about a third of Nike apparels are produced in Vietnam, where COVID-19 has long blocked production. Due to the lockdowns in this country, Nike estimates that it reduced production by about 130 million units during the first year of the pandemic alone.

Since the first months of the crisis, Nike has planned the return to long-term growth in four stages: (1) 'containment', (2) 'recovery', (3) 'normalization', and (4) 'return to growth'. The first phase, 'containment of the outbreak', necessarily varies by country. Stores are closed, but e-commerce growth is strong. Nike develops contact with clients who are spending a lot of time indoors, providing them with digital services, an approach that proved to be effective especially in China, Japan, and South Korea. In the second phase, the main indicator of the 'recovery' is that retail traffic is coming back, physical stores are reopening, and consumers are returning to the stores. In the 'normalization' phase, market and demand conditions begin returning to precrisis levels. The time to return to normal is different from country to country. Business conditions in China soon returned to prepandemic-outbreak levels. In the final stage, 'returning to growth', Nike planned to enhance its position in selling online and offline and giving priority to major cities such as New York, London, and Shanghai (Pacheco, 2021).

have instead been years of significant profits. This is the case of the Japanese makers of industrial equipment, toward whom the demand for automation has greatly increased. This happened first amid the disruption of the human workforce by COVID-19 and afterward when labor costs significantly increased (Box 7.5).

7.4.3 Shortages

Three sectors have shown the profound effects that can emerge from severe shortages: the car industry, the bike industry, and the music industry.

- **The Car Industry**

In the automotive sector, the most serious consequence of the pandemic, apart from changes in demand, has been the lack of semiconductors. With the arrival of the pandemic, many factories producing this vital component have closed, drastically reducing the supply.

What has happened in the semiconductor sector is significant in showing the effects of the pandemic on consumption and competition and in

Box 7.5 The Magnificent Four

In the last 10 years, the global supply of industrial robots has tripled, with Japanese manufacturers supplying 45% of the new equipment. The four main manufacturers — Keyence, Fanuc, SMC, and Lasertec — increased market capitalization by two and a half times in 5 years (2017–22). The owner of Keyence has become the richest man in Japan. The four, which have operating margins of more than 20%, also owe their success to very effective and innovative sales policies. Keyence has no middleman to sell its product to, relying instead on its own sale force consisting mainly of engineers. As in SMC, these engineers spend a lot of time on the factory floors of potential customers identifying 'niggles and tweaks', problems that otherwise would not be identified. It is no surprise that Japan has achieved excellence in automation. The 'just in time' manufacturing pioneered by companies such as Toyota and Panasonic in their obsessive search for efficiency has led to devising every means possible to replace man by machines. Initially, it was a source of competitive advantage, but then, starting from the 1990s when Japan's working age population began to shrink, it became a necessity (The Economist, 2022).

highlighting the difficulty of companies to respond due to future uncertainty about many variables. How long will this semiconductor shortage last, which is the consequence of the pandemic coronavirus that has hit an industry having a structure prone to cyclical and fluctuating activity?

The semiconductor sector has always been cyclical, but the pandemic has amplified demand swings. Locked-down consumers shopping online have increased the demand for personal computers: Microsoft and Sony have launched new video-game consoles, while the spread of video-calling, video-streaming, and video gaming has increased the use of data centers. The rise of remote work has caused the demand for high-end chips from cloud-computing operators to skyrocket.

Shortages affect every type of chips, from those with higher technological content and higher prices that power smartphones to microprocessors and simple sensors at very low prices. Shortages also affect a wide variety of industries, from games consoles to televisions and home broadband routers. Large semiconductor manufacturers such as Foxconn, Nintendo, Intel, and Samsung Electronics have announced the temporary collapse of production.

The critical point for the car industry came when, in the spring of 2021, manufacturers reduced semiconductor orders because of lower demand for cars due to the pandemic. Supplies fell further in the summer when parts production was suspended in Vietnam and Malaysia following government restrictions to curb the Delta variant. When consumers returned to dealers to buy new cars earlier than expected, carmakers found that the supply of semiconductors was very limited. Production had been hoarded by consumer electronics manufacturers, who have a higher technological content, and therefore are a greater source of profits for semiconductor manufacturers. The shortage has taken on such dimensions that most carmakers, including Ford and General Motors, have been forced to idle factories or to reduce work shifts.

It is not easy for semiconductor manufacturers to add operational capacity as the increase in overall demand (strengthened by that from new manufacturers) would require. Plants built with the latest technologies have very high costs (in the tens of billions of dollar range). Even the low-cost plants that work with old technologies are based on the latest generation equipment that is supplied by only a few companies.

In the short term, to increase resilience car companies have decided to accumulate stocks of key parts as much as possible (also subtracting them from others). In practice, they have abandoned 'just in time' to move on to 'just in case' (see below). With a long-term horizon, the major carmakers have adopted two policies to secure supplies:

(1) changing their procurement policy by deciding to make purchases directly from Tier 2, Tier 3, and Tier four suppliers, whereas previously they only bought from Tier 1. This policy has required the negotiation of new supply contracts to replace those stipulated before the pandemic;

(2) opting for long-term contracts, strategic alliances, or joint ventures with suppliers at various levels. Among the companies adopting this policy is General Motor, whose CEO Barra said: "We're re-evaluating, and having direct relationships with tier two, three and four suppliers" (Wainewright, 2021).

The sharpening of the crisis, which produced in the first year of the pandemic at least one million fewer cars than expected, has forced some carmakers to turn to extreme measures. Media outlets announced that Tesla was considering paying in advance for the purchase of chips and the possibility of buying a semiconductor plant.

Tier one manufacturers have also adopted procurement policies like those carmakers adopt for their suppliers (Box 7.6).

> **Box 7.6 "Put money on the table"**
> Don't forget that the microchip production process involves hundreds of steps, requiring up to 4 months from design to mass production. The months-long process needed to make a chip has meant global demand was far outstripping supply. According to Bosch, car makers can no longer make 'last-minute' decisions based on fluctuations in demand. To avoid repeating chip shortages that can cause great and continual trouble to the industry, carmakers must "put money on the table," which means giving rock solid guarantees that orders will be executed. For its part, Bosch has built a new semiconductor factory in Dresden (Germany) with the aim of becoming independent of chip suppliers.

- **The Bike Industry**

Another sector where supply chain shortages have blocked production for a long time is the bicycle sector. The bike industry had supply problems mainly because consumers preferred to ride a bicycle rather than take the risk of being infected on public transport. Shortages have been heightened because:

(1) the production of critical parts is concentrated in a handful of companies including Japan's Shimano, SRAM in the United States, and Italy's Campagnolo;

(2) this group of companies were unwilling to substantially expand production capacity fearing that the boom in demand could soon fade away, not lasting longer than the pandemic.

The shortages have highlighted the strong dependence of the industry on one firm, Japan's Shimano, which controls around 65% of the market for high-end components. European and U.S. producers had to face lead times from order to delivery that skyrocketed over 400 days for hydraulic brakes and wheels. The leadership of Shimano in the supply chain is secured by the quality of its production and by the high barriers to entry in the market (due to unrivalled high economies of scale).

Industry experts have warned that such a strong demand "cannot last forever", predicting it would come down to prepandemic levels in 2023 when indoor sports activities would make a full comeback and the market would have absorbed the huge volume of bikes sold in the previous years.

- **The Music Industry**

The pandemic has not saved the music industry. In the years immediately preceding the pandemic, the demand for vinyl records has rapidly increased as fans have come to appreciate even more having the music of their favorite bands in a physical form. In the late 1990s and early 2000s, many vinyl-pressing factories closed their doors. Due to COVID-19, the remaining factories had to shut down, causing demand of musicians to temporarily exceed production capacity. To make matters worse, the price of the plastic used to make long playing vinyl records has surged at unprecedented levels.

7.4.4 The increase in shipping costs

"The era of cheap shipping is behind us" (The Economist, 2021a). This is the phrase pronounced by the European head of Maersk, which sums up very well the expectations of operators in the sector at the beginning of 2022.

For some routes, shipping rates were 10 times the prepandemic levels. Sea freight costs between China and Europe have risen enormously due to a reduction in the number of container ships as the shipowners preferred the transpacific routes, which have higher rates. As a result, the cost of transport for businesses that use shipping firms has increased considerably.

For small products such as smartphones, the increase is very small, since the cost of transport is a small percentage of the price; however, this is not the case for lower-value goods for which the cost of transport (after the increases) represents a large part of the price. A company's manager that sells office supplies said: "They were moving a container whose contents were in the order of $15,000 in value. Well, if that now costs $15,000 to move, you have a problem, right?" (Varadarajan, 2021).

The increase in shipping costs is high even for the most voluminous products, the so-called bulky products such as, refrigerators, washing machines, and other large and small household appliances.

What were the causes of the increase in shipping costs? In the decade before the coronavirus, container shipping prices remained very low due to operational overcapacity, and operators barely managed to make profits. With the pandemic, the situation has radically changed.

Interdependent factors have significantly increased the costs of sea transport: (1) the high demand for the transport of consumer products (which account for the largest part of transport by sea); (2) the consequent congestion in the ports (clogged ports) also due to the COVID-19 restriction; (3) the difficulties in the handling of goods that have lengthened the waiting times for container ships (large numbers of which were stuck just outside the ports). In addition, the impairment of programming in the use of containers has spread to warehouses and ground transport.

In addition to this, when container ships arrived late at their destination, the planning regarding their subsequent use was disrupted, causing a ripple effect of disruption on freight, truck, and warehouse services[2].

To get around the shortage of shipping vessels, Walmart, and Home Depot, like other large importers, has decided to charter vessels directly to ensure regular supplies instead of waiting to find space in ocean carriers. Other companies, such as Peloton, a maker of price-end exercise bikes, have decided to resort to shipments by air. But even in this sector the fares have long remained high because, due to the drastic reduction in passenger flights, part of the cargo transport capacity of the sector (the lower part of the fuselage used for cargo) has disappeared.

Two main factors could keep shipping rates high in the future: (1) the consolidation of the industry (at present, the world's leading nine carriers control 85% of tonnage) and (2) tightened emission regulations could keep shipping rates high.

References

Financial Times. (2022a). Brussels curbs growth forecasts as inflation hits EU economy. *Financial Times.* www.ft.com/content/55bebb18-d458-4b75-b106-840b5c12a7a5.

Financial Times. (2022b). EU launches €43bn push for chip factories as shortages hit manufacturing. *Financial Times.* www.ft.com/content/afbee42b-ba06-49c7-a053-7263e1a4c228.

Hill, A. (2022). How Cirque du Soleil went from $1 billion to zero revenues in 48 hours. *Financial Post.* https://financialpost.com/financial-times/how-cirque-du-soleil-went-from-1-billion-to-zero-revenues-in-48-hours.

Ivanov, D., Dolgui, A., & Sokolov, B. (Eds.). (2019). *Handbook of ripple effects in the supply chain, 276.* New York: Springer.

Pacheco, I. (2021). Nike's supply crunch stunts growth again. *The Wall Street Journal.* www.wsj.com/articles/nikes-supply-crunch-stunts-growth-again-11640037479.

Romei, V., Arnold, M., & Ghiglione, D. (2021). Supply chain squeeze: First cars, now chairs and cupboards. *Financial Times.* www.ft.com/content/8e2b72f2-b937-4152-a61b-c18758160650.

Sheffi, Y. (2021). *What everyone gets wrong about the never-ending COVID-19 supply chain crisis.* MIT Sloan Management Review.

The Economist. (2021a). Why supply-chain snarls still entangle the world. *The Economist.* www.economist.com/business/a-return-to-container-shippings-pre-pandemic-days-is-a-long-way-off/21806844.

The Economist. (2021b). The chip shortage is a self-solving problem. Government subsidies will lead to overcapacity and waste. *The Economist.* www.economist.com/leaders/2021/08/07/the-chip-shortage-is-a-self-solving-problem.

The Economist. (2021c). The world economy's shortage problem. *The Economist.* www.economist.com/leaders/2021/10/09/the-world-economys-shortage-problem.

---

[2] There are vast consequences of the ripple effects in the supply chain which are difficult to control and resolve. This problem existed even before the coronavirus pandemic (Ivanov et al., 2019).

The Economist. (2022). Why Japan's Automation Inc is indispensable to global industry. *The Economist.* www.economist.com/business/2022/02/12/why-japans-automation-inc-is-indispensable-to-global-industry.

Treccani. (2022). *Black Friday.* https://www.treccani.it/.

Varadarajan, T. (2021). An insider explains the supply-chain crisis. *The Wall Street Journal.* www.wsj.com/articles/insider-explains-supply-chain-crisis-phil-levy-shipping-containers-ports-costs-inflation-logistics-11639757471.

Wainewright, P. (2021). *September 30. Some advice for businesses grappling with fragile supply chains.* https://diginomica.com/advice-businesses-fragile-supply-chains.

CHAPTER EIGHT

War in Europe: another blow to the global supply chains

8.1 Russia's invasion of Ukraine: another blow to the global supply chains

The invasion of Ukraine has added great distress to global supply chains. The war is different from the other disruptions because it marks the beginning of a phase of long and deep instability in the supply chains of key industries.

Russia's invasion of Ukraine "has put an end to the globalization we have experienced over the last 3 decades", wrote Larry Fink, the BlackRock founder and chief executive, in his shareholder letter in March 2022. The war, he wrote, marks "a turning point in the world order of geopolitics, macroeconomic trends and capital markets" (Masters, 2022). Many agree with this diagnosis. The invasion of Ukraine has added great distress to global supply chains.

These pages have been written while the war had been going on for months and had an uncertain future; yet a series of linked events destined to weigh deeply and for a long period of time on global supply chains have already emerged.

1. The first large-scale war in Europe since War World II, as well as the coronavirus pandemic, shortly before the fighting began has brought to the surface the vulnerability of supply chains. The longer they are, the more they extend over a variety of countries and are vulnerable to wage increases in Asian countries, rising energy prices, natural disasters, and armed conflicts.

    The Russia-Ukraine war, which has caused the largest commodity shock since 1973, has forced many companies to rethink the supply chains they have gradually built over the last few decades, reinforcing the need for most organizations to build more resilient supply chains.

The Digital Transformation of Supply Chain Management
ISBN: 978-0-323-85532-7
https://doi.org/10.1016/B978-0-323-85532-7.00005-0

Many sectors have been affected, from food to semiconductors. The war has certainly accelerated the shift from global to regional sourcing that had already begun, also inducing many Western companies to reduce their dependency on China for components and finished goods and on Russia for sources of energy and raw materials (Simchi-Levi & Harren, 2022).

As Deloitte noted in a report, "The principal reason that Russia plays above its weight is that it is a major exporter of some of the world's most important commodities" (Kalish, 2022). "Russia is a significant source of many of the 35 critical minerals that the US Department of the Interior (DOI) deems vital to the nation's economic and national security interests, including 30% of the globe's supply of platinum-group elements (including palladium), 13% of titanium, and 11% of nickel. Russia is also a major source of neon, used for etching circuits on silicon wafers" (Kirkpatric, 2022).

The war in Ukraine has sent shockwaves through the global supply chain with continuing and serious effects on the highly interdependent and interconnected world trade that exists today. The war's impact has revealed how wide the interconnection has become. According to reliable estimates, nearly 300,000 companies in the United States and Europe "have suppliers in Russia and Ukraine, a demonstration of how interconnected the world is today" (Simchi-Levi & Harren, 2022).

2. The war in Ukraine has highlighted the risks from Europe's dependence on Russia's energy supplies, particularly regarding gas and oil. The most obvious effect has come from the rise in the price of both commodities, which has fueled inflationary pressures. Other significant effects are seen in metals and ores, where Russia and Ukraine are relevant producers of commodities such as aluminum, steel, and platinum. Ukraine is a key exporter of metals, ores, ferroalloys, minerals, and engineering products. It also supplies about 50% of the world's neon gas, which is used to produce semiconductor chips.

As a report from the London Business School (London Business School, 2022) shows, two types of risks stand out for their effects on the structure of global supply chains: (1) the difficulty in finding substitutes, and (2) the spillover effect.

- **No easy way to find substitutes.** Modern manufacturing uses a wide variety of inputs that are not easily replaceable, which amplifies the effects of any kind of disruption. As we have experienced over the last few years, intertwined global supply chains in the semiconductor industry have suffered severe disruptions due to a variety of factors, from pandemic-related lockdowns to the switch in demand to a tsunami in Fukushima. The conflict in Ukraine is likely to have a lasting and deep negative effect on the semiconductor shortage, which will impact many industries from car to computer manufacturers.[1]

- **Spillover effect.** A second risk is that in modern, highly interrelated global supply chains an event such as the outbreak of a war could cause consequences that spread far beyond what emerges on the surface at first glance. "Spillover effect refers to the impact that seemingly unrelated events in one nation can have on the economies of other nations" (Kenton, 2022). Spillover effects are caused by intertwined global supply chains in today's highly interdependent and interconnected world[2].

For example, Russia and Ukraine are the main producers of wheat and corn (29% from the two countries together). Shortages in world wheat, barley, and corn markets have negative effects on the production of bread, pasta, and other products derived from cereals not only in countries that import in large quantities from Ukraine and Russia but also globally. Moreover, Russia is one of the main suppliers of raw materials to produce fertilizers. If exports of these raw materials from Russia cease, fertilizer prices rise. The same effect is caused by the increase in the prices of the energy needed to produce certain types of raw materials used in the production of fertilizers such as ammonia. Soaring energy prices are likely to cause fertilizer shortages with far reaching consequences since nearly half of global food production relies on fertilizers. The spillover effects would be further complicated by decisions to accumulate stocks because of the fear of possible future shortages (Box 8.1).

---

[1] As the report from London Business School explains: "Ukraine supplies more than 90% of the U.S.'s semiconductor-grade neon, a gas integral to the lasers used in the chip-making process. Russia, on the other hand, supplies 35% of the U.S.'s palladium, a rare metal used to create semiconductors" (London Business School, 2022).

[2] What Is the Spillover Effect? "Although there are positive spillover effects, the term is most commonly applied to the negative impact a domestic event has on other parts of the world such as an earthquake, stock market crisis, or another macro event". How the spillover effect works: "Spillover effects are a type of network effect that increased since globalization in trade and stock markets deepened the financial connections between economies. The Canada-U.S. trade relationship provides an example of spillover effects. This is because the U.S. is Canada's main market by a wide margin across nearly every export-oriented sector. The effects of a minor U.S. slowdown are amplified by the Canadian reliance on the U.S. market for its own growth" (Kenton, 2022).

Box 8.1 Production fallout from automakers.
The Russian invasion has had a large impact on European car manufacturers, bringing out the risks stemming from the existent global supply chain. The German automakers association, VDA, said the war in Ukraine has broken transport routes and financial transactions and caused shortages in a range of raw materials. The supply chains were under strong pressure from the impact of the war particularly on shipping, rail, and air freight, with Mercedes forced to cut shifts at European plants. As supplies of parts produced in Ukraine have run short, the automaker has reduced production at some of its plants. Trying to avoid a complete production stoppage, it decided to adjust shift planning at individual plants. Similarly, Volkswagen, BMW, and Porsche were forced to stop production at car factories in Germany as the production in Western Ukraine of crucial wire harnesses has been disrupted by the Russian invasion (Automotive News, 2022).

8.2 Lessons for business leaders

The previous chapters discussed decisions companies take to protect supply chains from possible risks and how in recent years various types of adjustments have been underway, of which reshoring is the common denominator. To mention just a few: (1) avoiding concentrating parts of supply chains in politically unstable countries/regions; (2) investing in alternative forms of sourcing that may include a mixture of local, regional, and global supply partners; (3) adopting 'just in case' as a replacement for 'just in time' to reduce the risks of supply chain disruption.

Between 2018 and 2022, due to the China-U.S. trade war and the supply chain disruptions caused by the pandemic, a variety of companies decided to relocate at least part of their supply chains. Reshoring became even more the new name of the game, a new watchword.

What has happened in the semiconductor industry is emblematic: in 1990, the U.S. and Europe produced 80% of their semiconductor needs; 30 years later this percentage had fallen to 20%. The supply difficulties caused by the pandemic have pushed many companies, in particular the American ones, to reverse the trend by making significant investments at home. Intel is an example of this new trend: in 2022, it announced a plan to spend $20 billion to build two semiconductor factories in Ohio.

Many companies were still reluctant to start reshoring, but after the invasion of Ukraine they have re-examined their options. They "are living through the era of disequilibrium", and all of a sudden 'just in case' sounds more reasonable than 'just in time', noted Sang Kim, a professor of supply chain management at the Yale School of Management. Kim noted that the war, "signifies yet another trigger for the movement toward the deglobalization of supply chains (Segal, 2022).

Other Authors have arrived at the same conclusion. "The Ukraine war and closer alignment of China and Russia will modify profoundly the exchange of energy, raw materials, industrial parts, and goods between the Western world, China, and Russia and promise to accelerate the reshoring trend" (Simchi-Levi & Harren, 2022).

Reshoring means looking for domestic locations or, if this is not possible, in neighboring areas that are politically non-hostile, internally secure, and reliable. For some industries, this is relatively simple; however, reducing dependence on China and other countries that are a source of thousands of components takes time and significant investments. In some sectors, such as agricultural commodities, it is a question of finding other regions where the commodities can be sown and grown.

As for the West, and Europe in particular, it was immediately evident that the longer the war in Ukraine lasts, the more the West would have to develop alternative sources. In the short term, there was no doubt about the need to deal with the emergency, but designing a long-term strategy is more difficult. Agricultural commodities can be supplied to Europe and Africa and parts of Asia from crops in South America, but with what investments?

Many thought that soon or later stability could be restored again (regardless of who wins the war or the kind of peace agreement), but for many companies, finding suitable solutions in the short term is the way to survive and build a bridge to future solutions.

To design new supply chains that can mitigate the risks of political disruption the government help is needed, regarding both the relevance of the investments and the need to coordinate the interventions among the various sectors involved (Simchi-Levi & Harren, 2022).

Simchi-Levi and Harren cite two examples of a swing from globalization to localization mastered by governments. The first is the recent agreement by Électricité de France (EDF) to purchase part of GE's nuclear power business, which GE had bought from Alstom in 2015. France plans to increase the production of its nuclear power plants, which already generate 70% of its electricity (Alderman, 2022). To do so, it has decided it needs better control over the entire supply chain for such plants. The second example is the decision of the U.S. and Dutch governments to block ASML, the world's largest producer of lithography equipment used to make computer chips, from selling its most advanced machines to China (these machines are crucial elements for semiconductor manufacturing equipment).

In a report about the impact on supply chains from the Russia—Ukraine war, Deloitte has collected data showing that the effects are very broad (Kirkpatric, 2022). The cascading structure of global supply chains (from Tier 1 to Tier 3 and sometimes even Tier 4) has exacerbated the effects of the crisis triggered by Russia's war. Quoting data from Dun and Bradstreet, the report by Deloitte points out that: (1) there were fewer than 15,000 Tier 1 suppliers (of the global supply chain) in Russia, but the country had 7.6 million Tier 2 suppliers globally; (2) more than 374,000 businesses, 90% of which are in the United States, rely on Russian suppliers.

The same report compares this data with Deloitte's 2021s survey, which showed that 70% of chief procurement officers "believed they had good visibility into risks in their Tier 1 suppliers, but only 15% had the same confidence about Tier 2 and beyond" (Kirkpatric, 2022). This shows that the risks of disruption have been greatly underestimated.

The invasion of Ukraine tests the rules of protection of global supply chains adopted by companies in the years immediately preceding the invasion. To address the risks arising from the Russia-Ukraine conflict, Deloitte's report proposes five important actions, which can be summarized as follows (Table 8.1).

8.3 How to respond to war disruptions

As the unprecedented humanitarian and economic disaster after WWII continued, consulting firms, researchers, and experts in various fields contributed to preparing responses to the disruptions in the supply chains caused by the war. The short- and medium-term responses are generally no different from those adopted to mitigate the effects on supply chains of other disruptions of recent years (trade wars, natural disasters, geopolitical clashes). These disruptions are examined in full in Chapter 9.

Table 8.1 What companies should do to mitigate the impact on supply chains from the war in Ukraine.

A set of actions	Reason why
Verify that the company has an appropriate risk management system	• As already occurred during the pandemic, upon the outbreak of war in the Ukraine, most companies had no specific plan to deal with the risk of such a large-scale war in Europe. • The risk management system must monitor the entire supplier network.
Use technology to manage risks at the Tier 1 level	• Visibility is a fundamental pillar of a resilient supply chain. Deloitte's survey indicates that few companies (26%) felt they could predict risks in their Tier 1. • To increase the risk identification capacity it is necessary to set up "control towers" based on artificial intelligence, machine learning and advanced analytics. • The aim is to highlight those suppliers and/or commodities that represent a high risk for a company's direct suppliers and the entire supplier network (suppliers' suppliers).
Activate alternate sources of supply	• Need to quickly build alternative sources of raw materials and components and accumulate stocks of both. • It is also important to move quickly to reinforce supplier relationships and secure additional inventory and capacity along the entire supply chain.
Evaluate onshoring and 'friend-shoring'	• Reshape global supply chains with a more regional, even local, structure. The Ukraine conflict will accelerate that movement. • Bringing supply chains home can offer governments and companies more control over supply chains and remove the volatility of foreign dependence.

(Continued)

Table 8.1 What companies should do to mitigate the impact on supply chains from the war in Ukraine.—cont'd

A set of actions	Reason why
	• As traditional supply routes were disrupted by the Ukraine conflict, the need for logistical flexibility in the design of new global supply chains has become an essential requirement. For instance, air-routes have been changed to avoid the closed air space over Russia and Ukraine, and freight trains that were connecting China to Europe through Russia, Ukraine, or Belarus are no longer available
Conduct global scenario planning	• Both the duration and extension of the crisis are uncertain. To define the best medium- to longer-term course of action, companies should assess scenarios based on the nature of their exposure to the conflict.

The effects on the global supply chains from the Fukushima disaster had been absorbed (albeit slowly) and, thanks to the rapid discovery of vaccines, those caused by COVID-19 were on the verge of being taken toward a 'new normal' when the war broke out in Ukraine. The war is not a disruption like the others because it marks the beginning of a phase of long and deep instability in the supply chains of key industries.

• **Instability makes it difficult to design supply chains.** The complexity and interconnections of supply chains are such that it is difficult to adapt them to the effects of the disruptions caused by the instability from the war in Ukraine. Supply chain relationships are hard to disentangle. "Perhaps the conflict will push supply chain relationships between countries with like - minded values - but who is to say a country that shares common values today may not turn hostile in the future?"

(Ganeshan & Boone, 2022).[3] Hungary's decision not to join the Russian oil and gas embargo decided on by European countries is an example of how difficult it is to make predictions in a phase of strong geopolitical instability.

- **The vulnerability of supply chains has distant roots.** In an article published in *Supply Chain Management Review*, the two Authors conclude that it is not possible to predict what kind of solutions the war in Ukraine will have (Terino & Guarraia, 2022).

   Many think it will last a long time and that it could trigger tensions in other geographical areas. This is certainly another link in a chain of events (from natural disasters to the resurgence of inflation) that have made supply chains vulnerable. The effects of the war in Ukraine must also be monitored by many companies whose supply chains are not directly involved.

   The chart below shows how the frequency of and impact on supply chain disruptions were increasing well before the conflict in Ukraine (Fig. 8.1).

- **Common rules to overcome the challenges**. The war in Ukraine has encouraged a lot of research and proposals on what businesses should do to successfully deal with the consequences of the conflict on supply chains. They have in common the need to draw up scenarios, build resilience, assess and mitigate risks, and reinvent supply chains. A few valuable examples will suffice.

   - Since business leaders are facing an increasingly unstable business environment, they must respond with immediate actions while preparing their organizations and looking far ahead. Bain and Company describe that frame of mind as "respond and reposition" (O'Keeffe et al., 2022).

      To respond in the short term, companies must take decisive actions, continuously adapting them to the evolving situation. The answers given by the various functional areas of the enterprise must be coordinated to avoid gaps. The weakness of one point can compromise

---

[3] To mitigate the impact of supply chain disruptions, the two authors propose two types of actions that are extensively discussed in the literature on the subject (see Chapter 9 below). The first calls for government intervention to introduce policies that increase the resilience of supply chains critical to an industry. The second suggests that companies identify whether there are other suppliers of key components, accumulate safety stocks, and favor suppliers closer to the final markets from a geographical point of view.

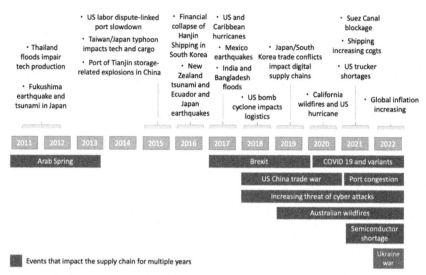

Figure 8.1 *The Increasingly Relentless Magnitude of Supply Chain Disruptions.* The figure illustrates the increasingly relentless magnitude of supply chain disruptions.

the entire company. "After all, a company is only as resilient as its weakest link". In the medium-to-long term, companies need to strengthen their supply chains to deal with future crises ('reposition'). Of course, every company has its own uniqueness: the war and its global effects pose widely different challenges for different industries and companies.

- In the report "From Disruption to Reinvention - The future of supply chains in Europe", Accenture wrote that a new economic order is upon us and that supply chains will require reinvention. The consulting company recalls that supply chains have been designed primarily to reduce costs, but under the new scenario they must also be resilient and agile to respond to the unprecedented uncertainty of recent years (Accenture, 2022). A focus on three key areas is highlighted: Resilience, Relevance, Sustainability. Relevance entails that "Supply chains will need to be customer-centric and agile so they can quickly and cost-effectively adapt to changes in demand. Capturing new data sets, including real-time data, from inside and outside the organization and across the value chain will be critical."

- In the article mentioned above, Terino and Guarraia suggest companies implement a series of "no-regret supply chain actions" to protect their businesses in the short term and strengthen resilience in the long term. First and foremost, there must be the identification and assessment of risks along the value chain, followed by the identification of the points of greatest risk and how to monitor them; the determination of specific policies for the most acute risks; and the mapping of the supply chain to build traceability from the top to the bottom tier. However, the time needed to change policy must never be forgotten; for example, choosing and operationalizing alternative supply sources and transport routes takes time to adapt to required levels of production.

8.4 Take a step back to go further on global supply chain rebound

Predicting what the evolution of global supply chains will be under the shocks of recent years is difficult, but a long-term trend can be grasped. The war at the center of Europe is also the confirmation that the world tends to divide into blocks, which, among the many consequences, provides a further strong push to the rewriting (mainly reshoring) of supply chains and the increase in costs in their management, and therefore to the loss of part of the advantages obtained in the past through globalization.

In the short and medium term, it is possible to mitigate the effects of supply chain disruptions (as mentioned above), but if you look far ahead the scenario under which many global supply chains have been built is destined to change drastically. Much will never be the same again after Russia's invasion of Ukraine.

How is this conclusion arrived at? According to an analysis of The Economist (2022), the conflict in Ukraine is pitting large autocracies (Russia and China at the forefront) against liberal democracies (so-called Western countries).

This clash had already occurred during the Cold war, but the balance of power was different: "But this time autocracies are bigger, richer and more technologically sophisticated. Their share in global output, trade and innovation has risen, and they are key links in many supply chains. Attempts to drift apart, therefore, will bring new consequences, and costs, for the world economy." The war in Europe can accelerate "another profound shift in global trade flows" (The Economist, 2022).

After World War II, the article reminds us, democracies dominated international trade. In 1960, the U.S., Britain, Canada, France, Italy, and Japan together accounted for about 40% of global exports. Autocracies, on the other hand, had a very modest weight in the world economy. The Soviet Union accounted for 4% of global trade and China "barely featured in the statistics." The West fought an ideological battle with communist countries but was vastly superior economically and technologically. In addition, the two blocks were clearly separated. Trade and foreign direct investments were very modest.

In the late 1970s, autocratic regimes (especially China) began to participate in international trade. Two strong thrusts came in the 1980s with the decision of the new Chinese leader Deng Xiaoping to open China to the advantages of globalization, then in its initial stages, and in 1991 with the breakup of the Soviet Union.

Western countries generally pushed for trade liberalization to reap economic benefits, in the belief that bringing more countries into the global trading system would have encouraged democracy in a more peaceful world. In the 1990s the overwhelming growth of globalization began. International trade and foreign direct investments grew rapidly and Russia started to export oil to the West. In the following two decades, Chinese exports to the U.S. skyrocketed. Living standards went up around the world and extreme poverty decreased significantly. Autocracies and democracies started to bond with each other.

However, an expected benefit from globalization was missing: political liberalization. Classifying political regimes "is not an exact science," observed the Authors of the quoted article; nevertheless, it helps in revealing a broader trend: "the waning might of liberal democracies." The diminishing economic and political power of liberal democracies such as those in Western Europe, the U.S., and Japan is clear for all to see. "World in Data, a research organization, puts countries into four groups, ranging from most to least free: 'liberal democracies', such as America and Japan; more flawed 'electoral democracies', such as Poland and Sri Lanka; 'electoral autocracies', such as Turkey and Hungary; and 'closed autocracies', such as China and Vietnam, where citizens have no real choice over their leader.

Globalization and autocracy are locked together. For how much longer?" (The Economist, 2022). Liberal and electoral democracies together represent 30% of world population. Most of the supply chains of Western multinational companies are in the other part of the world represented by closed and electoral autocracies.

Using data from the World Bank and the IMF, the Authors divide the global economy into two. They estimate that closed and electoral autocracies today have more than doubled their share of global GDP since the end of the cold war. Over that period, their share of global exports has greatly increased, with the combined market value of their listed companies rising to 30% of the global total (3% in 1989). In the fields of innovation and investment, autocracies are becoming a stronger rival to democracies. "In 2020 their governments and firms invested $9trn in everything from machinery and equipment to the construction of roads and railways. Democracies invested $12trn" .. "Nonetheless autocracies have become integrated with democracies to an extent that would have been unthinkable during the cold war." (The Economist, 2022). With this situation, being part of very extensive global supply chains in autocracies, or relying on them, means being vulnerable.

Conclusion. The trend which the war in Ukraine strengthens and accelerates is the separation between the world's most powerful democracies and autocracies, which decades of globalization had led to intertwine. Both tend to form separate blocks. Liberal democracies prefer alliances in regional trade. Autocracies also tend to form their own alliances (i.e.: Russia and China). A common tendency of the two blocs in the supply chain perspective is that at the same time large countries tend to become more independent (i.e.: the U.S., on the one hand, and China on the other).

After mitigating the short- and medium-term effects of the war, companies in liberal democracies must look at the long term to design their supply chains in a new way. To succeed, they will have to face strong tensions to unravel the supply chain problem.

References

Accenture. (May 23, 2022). *From disruption to reinvention—The future of supply chains in Europe was published at the world economic forum's annual meeting in davos.* World Economic Forum's Annual Meeting, Davos. Accenture. www.accenture.com/us-en/insights/strategy/ukraine-future-supply-chains-europe.

Alderman, L. (2022). France announces major nuclear power buildup. *New York Times.* www.nytimes.com/2022/02/10/world/europe/france-macron-nuclear-power.html.

Automotive News. (2022). *Here's how Russia's invasion of Ukraine is impacting the auto industry.* Automotive News Europe. www.autonews.com/automakers-suppliers/heres-how-russias-ukraine-invasion-impacting-auto-industry.

Ganeshan, R., & Boone, T. (2022). *How the war in Ukraine impacts global supply chains.* IPS, Economy and Ecology. www.ips-journal.eu/topics/economy-and-ecology/how-the-war-in-ukraine-impacts-global-suppy-chains-5894/.

Kalish, I. (March 15, 2022). *How sanctions impact Russia and the global economy.* Deloitte Insights. https://www2.deloitte.com/us/en/insights/economy/global-economic-impact-of-sanctions-on-russia.html.

Kenton, W. (2022). *Spillover effect.* Investopedia. www.investopedia.com/terms/s/spillover-effect.asp.

Kirkpatric, J. (March 25, 2022). *Supply chain implications of the Russia-Ukraine conflict.* Deloitte Insights. https://www2.deloitte.com/xe/en/insights/focus/supply-chain/supply-chain-war-russia-ukraine.html/#endnote-1.

London Business School. (2022). *Global supply chains face disruption following Russia's invasion of Ukraine.* Forbes. www.forbes.com/sites/lbsbusinessstrategyreview/2022/03/24/global-supply-chains-face-disruption-following-russias-invasion-of-ukraine/?sh=398b3d342ce0.

Masters, B. (2022). BlackRock chief Larry Fink says Ukraine war marks end of globalisation. *Financial Times.* Financial Times www.ft.com/content/0c9e3b72-8d8d-4129-afb5-655571a01025.

O'Keeffe, D., Harris, K., Schwedel, A., & Devlin, T. (April 6, 2022). *Crisis in Ukraine: Respond and reposition.* Bain Company. www.bain.com/insights/crisis-in-ukraine-respond-and-reposition/.

Segal, E. (2022). *Supply chain crisis worsens as Russia's war against Ukraine continues.* Forbes. www.forbes.com/sites/edwardsegal/2022/04/02/supply-chain-crisis-worsens-as-russias-war-against-ukraine-continues/?sh=211403d46e49.

Simchi-Levi, D., & Harren, P. (2022). How the war in Ukraine is further disrupting global supply chains. *Harvard Business Review.* https://hbr.org/2022/03/how-the-war-in-ukraine-is-further-disrupting-global-supply-chains.

Terino, J., & Guarraia, P. (2022). War in Ukraine: Responding to supply chain disruption. *Supply Chain Management Review.* Supply Chain Management Review www.scmr.com/article/war_in_ukraine_responding_to_supply_chain_disruption.

The Economist. (2022). Globalisation and autocracy are locked together. For how much longer? *The Economist.* www.economist.com/finance-and-economics/2022/03/19/globalisation-and-autocracy-are-locked-together-for-how-much-longer.

PART FIVE

How businesses reacted to disruptions of supply chains

CHAPTER NINE

Business models at a crossroads: the post-crisis cleanup

9.1 The risks of supply chain disruptions

How to deal with the risks of supply chain disruptions has been one of the most debated topics during the coronavirus pandemic (Monson, 2020; Szlezak et al., 2020; Govindan et al., 2020). An article in *Harvard Business Review* suggested that companies first identify hidden risks and then examine and protect their vulnerabilities as those risks emerge[1].

Modern products are very complex and incorporate components that are critically important. It is therefore difficult for a company to produce everything on its own. In most industries, companies buy from external suppliers, who in turn rely on other suppliers. This policy offers advantages as it gives flexibility in the choice of components and allows companies to enrich their products with the latest technologies. However, companies will inevitably become vulnerable when there are only one or few suppliers of a given component in the network. If a company produces in a single plant and in a single country, the risk of disruption during the coronavirus pandemic is very high.

A case in point concerns Coronavirus repercussion (Box 9.1).

9.1.1 Identify the vulnerability

To understand in which nodes the greatest risks exist, it is necessary to explore the entire supply chain network. This is easier said than done because there are many causes and consequences and because COVID-19 (being an infectious disease) has spread its effects and vulnerabilities everywhere in the supply chain. After the 2011 Fukushima tsunami, a Tier 1 global semiconductor explored its vulnerability to third- and fourth-tier

---

[1]"The challenge for companies will be to make their supply chains more resilient without weakening their competitiveness. To meet that challenge, managers should first understand their vulnerabilities and then consider a number of steps, some of which they should have been taken long before the pandemic struck" (Shih, 2020).

The Digital Transformation of Supply Chain Management
ISBN: 978-0-323-85532-7
https://doi.org/10.1016/B978-0-323-85532-7.00008-6

> ## Box 9.1 Coronavirus fallout
>
> Samsung Electronics is the world's leading manufacturer of smartphones and computer chips. At the end of February 2020, it was facing a sudden and potentially dangerous disruption: it had quarantined 1500 workers at plants in Daegu, one of the country's most important cities, after some workers had tested positive for the virus. South Korea's economy is largely dependent on the Samsung conglomerate, of which Samsung Electronics is a member. The conglomerate is the largest company in the country with revenues that in 2019 accounted for 12.5% of GDP. For years, Samsung had pursued a policy of diversifying production, first in China and then in other Asian countries, including India and Vietnam. However, the most important segment - smartphones and computer chips - depends on Korean plants, especially for leading-edge technologies. Analysts say the risks are mitigated by the fact that most productions are automated and the engineers have always worked in highly controlled, clean rooms with sophisticated protective equipment. The fact remains that disruption of even a few days in Daegu's plants could create chaos in the global memory chip and smartphone markets (Jung-a & White, 2020).

suppliers. It took a team of 100 specialists over a year to simply locate which companies were participating in the supply chain.

Since research takes time and has high costs, companies often limit themselves to identifying the most important suppliers based on the weight they have on the total value of purchases. Experts warn, however, that: "a surprise disruption that brings your business to a halt can be much more costly than a deep look into your supply chain is" (Shih, 2020).

A significant example concerns the closure of Chinese factories in the pharmaceutical field (Box 9.2).

The journey of pasta from farms to consumers is an interesting example to explain the complexity of steps and processes that companies must manage (Terazono & Evans, 2020).

The pasta supply chain passes through many countries of the world. The pasta consumed in Great Britain starts the journey after wheat harvesting in Canada, then travels to Italy to be processed (for example, by Barilla), and afterward is exported to many European countries, reaching the final point of sale passing through wholesalers, distributors and, finally, supermarkets, many of which are in Great Britain.

Box 9.2 A remote supplier

Until the third week of January 2020, only a few pharmaceutical company executives were concerned that a very large share of the world's antibiotic supply depended on a small group of Chinese factories. This group included a cluster in Inner Mongolia, a wind-beaten northern province with inhospitable cities nestled in large desert areas. Then came the COVID-19 epidemic and the quarantine that closed factories in Inner Mongolia and, gradually, entire cities across China.

The risks of supply chain disruption because of worker infections depend on the phase of the supply chain. Risks are very low in production and harvesting because the processes are mainly mechanical. The transport to ports by rail and the handling phase is operated by largely automatic equipment as well. Risks exist for the subsequent steps, from processing in Italy to transportation to other countries, and then its arrival to the personnel at the points of sale in Great Britain. During the most acute phase of the coronavirus pandemic, there was a further risk as authorities decided to close their borders to cope with the spread of the virus. A strong disruption in the U.K. occurred because of a lack of truck drivers due in part to Brexit.

Disruption risks could be divided into three categories: low, medium, or high-risk (Shih, 2020). If supplies of a certain component of a product begin to fail, how long can the company continue its production? How long does it take for out-of-stock supplies to resume? Are there alternative sources?

The answers depend on the extent to which the manufacturing capacity is flexible and can be reconfigured, but above all, they depend on the degree of specialization of the supply. In the electronics sector, there are many examples of components produced in a few highly specialized plants and concentrated in a few countries. Having a map of the risks the company runs in the supply chain, there are two main ways to deal with them: diversification of sources (between supplier companies and producing countries) or the accumulation of stocks (these two topics are covered below).

9.2 Be more 'resilient'

The main strategies to make supply chains more 'resilient' without weakening their competitiveness are the following. (1) "It's quicker to build inventories than factories"; (2) reshore or onshore: back to the country of final assembly; (3) diversification of supply bases; (4) a new business model; (5) beyond traditional business intelligence: the need to accelerate technological innovation; (6) rethink the trade-off between product variety and flexibility of production capacity.

9.2.1 "It's quicker to build inventories than factories"

The easiest way to give 'resilience' to a supply chain is to increase the total level of stocks by adding an additional stock (called a safety stock) to the level necessary to feed the normal flow of production. The size of this stock should be in proportion to the probable duration of any interruptions in production (Alicke et al., 2021).

Adding a safety stock breaks the rules of 'just in time' and lean management, but it can protect the whole supply chain. 'Just in time' reflected the goal of prioritizing cost reduction in inventory policies, supplier selection, and plant construction and localization. Particularly regarding inventories, the goal was to minimize working capital and thus inventory levels and to enter into flexible contracts to respond quickly to changes in demand (See 'just in time' vs. 'just in case' below). In addition, enterprises transferred production to countries with low labor costs, determined order volumes according to the principle of maximizing economies of scale, and limited locating production in countries with high taxation.

The pandemic has questioned the validity of these objectives and rules. Manufacturers have discovered that in times of strong variability, lean supply chains can mean inadequate access to essential components as well as low costs.

Stockpiling is easier than building new plants. If there is no possibility of creating alternative sources in the short term, the accumulation of stocks along the supply chain is the simplest policy to prevent disruptions, thereby avoiding a loss of sales and high costs to find raw materials or components in a short time. However, this involves the investment of working capital and runs the risk of obsolescence for what has been accumulated.

A follow-up McKinsey survey (Alicke et al., 2021) has highlighted that, during the hardest period of the pandemic, 61% of companies had increased their inventory of critical products and 55% had taken action to ensure they had at least two sources of raw materials. An inevitable consequence has been the increase in warehouse costs. To give stability to procurement policies, some companies entered into long-term contracts with key suppliers.

A case in point concerns the decision of Toyota to build the safety stocks of chips (Box 9.3).

9.2.2 Reshore or onshore. Back to the country of final assembly

Reshoring and onshoring have the same meaning. They convey a concept in which a manufacturing business that moved overseas (delocalization) has decided to go back to the country from which it was originally transferred. In other words, to reshore means to reintroduce manufacturing production to a place (a country) in which it was previously developed.

The coronavirus pandemic prompted a review of delocalization policies. Bringing back to the countries of origin the production once

Box 9.3 Toyota

The Japanese manufacturer exemplifies the problem of the limits of safety stocks. After an earthquake, a tsunami, and a nuclear reactor meltdown in Fukushima in March 2011, the company reviewed its vulnerabilities. It discovered that the automotive industry's supply of semiconductors was insufficient to meet demand because vehicles "largely depended on simpler chips of older designs made in older chip factories that were not receiving continuous investment" (Sheffi, 2021).

Therefore, Toyota and its suppliers decided to build safety stocks of chips. During the first half of 2021, while most automobile manufacturers were announcing significant production cuts and plant closures, Toyota factories were working at full capacity, using their amassed inventory of chips. Because of this decision, during the second quarter of 2021, for the first time ever Toyota took the top position in the U.S. for the number of vehicles sold. However, in a few months, the situation was upended. In September 2021, the company had to reduce its worldwide output by 40% because of the continuing chip shortage that it could not avoid.

transferred to low-cost countries, or to countries rich in raw materials, has become an industrial policy buzzword across the Western world. The supply chain disruptions caused by the pandemic brought back to the foreground objectives such as 'national economic resilience' and the 'reshoring' of critical manufactured goods from vaccines to semiconductors to textile products.

In the European Community, many manufacturers and retailers abandoned a policy adopted for years and began to prefer having suppliers closer to consumers. In some sectors (such as pharmaceuticals), companies have received government support for this policy. Almost everywhere in the most economically advanced countries, bringing home production and jobs has been advocated by academics and political parties.

In France, candidates for the 2022 presidential elections were competing to propose solutions to reverse decades of decline in manufacturing production. The government has made it known that more than 10,000 industrial companies received financial support from France's EU recovery package and that more than 620 of them are being given help specifically to reshore their activities. In the latter part of the last century, the French industrial sector was depleted by the massive transfer of production to Asia and Eastern Europe, where labor costs were lower and labor rules were less restrictive (White & Mallet, 2021).

Due to the rising costs of managing the global supply chain, some companies have been pushed to reconfigure their value chain activities, including the relocation of plants and the change of supply bases in their home country (Robinson & Hsieh, 2016). Sometimes companies operating offshore have to deal with a variety of operational issues and adverse changes in the local environment (costs, suppliers, regulations, political issues, for example), difficulties in ensuring the planned quality levels, and supply chain disruptions (Ancarani et al., 2015). "The current hot topic in global supply chains is whether and where manufacturing is moving, expanding, or contracting across the globe" (Ellram, 2013).

Gray et al. identified four reshoring options (Gray et al., 2013):

(1) in-house reshoring, which refers to "relocating manufacturing activities being performed in wholly owned offshore facilities back" to exclusively owned national facilities;

(2) reshoring for outsourcing "by relocating manufacturing activities being performed in wholly owned offshore facilities back" to national suppliers;

(3) reshoring for insourcing "by relocating manufacturing activities being performed by offshore suppliers back" to fully owned national structures;

(4) reshoring by outsourcing "by relocating manufacturing activities being performed by offshore suppliers back" to national suppliers.

9.2.3 Diversification of supply bases

Sourcing diversification is the preferred hedge to supply chain disruption risks.
(Whitney et al., 2014).

A first way to diversify the supply chain in the face of disruption risks is to add supply bases in other geographical areas not subject to the same risk as those already operating. For example, when the trade war between China and the U.S. made matters worse, many companies shifted production from China to Vietnam, Indonesia, and Thailand (geographical diversification of supply bases)[2].

A second way to diversify, known as regionalization, is to produce high volumes of components and finished products within the regional area where the latter is sold. For instance, North America might be served by Mexico and Central America, and Western Europe could rely on Eastern EU countries. This policy may be appropriate for products whose raw materials are easy to find, but it may be impossible for other specialized products such as machinery, which have strong technological content.

Since the beginning, the pandemic has wreaked havoc on supply chains, and the turmoil continued in the following years as well. The story has laid bare the vulnerability of many supply chains. World trade has been hit by congested ports, a shortage of truck drivers, and delays in railway yards.

Companies that had concentrated production in one or a few geographical areas suffered serious supply chain disruptions due to factory lockdowns and shipping bottlenecks. Furthermore, the increase in the cost of transport has partially canceled the advantages of producing in low-cost countries even very far from the end markets. These and other reasons, such as the worsening of relationships between the U.S. and China or taking advantage

---

[2]The earthquake that struck Fukushima in 2011 revealed to businesses worldwide how dependent they were on parts production in the region. Diversification in other areas would have mitigated the risk. Not everyone agrees, but for many the pandemic, precisely because it is different from other shocks to supply chains, has increased the need for geographical diversification.

of government incentives for manufacturing reshoring, have prompted the transition from global to regional networks.

Regionalization has soon become a priority. It stands for producing closer to the sales markets as a way to reduce the risk of disruption in transport. Almost 90% of respondents to a McKinsey survey in 2021 said they expected to pursue some degree of regionalization during the next 3 years. The degree of 'regionalization' is different among industries: it is very high in pharmaceuticals where it exceeds 60%, and around 22%—25% in the automotive, aerospace, and defense sectors, while it is very low in chemicals and commodities. Some of these differences among industries can be attributed to the structural characteristics of the industries involved (Alicke et al., 2021).

One proof of the trend toward the regionalization of supply chains is the increase in construction orders for small-size container ships. In some countries, such as the U.S. and Japan, governments have openly encouraged the reshoring of production through various types of incentives. Some companies have explored the possibility of collaborating with rivals to make new diversification by geographical areas cost-effective. For example, Volkswagen and BMW have identified common components among various models and brands so that suppliers have sufficient volume to manufacture regionally.

Regionalization has its weaknesses. First of all, it is not easy to build a new supplier network in a new regional area. This could take substantial time and investment. Moreover, in the long run, it can be a mistake to leave one country completely and transfer production to another. Today, this country may produce and export only one component, but soon it could become a country that buys the finished product to which that component contributes (and whose production the company has decided to transfer elsewhere). It would therefore be necessary to be present to follow the evolution of demand and collect information on market factors that power a business's competitive advantage.

A significant example of diversification of supply bases is Hugo Boss (Box 9.4).

It is not just logistics that orients the localization of supply chains. Government efforts to reduce global warming and those of firms trying to benefit from them also go in the same direction.

Firms along the supply chain try to take advantage of government policies that aim to protect the environment. Reducing the parts and finished

> ### Box 9.4 Hugo Boss moves production closer to home
>
> Deciding to enlarge its factory in Izmir, Turkey, the German fashion house has expanded production capacity closer to its base in Europe to reduce its dependence on South-East Asia at a time when global supply chains were under severe pressure. Chief executive Daniel Grieder said that "supply chain disruptions were creating 'unbelievable challenges' for Hugo Boss and its rivals, with supply shortages, delays and higher shipping costs" (Storbeck, 2022).
>
> The company also had sites in Germany, Poland, and Italy, which, combined with Turkey, account for about 20% of its clothing production. Another 30% of its garments are sourced from suppliers in or close to Europe. Hugo Boss said this share would rise further over the coming years. Much of the industry relies heavily on production in South-East Asia, where labor costs are far lower. Grieder, an industry veteran who was poached by rival fashion brand Tommy Hilfiger, declared that the shift would be permanent. "Our future strategy is to produce even more garments close to those markets where they will be sold", he said (Storbeck, 2022). Products for the Americas would be made there; likewise, for Europe and Asia, he said, adding that this would be a 'huge switch' for the company.

products that are transported to various parts of the world reduces CO2 emissions. Fewer transport activities generate lower emissions, which in turn generate less carbon footprint (the amount of carbon dioxide released into the atmosphere). The same results can be achieved by moving manufacturing activities to areas where renewable energy (such as hydropower) is abundant and the products manufactured there can find an attractive demand (Masters & Edgecliffe-Johnson, 2021).

It should be remembered that, in several sectors, new technologies allow companies to replace the production of parts and components in a few large plants with a network of smaller plants distributed over the territory, which during a pandemic can limit the risks of supply chain interruption thanks to geographical diversification. The benefits derived from financial incentives offered by the governments of various countries must also be considered. The global agreement to increase the taxation of companies operating in a country to at least 15%, which was signed at the end of 2020, is an impetus to reinventing new global supply chains. With them, part of the literature on outsourcing and offshoring will be considered old.

9.2.4 A new business model

When should the business model be changed? Reply: when internal or external factors make it obsolete and are not compliant with company goals.

To respond to the pressures of the pandemic on supply chains, some companies have changed their business models. Among the four main elements that make up a business model - customers, suppliers, production process, and key resources – these companies acted mainly on the third and fourth: the production process and the factors of production: they reinvented products or services to make the procurement of needed materials and parts less vulnerable to the disruptions of supply chains. Passenger aircraft were being refitted for freight, and some retailers, like Walmart, have taken to chartering entire ships exclusively for their own cargo.

The shift toward a business model has been accelerated in some industries by the search for digital solutions, as occurred in the shipping industry. As KPMG remarked: "The new business environment demands the shipping industry to shift from the traditional business model of selling capacity, to one that offers value to customers. With the increasing need of global supply chains for seamless flow of goods and services, digital business is a key enabler for shipping companies today" (Papageorgiou, 2020).

9.2.5 Beyond traditional business intelligence. The need to accelerate technological innovation

Under the pressure of the coronavirus pandemic and as a result of new technologies, forecasters and economists quickly changed their approach. "There are no lessons from history. We can't find the patterns looking to the past. We have new weapons to forecast. We have frequently listened to those words". Professor Varadarajan sums up very well what has changed. "We now use much more short-term historical data and new predictive analytics tools, such as neural-network analysis, to create accurate short-term forecasts. In 40 years of helping firms forecast supply-chain problems, I have never had the abundance of data and the powerful and predictive tools that we employ now", he emphasized (Varadarajan, 2021). All of this has contributed to mitigating the supply-chain problems.

The introduction of technologies that in real-time communicate the position of moving parts (i.e.: the strong use of advanced analytics) helps to quickly identify supply chain delays and provide advance warning of potential bottlenecks. Furthermore, if we have reliable and timely information on the supply chain, we can lower the buffer stocks and save working capital.

The success in supply chain management is partly related to the use of modern digital tools, especially advanced analytics[3]. There is a growing interest in greater technological innovation in the management of the supply chain, particularly regarding logistics (Shih, 2020). Companies are also looking for technological innovations to manage disruptions caused by lockdowns.

The introduction of new technologies has been accelerated by the crisis brought on by the pandemic. The main reasons are more security and flexibility, on the one hand, and enhanced efficiency in production processes on the other.

(1) Technologies to find ways to operate with more security and flexibility have gained in popularity. Driven at the beginning by the need to lower costs and achieve greater reliability in production, the demand for automation during the coronavirus outbreak has grown exponentially. One of the main reasons was the need for social distancing in factories to protect the health of workers. Software, sensors, Robotics, and Artificial Intelligence (AI) applications have increased dramatically, the latter helping to carry out remote checks on the 'robustness' of the supply chain.

(2) New technologies in production processes can reduce energy consumption, are less capital-intensive, and can lower management costs. Blockchain technology is used by more companies to face the effects of the coronavirus on supply chains. Companies have discovered that in this way they can reduce both delivery times and costs and make products more traceable along the supply chain.

Supply-chain startups are drawing increased attention from investors as retailers and manufacturers struggle to overcome shortages, delays, and bottlenecks in the ongoing coronavirus pandemic. Project44 is an example of the growing interest in digital upstarts that help shippers navigate congested supply chains (Box 9.5).

The pandemic has accelerated the search for how to leverage new technologies to improve efficiency and productivity, for instance, in the shipping industry. The complexity of this industry has delayed the digitization of operations in comparison with other industries, although the situation has changed very quickly. According to a survey by Wärtsilä Marine Business, two-thirds of shipping companies started on their digital journey in

---

[3]"Advanced Analytics is the autonomous or semi-autonomous examination of data or content using sophisticated techniques and tools, typically beyond those of traditional business intelligence (BI), to discover deeper insights, make predictions, or generate recommendations" (Gartner Glossary, 2022).

> **Box 9.5 Project44**
>
> The Chicago-based company develops supply-chain analytics software for shipping and logistics companies, representing an example of the importance given to technology in managing products as they cruised supply chains around the world. The company offers software platforms from which logistics companies can have a detailed view of where their products are, optimize supply chain networks, and reduce shipping times and costs. Project44 collects data from carriers and shippers, allowing businesses to make transportation changes in response to hold-ups or swings in market demand. The company has been valued at $2.2 billion, and its customers include Amazon and Home Depot, which use the provider's technology to track cargo as it moves through distribution networks (Vartabedian, 2022).

2021–22. Technologies such as the Internet of Things (IoT), Big-Data, and Artificial Intelligence (AI) are used more and more frequently in the shipping industry to boost efficiency, drive down costs, and reduce vessel downtime. Digital technologies have transformed the role of ships from being a central mechanism to being an enabler of value creation. This is what KPMG defines as "Maritime 4.0: Disruption by digital innovation" (Papageorgiou, 2020). The connected vessels have given way to integrated value chains, and the latter, in turn, to the infrastructure and operations of both the vessels and the world's maritime cities that service them: vessels andand smart ports. New technologies "will create smarter, more connected distributed networks and will provide performance monitoring as well as real-time visibility of the vessels" (Papageorgiou, 2020).

9.2.6 Rethinking the trade-off between product variety and the capacity for flexible production

"More choice is not always better" (Schwartz, 2006). Increasing the variety of products offered means reaching more segments and meeting the expectations of a greater number of customers. However, the variety comes at a cost. What is the degree of variety that should not be exceeded? During the pandemic, doubts have increased. The demand for many products has undergone significant shifts from one version of a product to another, from one segment to another, from one period of time in sales to another. Many businesses have had confirmation that adding variety means adding complexity to forecasting, production, and distribution, and that rewards are difficult to achieve and maintain. The lesson: companies should reconsider the pros and cons of producing numerous product variations.

9.3 Refitting the business

'Resilience' can be designed into a supply chain through a broad identification of vulnerabilities and by taking the necessary measures to address and contain them. The best way to achieve this is to give broad visibility to both upstream and downstream supply chain participants. Creating visibility requires a high level of collaboration within the supply chain and the development of behavior/rules of conduct in which a supplier is encouraged to audit its own suppliers (Manners-Bell, 2018).

A supply chain's disruption can occur during many phases. A flood or fire or other natural disasters can temporarily idle the warehouse or transportation system, or a logjam in a busy port can shut down processing plants because of a lack of supplies. According to Manners-Bell, one of the ways to formally approach risk management is through the adoption of the ISO31000 standard. Using this standard, the company can improve its ability to identify opportunities and threats and better allocate resources to address risk. The standard helps managers answer four questions: What can happen and why? What are the consequences? What are the probabilities of their future occurrence? Are there any factors that can mitigate the consequence of the risk or reduce its probability?

An interesting example of supply chain risk management concerns Cisco (Box 9.6).

9.3.1 'Resilience' versus 'robustness'

Miroudot distinguishes between 'resilience' and 'robustness'. 'Resilience' refers to the ability to return to normal operations after a disruption, while 'robustness' refers to the ability to maintain operations during a crisis.

Starting from that distinction, the Author states that geographical diversification is the best rule for building 'robustness' during a pandemic. In a pandemic, the Author observes, it is necessary to restore production quickly if some of its parts are disrupted ('resilience'), but 'robustness' is more relevant. The most effective way to build 'robustness' is to diversify suppliers over various geographic areas. "Producing in a single country, even if it is

Box 9.6 Supply chain risk management at Cisco's

The high-tech manufacturer Cisco is widely regarded as having one of the best supply chains in the industry. To give 'resilience' to the organization, Cisco has adopted a 'proactivity' approach in which 'resilience' is embedded in design and processes. This involved establishing a 'control tower' staff whose responsibility is to continuously monitor the situation and respond promptly to harmful events. Cisco's experience in its response to the postrecession shock in 2010 highlighted the need to improve collaboration with suppliers. In particular, the company felt the need to take on the mission of regaining its status as a supply chain innovator.

Cisco was managing over 8.000 products, with 95% of production outsourced and with more than 90 locations around the world. To mitigate the risks, Cisco set up supply chain risk management teams organized by region and function. These teams monitor the system of suppliers and partners, evaluate the effects of possible disruption on Cisco's operational activity, and evaluate the ability of each partner to positively address this disruption. If necessary, they make the necessary decisions to move production to a new site or establish relationships with a new supplier. To monitor and evaluate the situation at each stage, the various teams collaborate through a common internet portal through which a wide variety of tools such as crisis response e-mail lists, videos, and communication services are used. After the crisis is over, Cisco begins an analysis process to establish what has worked, what needs to be improved, and what early signs of a crisis need to be picked up and analyzed.

In 2011, Cisco's anticrisis model was put to the test when a tsunami struck Japan causing a disaster at the Fukushima nuclear power plant. Within 30 min of the first earthquake alert, a dedicated supply chain incident manager was informed of the event, and he alerted the supply chain risk management team leader. Within 12 h, the supply chain incident management team was activated and able to take snapshots of the possible impacts on suppliers' activities and their conditions across the region. These snapshots were updated daily based on the evolution of the crisis. Cisco's managers were able to profile each supplier site from various 'resilience' perspectives, such as the expected time-to-recover for the site and whether the supplier was the only source of supply or there were alternatives.

Not everything worked out perfectly: Cisco underestimated the importance of continuously updating the production site map and underestimated the need to act closely with manufacturing partners. The lessons they learned served to better deal with the subsequent disasters created by the flood in Thailand.

the country of origin of the company, does not guarantee robustness" since any geographical area can be affected by pandemics. "It is a mistake to equate self-sufficiency with 'robustness' - putting all the eggs in one basket is still not a good idea" (Miroudot, 2020).

In times of COVID-19, there are difficulties in achieving geographical diversification. For certain product components, it takes months to find a supplier, discuss specifications, assess production quality, and make sure their procedures are reliable and repeatable. Even more complex is achieving reliable geographical diversification in a short time. "You'll probably go bust before it arrives", comments an industry expert. "Just imagine that you've decided to have three suppliers for a component. You'd have three sets of tooling, three teams that need to go in and work with them and support them. The costs would be astronomical and those would make you uncompetitive. So you might have a more 'robust' supply chain than the other guys but no one's going to buy your cars because they're too expensive" (Neill, 2020).

9.3.2 Types of 'resilience'

"When severe storms hit in tropical climates, buildings may fall, but most palm trees survive. They bend but don't break. They have 'resilience'. Can your organization say the same?" (Polman & Winston, 2021a). Thus begins an article by Polman and Winston that argues that, in order to deal with the coronavirus crisis and its aftermath, companies must build two blocks of 'resilience'.

(1) "Financial flexibility, portfolio diversity, and organizational agility". The coronavirus pandemic, having given rise to factory closures, bottlenecks, and shortages, has pushed the financial equilibrium of many companies to the crisis point. Only those with financial flexibility, financial 'resilience', and solid balance sheets have resisted. Companies that offer a variety of product mixes can dampen ups and downs better than others that have a single business. The search for diversification, and above all portfolio diversity, is the way to remain competitive and 'resilient'. The third factor of 'resilience' can be obtained by acting on the organizational structure with organizational agility as its objective. The Authors cite, for example, the increased agility achieved by Unilever when it decided to change its organization. The previous organization was based on decentralization by product categories and geographical areas that became excessive. After deciding to move to an organization based on broad product lines and the reduction of management layers, greater agility and greater outward-looking ability were achieved. Empowering on-the-ground employees to deal with looming problems better prepares you to deal with any surprises.

2) "Financial, portfolio, and organizational strength". These three elements are important, but the larger opportunity arises from making a company more broadly crisis-resistant for the long term "because doing so serves multiple stakeholders, not just shareholders". The Authors argue that the strongest organizations today and in the future "will thrive by giving more than they take from the world" (Polman & Winston, 2021a). They call this kind of company "net positive" because "it seeks to improve the well-being of everyone it touches through its operations, value chain, products, services, and influence". Polman and Winston lay out how to build a business with a "net positive" goal in their seminal book (Polman & Winston, 2021b).

9.3.3 Three steps to prevent supply chain disruption

"Sometimes, the best way to understand how a system works is to observe how it breaks", Swabey states in an article that collects the opinions of several experts. Supply chain disruptions have many antecedents (Swabey, 2021). Even going back only two decades, we find examples such as the impact of the terrorist attack on the Twin Towers in 2001, Hurricane Katrina in 2005, and the Eyjafjöll volcano eruption in 2010.

'Just in time' (JIT), widely adopted by companies, has contributed to the vulnerability. Based on the principle of accumulating only as many stocks as necessary to meet the demand of orders already acquired, JIT showed vulnerability in the second year of the pandemic when it was very difficult to predict demand and have security of supply times (see 'just in time' vs. 'just in case' below).

What can be done to avoid future disruption? According to the experts who contributed to Swabey's article, there are three main actions: reconfiguring supply chains, greater transparency, and short-term predictions in demand.

(1) Reconfiguring supply chains. This means redistributing among countries the various phases of the supply chain, adding more redundancy and bringing them closer to the final assembler: "bringing production closer to home". If the supply chain becomes shorter, it is easier for

companies to adjust supply to any changes in demand. If you have suppliers in Asia and the supply chain ends in the UK, it takes an average of 6 weeks for the parts to be transported. This prevents you from reacting in a short time to any shocks. "But if you're closer to your consumers, you can respond more quickly" (Swabey, 2021)[4].

(2) More transparency. The second answer is to give maximum transparency to the supply chain using digital technology to allow the various companies (participating in the supply chain) to detect disruptions "sooner or even anticipate them". However, it is not easy to do this when the supply chain flows from the final manufacturer to a Tier 1 and from these to a Tier 2, Tier 3, and often a Tier 4. The collaboration between the final manufacturer and its Tier 1 suppliers is effective, but less in the next steps.

Supply chain transparency can be attained using Blockchain technology by revealing the origin of parts, components, and materials. 'Digital twins', which combines IoT and Machine learning, is considered the next step in supply chain transparency, allowing companies to forecast the impact of supply chain shocks and "explore hypothetical responses". Tesla is an example of a company that has adopted 'Digital twin' technologies to improve its products and offer better customer service. Tesla builds a 'Digital twin' for every car it produces, and logistics provider DHL Supply Chain maintains 'Digital twins' of its warehouse operations. By feeding real-time data from IoT sensors into digital models of their supply chains, companies can predict and assess the impact of supply chain shocks and find suitable responses. Large enterprises also need to invest in boosting the technology capabilities of their suppliers if they are to take full advantage of supply chain digitization.

(3) Short-term predictions in demand. The third approach assumes that even peaks in demand can cause disruption, not only suppliers' decisions. Supply chain 'resilience' can be achieved by demand sensing (a forecasting method that leverages new mathematical techniques) and by analyzing market data to make short-term predictions about demand.

---

[4]This response can be supported by 3D printing, which allows companies to move production closer to their customers. Oil and gas giant Shell maintains a 'digital warehouse' containing designs of spare parts for its production machinery (van Keulen, 2021).

9.3.4 The case of the pharma industry

In the last two decades, the pharmaceutical sector has had very strong growth (revenues have increased more than six times in value). One of the consequences is that supply chains have become increasingly global and complex, and the risks of disruption have increased. "For some products, this results in supply chains that are so complex that they start in Asia and circumnavigate the globe twice" (Foster et al., 2021). According to the McKinsey Global Institute survey, 50% of respondents indicate that the fact they have only one source of supply is a critical vulnerability, and 25% say they have little or no visibility into the supply chain.

Supply chain risks are unavoidable, but companies can mitigate the disruptive effects by using appropriate strategies for building 'resilience'. What are the risks we face? Since the supply chains are geographically very extensive, natural disasters and international trade tensions are two of the many risks that pharma companies are running. Moreover, although the pharma industry has supply chains that are more global than those of other industries, it is strongly dependent on several geographical areas, and therefore particularly exposed to the risk of shortage. As McKinsey reports, "86% of the streptomycin sold in North America and 96% of the chloramphenicol sold in the European Union come from China" (Foster et al., 2021).

Supply-chain 'resilience' in the pharma industry requires four elements.

(1) "Complete transparency". The company must have a map of its suppliers to have an 'end-to-end view' of the supply chain and be able to quickly identify its vulnerabilities. Not having this visibility, or transparency, involves a serious risk for pharma companies. There are numerous and documented accusations that its companies engage in unfair labor practices, above all by resorting to suppliers that use child labor.

(2) "Routine stress-testing and reassessment". If the company has continuous visibility into its supply chain, it can also constantly assess the likelihood of the occurrence of different risks. Scenario planning and simulation models can help identify vulnerabilities, estimate their potential impact, and target measures to mitigate related risks. For example, during the COVID-19 pandemic, a leading pharma company "used a digital twin simulation to understand the impact of production slowdowns and shutdowns on the supplies of patient medication. This helped the company realize that it had more time than it had anticipated

to design and implement safer ways of working at its manufacturing plants, allowing it to take more time to get the best solutions" (Foster et al., 2021).

(3) "Reduce exposure to unexpected impact". Extending the network of suppliers is one of the simplest strategies for building 'resiliency'. The vulnerability increases if the company relies on a single supplier for raw materials or for a critical component, or if the suppliers are concentrated in a single geographical area. As mentioned above, the abandonment by various companies of the JIT method to switch to forms of JIC is aimed at reducing the exposure to shocks. New technologies have contributed to advances in this field, for example, by enabling quick changes among suppliers and the use of advanced analytics.

(4) "Supply resilience must be lowered across the entire organization". It must be an integral part of both long-term plans and day-to-day operational programs. Management must be able to see the risk to its organization and evaluate and lessen its impact.

9.3.5 'Just in time' versus 'just in case'

'Just in time' is a milestone in the search for greater efficiency of production processes. It was introduced to the car industry by Toyota, giving the Japanese manufacturer its biggest strength and an edge over global rivals, who imitated it and made it an inescapable rule for production efficiency. Like other management principles, 'just in time' has been questioned due to the effects of the coronavirus pandemic on business management, and many have preferred replacing it with 'just in case'. Before discussing the reasons for this replacement and evaluating its effectiveness, let us examine the logic of the two management concepts.

'Just in time' (JIT). In its narrowest sense, it means producing only what the customer requests in the time required by the customer. The aim is to reduce the costs associated with the accumulation of stocks (investments in working capital and investments in space in warehouses and along production lines). It requires an organization that involves the replenishment of raw materials, parts, and components exactly when they are needed for the production process to take place. JIT is part of the wider choices of 'lean manufacturing', which suggests the reduction or elimination of seven types of waste in production activity: overproduction, waiting, transporting, inappropriate processing, unnecessary motions, and unnecessary inventory.

JIT has been widely used in the automotive construction industry. To reduce stocks, it is necessary to use a 'pull' system (produce only what has already been sold or what you plan to sell in a short time) instead of a 'push' system (produce finished products waiting to be sold for the warehouse). With the 'pull' method, the replenishment of stocks is ordered only when it is necessary to meet demand. The goal is to keep the stock level very low along the entire supply chain, thereby reducing its cost (lower investment). In essence, the method is based less on production forecasts and more on responding quickly to demand when it arises.

Certain conditions are required for efficient JIT. First, participants in the supply chain must be linked by long-term partnership relationships and not by 'arm's-length' relationships. These relationships can act on the growth and stability of suppliers. The more the relationships are shorter-term and transaction-based, the more the chances are reduced of creating win–win relationships. Second, communications about demand must be clear and timely to reduce volatility and uncertainty. These conditions were not experienced during the coronavirus pandemic.

A case in point concerns the pandemic and the disruptions in the supply chains of Toyota (Box 9.7).

'Just in case' (JIC). While 'just in time' produces only in response to customer orders ('pull') without accumulating safety stocks, 'just in case' produces to maintain sufficient stock to cope with any fluctuations in demand ('push'). 'Just in time' lowers average stock levels but is vulnerable to the effects of a sudden increase in demand, supply chain disruptions, or

Box 9.7 Toyota

Toyota has become vulnerable to the effects of the pandemic due to superiority over rivals that have never been fully matched, owing, in particular, to lean management and 'just in time'. The pandemic, creating continuous disruptions in supply chains and driving up inflation, has caused manufacturers to accumulate stocks. Production at many of Toyota's plants in Japan has long been suspended due to chip shortages from the Japanese manufacturer's suppliers in South-East Asia, who were running short of components in 2021–22. Typically for automakers the size of Toyota, a day of lost production can cost up to $10m (Rassoul, 2022), to which must be added the advantages lost with JIT such as the reduction of space in warehouses and along production lines (parts waiting to be used).

logistics scheduling errors. 'Just in case' has higher average stock levels (compared to JIT) since it aims to anticipate any disruptions in the supply chain. However, it has lower production costs thanks to the possibility of choosing the most convenient production batches. Using 'just in case' rather than 'just in time' processes means adopting more 'resilient' but less efficient production processes that could raise costs, but it is a form of insurance against disruption.

"Suddenly the pandemic has struck the supply chains" (Financial Times, 2021). Some media articles clearly described what befell the supply chains and what the effects were on 'lean manufacturing' as the pandemic spread around the world.

In mid-2021, a shortage of semiconductors spread through supply chains around the world. The shortage extended to the production of televisions, home appliances, and smartphones. Automakers were also hit hard. As 'just in time' moves ships, trains, and trucks across continents, it has suffered. Lean management methods tolerate little margin for error. The model had shown proof of the 'resilience' and the ability to adapt to new conditions but did not overcome the disruptions caused by the pandemic. At present, companies are paying the price for prioritizing 'just in time' rather than 'just in case'. "Protecting supply chains in the future will need a change in mindset as well as a willingness to spend" (Financial Times, 2021).

'Just-in-time' production reduces ongoing costs; however, it provides little protection against disruption. Carmakers and others are paying the price in production delays, lost sales, and reputational damage. Managing high inventories is a form of guarantee against these later costs. In the car industry, the disruption has been magnified by whipsaws in demand. In the first lockdown, companies cut back on orders for parts, components, and modules to avoid a buildup of excess stocks, failing to foresee that the success in vaccinations would have led to a much faster recovery than expected and that, forced them to entertain at home and work remotely, people would increase purchases of electronics. 'Just in time' has the advantage of reducing costs (less investment in working capital), but it is vulnerable to disruptions in the supply chain.

Another article has highlighted that the "pandemic changed everything. Things are different now. 'Just in time' inventory didn't work anymore. We need to shift to 'just in case'". Arguing from a long-term perspective, the Authors stated: "We are facing a change from a buyer's to a seller's market" (Masters & Edgecliffe-Johnson, 2021). This shift has involved bringing more stability to the supply chain and changing relationships with partners, as well as paying before receiving goods, extending contract lengths with key suppliers, and establishing partnerships rather than entering into a contractual arrangement with semiconductor manufacturers[5].

But not everyone agrees with blaming JIT as the propelling force behind the pandemic shortages. Among those who think differently, Sheffy makes three observations with solid foundations (Sheffi, 2021).

(1) "The rationale for JIT is not cost reductions, it is to make products with far fewer defects". As mentioned above, the logic of JIT is to reduce inventories in each stage of production by pulling, 'just in time', only what is needed from one production stage to the next. Defects in the parts and in the production process are quickly detected. If necessary, the production chain is temporarily stopped. Therefore, the main objective was to avoid wasted scrap, rework, and warranty claims rather than reducing the modest costs of stock maintenance. "Thus, JIT is a story of boosting quality and customer satisfaction rather than a story of penny-pinching".

(2) "JIT has knock-on benefits because it also enables flexibility". Since there are no stocks accumulated in advance of the needs of the production process, any mismatches between demand and supply can be easily adjusted. This makes the company far more adaptive to changing market conditions. "JIT creates resilience, not fragility".

(3) By contrast, building up stocks becomes "a financial liability and environmental waste" if the demand for a product falls. This applies especially to fashion and perishable products, which quickly lose value and the possibility of being sold without avoiding losses.

To conclude, borrowing the words of Sheffi: "Abandoning JIT would do little to help current supply chain problems. Companies do keep significant amounts of inventory, even with JIT. However, such so-called safety stock helps insulate a company only from short-term fluctuations".

9.3.6 Why do disasters often find MNCs unprepared?

Multinational companies are in the best position to know what is happening and what could happen in the world. They also have the most experience in natural disasters, from earthquakes to epidemics, since their supply chains

---

[5]Moreover: "The changes are being driven by the pandemic and the supply chain shock that followed. But they also reflect the geopolitical tension between China and the west and the pressure on companies to reduce their carbon footprint. Tens of thousands of tiny changes are fundamentally reshaping the way things are designed, manufactured and sold" (Masters & Edgecliffe-Johnson, 2021).

extend their networks to a wide variety of economies, cultures, and social structures, and they are in contact with a vast array of situations. They also have the resources to deploy tools that can effectively scrutinize what is happening or could happen.

Why do disasters often find the MNCs unprepared? Psychologists have an answer. The problem is often not the inability to predict but the inability to react to the perception of risk. This may explain why organizations that have great means to scrutinize the horizon and protect themselves from large risks, such as NCPs, have been slow to react to the effects of the pandemic.

Why did the news at the end of January 2020 that, in Rome, two tourists from China had tested positive for the SARS COVID-2 virus does not arouse alarm in Italy? A few days earlier, the Italian authorities had even sent medical material to China as a sign of solidarity to face the epidemic that had exploded in a region of that country at the end of the previous year. Only on February 20, following the first deaths in the Codogno area, were drastic measures taken in Italy.

This behavior, which psychologists call "in-group bias", led Europeans and Americans to think that what had happened in Hubei was not a matter of great concern. It is common knowledge that epidemics spread without respecting political boundaries, but "in-group bias" has made people forget this[6]. Psychologists define this behavior as driven by "psychological bias".

If an event is out-of-the-ordinary, we have difficulty reacting to it. We are inclined to evaluate the possibility of an event occurring in terms of probability and based on our supposed ability to predict the extent to which it may occur. We are therefore inclined to ignore or underestimate what has not occurred previously. Many of the consequences of the coronavirus are to be attributed to this trend of ours (Harford, 2020).

We are led to think that a series of growing data moves according to an arithmetic progression (by a certain amount) and not in geometric progression (based on a ratio). The pandemic in various countries has spread in geometric progression, surprising people and organizations. The burden on healthcare organizations has risen very rapidly, thereby reducing defense capabilities.

Why were many authorities, public organizations, and businesses unprepared for the arrival of COVID-19? There was no lack of warning signs.

---

[6]"In-group" is a small group of people whose common interest tends to exclude others. A broader definition is that "in-group" refers to a social group whose members are very loyal to each other, share many interests, and usually try to keep other people out of the group.

Why did so much time pass between the perception of danger and the response to it? "Analysis paralysis" and the "ostrich effect" are the explanations that psychologists give to the lack of an answer to the arrival of a danger we notice. "Analysis paralysis is an inability to make a decision due to overthinking a problem" (Chen, 2022)[7] It is a situation in which a person or group of people in an organization may have too much data and have difficulty deciding within the proper time. The example often given to represent a situation particularly prone to "analysis paralysis" is a person who must decide whether to make an investment and to what extent. It is common for individuals to examine many options until it is impossible to make a choice (time is up).

In behavioral finance (the field of study of the effects of psychology on investors and financial markets), the "ostrich effect" is a cognitive bias that causes people to avoid information they perceive as potentially unpleasant. For example, the "ostrich effect" can prompt an investor to deliberately ignore negative information. Many of us tend to underestimate the possibility of a disaster happening that could affect us and to ignore its negative effects. Faced with a natural disaster, such as a pandemic or a man-made disaster, we are not as prepared as we should be. People are slow to recognize danger; they are confused, and undecided about what to do until it is too late.

Our behavior also depends on the fact that in the face of an unexpected event we are led to observe what others do and to follow them. Darley and Latané studied this phenomenon. The "bystander effect" is the behavior of those in an emergency situation who draw reassurances from the presence of others (Latané & Darley, 1970). The two psychologists pumped smoke into a room where a group of people (unaware that they were the protagonists of an experiment) were answering a questionnaire. When there was only one person in the room, he reacted quickly to the first smoke signals and warned those in charge. When there were at least three people in the room, they were all reluctant to ask for outside intervention, and so no one intervened. They were reassured by the presence and nonreaction of others. In behavioral finance, this phenomenon is known as the "herd instinct", which

---

[7]"Analysis paralysis (or paralysis by analysis) describes an individual or group process when overanalyzing or overthinking a situation can cause forward motion or decision-making to become 'paralyzed', meaning that no solution or course of action is decided upon within a natural time frame" (Wikipedia, 2022). Analysis paralysis can be a difficult challenge to overcome, especially when making an important decision.

occurs when investors do what others do instead of doing their own analysis of the situation.

Why are we vulnerable to surprises? Watkins and Bazerman, based on their research on surprises that could have been predicted in organizations but were not, conclude that this inability depends on the existence of barriers. Some are psychological in nature, originating from "cognitive defects" that cause people to ignore the approach of a threat. Within organizations, there may be barriers that hinder both communications between various functions and the assumption of responsibility. Individually or in a coordinated way they can weaken the organization.

In an article published in *Harvard Business Review*, Watkins and Bazerman (2003) point out that, in 1995, a small group of Greenpeace activists in the North Sea boarded an old and obsolete oil rig, the Brent Spar, that Shell was about to sink. The activists wanted to block Shell's decision because the platform contained radioactive waste, which could seriously pollute the environment. Shell got the courts to order the activists to leave the platform. The multinational succeeded in attracting media attention and creating an incident that obscured Shell's image to the point of inducing a boycott of its products in some countries. The Authors argued in the article that: 1) even the largest and most experienced companies can be taken by surprise; and 2) when unprepared to face surprises, companies may react in a disorderly manner, ending up exacerbating disasters (Watkins & Bazerman, 2003).

References

Alicke, K., Barriball, E., & Trautwein, V. (2021). *November 23). How COVID-19 is reshaping supply chains.* McKinsey. www.mckinsey.com/business-functions/operations/our-insights/how-covid-19-is-reshaping-supply-chains.

Ancarani, A., Di Mauro, C., Fratocchi, L., Orzes, G., & Sartor, M. (2015). Prior to reshoring: A duration analysis of foreign manufacturing ventures. *International Journal of Production Economics, 169*, 141—155. https://doi.org/10.1016/j.ijpe.2015.07.031

Miroudot. (2020). In R. Baldwin, & S. Evenett (Eds.), *Resilience versus robustness in global value chains: Some policy implications.* CEPR Press.

Chen, J. (2022). *Analysis paralysis.* www.investopedia.com/terms/a/analysisparalysis.asp#: ~:text=Analysis%20paralysis%20is%20an%20inability,an%20inability%20to%20pick% 20one.

Ellram, L. M. (2013). Offshoring, reshoring and the manufacturing location decision. *Journal of Supply Chain Management, 49*(2), 3—5. https://doi.org/10.1111/jscm.12023

Financial Times. (2021). *Chip shortage shows the pitfalls of just in time.* Financial Times. www.ft.com/content/8fd09156-434c-45c6-8d26-3765b98f1980.

Foster, T., Patel, P., & Skiba, K. (2021). September 23). *Four ways pharma companies can make their supply chains more resilient.* www.mckinsey.com/industries/life-sciences/our-insights/four-ways-pharma-companies-can-make-their-supply-chains-more-resilient.

Glossary, Gartner (2022). *Advanced Analytics, Gartner*. https://www.gartner.com/en/information-technology/glossary/advanced-analytics.

Govindan, K., Mina, H., & Alavi, B. (2020). A decision support system for demand management in healthcare supply chains considering the epidemic outbreaks: A case study of coronavirus disease 2019 (COVID-19). *Transportation Research E: Logistics and Transportation Review*, 138. https://doi.org/10.1016/j.tre.2020.101967

Gray, J. V., Skowronski, K., Esenduran, G., & Johnny Rungtusanatham, M. (2013). The reshoring phenomenon: What supply chain academics ought to know and should do. *Journal of Supply Chain Management, 49*(2), 27−33. https://doi.org/10.1111/jscm.12012

Harford. (2020). Tim harford: Why we fail to prepare for disasters. *Financial Times*. www.ft.com/content/74e5f04a-7df1-11ea-82f6-150830b3b99a.

Jung-a, S., & White, E. (2020). Coronavirus disruption at Samsung could threaten S Korea economy. *Financial Times*. www.ft.com/content/4a42e9a8-57b6-11ea-a528-dd0f971febbc.

Latané, B., & Darley, J. (1970). Bystander intervention in emergencies: Diffusion of responsibility. *Journal of Personality and Social Psychology, 8*, 377−383.

Manners-Bell, J. (2018). *Supply chain risk management*. KoganPage.

Masters, B., & Edgecliffe-Johnson, A. (2021). The shift from 'just in time' to 'just in case'. *Financial Times*. www.ft.com/content/8a7cdc0d-99aa-4ef6-ba9a-fd1a1180dc82.

Monson, C. (2020). What small businesses need to survive the coronavirus crisis. *Harvard Business Review*. https://hbr.org/2020/03/what-small-businesses-need-to-survive-the-coronavirus-crisis.

Neill, J. (2020). *Why supply chain diversification isn't all that easy"*. Washington Latest. May 11 https://washingtonlatest.com/why-supply-chain-diversification-isnt-all-that-easy/.

Papageorgiou, M. (2020). *Digital Transformation in the Shipping Industry Is Here*, 50−52. https://assets.kpmg/content/dam/kpmg/gr/pdf/2021/02/gr-digital-transformation-shipping-papageorgiou-nafs-magazine.pdf.

Polman, P., & Winston, A. (2021a). *6 types of resilience companies need today*. https://hbr.org/2021/11/6-types-of-resilience-companies-need-today.

Polman, P., & Winston, A. (2021b). *Net positive: How courageous companies thrive by giving more than they take*. Harvard Business Review Press.

Rassoul, M. (January 21, 2022). *Toyota: Just in time now just means more disruptions*. https://thefifthskill.com/toyota-just-in-time-now-just-means-more-disruptions/.

Robinson, P. K., & Hsieh, L. (2016). Reshoring: A strategic renewal of luxury clothing supply chains. *Operations Management Research, 9*(3−4), 89−101. https://doi.org/10.1007/s12063-016-0116-x

Schwartz, B. (2006). Global supply chains in a post-pandemic world. *Harvard Business Review*. https://hbr.org/2006/06/more-isnt-always-better#:~:text=Summary.&text=Offering%20customers%20too%20many%20product,find%20just%20the%20right%20thing.

Sheffi, Y. (2021). What everyone gets wrong about the never-ending COVID-19 supply chain crisis. *MIT Sloan Management Review, 63*(1), 1−5.

Shih, W. C. (2020). Global supply chains in a post-pandemic world companies need to make their networks more resilient. *Harvard Business Review, 2020*(September-October), 1−9. https://hbr.org/download/subscriber/reprint/R2005F-PDF-ENG.

Storbeck, O. (2022). Hugo Boss moves production closer to home to shorten supply chain. *Financial Times*. www.ft.com/content/0eaecd94-ef71-4078-9f99-43cd203b246c.

Swabey, P. (October 6, 2021). *Can digital technology prevent supply chain disruptions?"* Techmonitor. https://techmonitor.ai/leadership/strategy/can-digital-technology-prevent-supply-chain-disruptions.

Szlezak, P., Swartz, P., & Reeves, M. (2020). Taking stock of the covid-19 recession. *Harvard Business Review*. https://hbr.org/2020/08/taking-stock-of-the-covid-19-recession.

Terazono, E., & Evans, J. (2020). How coronavirus is affecting pasta's complex supply chain. *Financial Times*. www.ft.com/content/5456bc24-6dd4-11ea-9bca-bf503995cd6f.

van Keulen, N. (2021). *A digital future for spare part management*. Shell. https://www.shell.com/energy-and-innovation/digitalisation/a-digital-future-for-spare-part-management.html.

Varadarajan, T. (2021). An insider explains the supply-chain crisis. *The Wall Street Journal*. www.wsj.com/articles/insider-explains-supply-chain-crisis-phil-levy-shipping-containers-ports-costs-inflation-logistics-11639757471.

Vartabedian, M. (2022). Project44, a supply-chain tech startup, raises $420 million. *The Wall Street Journal*. www.wsj.com/articles/project44-a-supply-chain-tech-startup-raises-420-million-11641920462.

Watkins, M. D., & Bazerman, M. H. (2003). Predictable surprises: The disasters you should have seen coming. *Harvard Business Review, 81*(3), 72–140. https://hbr.org/2003/04/predictable-surprises-the-disasters-you-should-have-seen-coming.

White, S., & Mallet, V. (2021). France: The battle over wind power stirs up the election. *Financial Times*. www.ft.com/content/29cb5f2b-9b09-49bf-b306-c3a782191f6c.

Whitney, D. E., Luo, J., & Heller, D. A. (2014). The benefits and constraints of temporary sourcing diversification in supply chain disruption and recovery. *Journal of Purchasing and Supply Management, 20*(4), 238–250. https://doi.org/10.1016/j.pursup.2014.06.001

Wikipedia. (2022). *Analysis paralysis, Wikipedia encyclopedia*. https://en.wikipedia.org/wiki/Analysis_paralysis.

Index

Note: Page numbers followed by '*f*' indicate figures those followed by '*t*' indicate tables and '*b*' indicate boxes.

Printed in the United States
by Baker & Taylor Publisher Services